Praise for *Maroon the Implacable*

"This book, *Maroon the Implacal* manual on how to make revoluti
—Amiri Baraka, poet, essa laureate of New Jersey

"The occult history of America concerns a space where Black, Red, and white together produce the culture of resistance—and the permanent uprising against hegemonic power and alienation. This space could be called the hideout of the Maroons, those few who have made the revolutionary exodus from the world of slavery to the 'inaccessible' wilderness of an alternate universe. If the Great Dismal Swamp is no longer a refuge, nevertheless the message of the Maroons lives on, and Russell Maroon Shoatz is today its untamed voice. Free Maroon the Implacable!"
—Hakim Bey, author of *TAZ: The Temporary Autonomous Zone*

"Russell Maroon Shoatz wrote the essays in this book during thirty cumulative years of solitary confinement under conditions that international law would consider 'cruel and inhuman.' The essays trace a remarkable political trajectory, starting with involvement with the gang world of Philadelphia, leading to membership in the Black Panther Party, and ending with full-hearted support for ecofeminism and a repudiation of the patriarchal violence he once embraced. At the core of the book is the theme of *marronage*—the will to escape from conditions of enslavement at any cost. This is what Russell Maroon Shoatz has done, not only physically, but in the world of ideas by escaping from the rigid patriarchal framework he inherited and revaluing and promoting the role of women in the history of liberation. This book is a document of this transformation carried out against tremendous odds and told with searing honesty."
—Silvia Federici, author of *Revolution at Point Zero: Housework, Reproduction, and Feminist Struggle* and *Caliban and the Witch: Women, the Body and Primitive Accumulation*

"Russell Maroon Shoatz's life reads like fiction composed by Victor Hugo. But this Jean Valjean for our time is the living truth, and his writings are a beacon for a new, revolutionary age. What a treasure has here been uncovered!"
—Joel Kovel, author of *White Racism: A Psychohistory* and *The Enemy of Nature: The End of Capitalism or the End of the World?*

"The message of Russell Maroon Shoatz, the message of the revolutionary maroon, is a message that we ignore only at our own peril and that of our world. Prison is designed to crush the soul, deaden the mind and destroy the spirit, but it becomes for some, like Maroon, a place for new awakening, deeper insights, and expanded solidarity. As Maroon shows, the awakened prisoner understands the contradictions of the state, capitalism, and patriarchy in a way that most of us, living in our larger and more comfortable prisons, can hardly begin to understand. We are living in Babylon, and Babylon must be destroyed. Our brothers and sisters in prison are uniquely gifted to help lead us out of captivity. The message of the revolutionary maroon is that 'exodus is the primary form class struggle takes today.' This idea, that we must learn to create and to live together in communities of liberation and solidarity, communities that openly defy and negate the brutal oppression of capital, state and patriarchy, is the precisely correct message for our time."

—John P. Clark, professor of environmental studies and philosophy at Loyola
University, author of *The Impossible Community: Realizing Communitarian Anarchism*

"He escaped from custody two times, and although recaptured and imprisoned under horrific conditions, Russell has not relinquished his spirit of resistance. He is the 'Maroon.' If more young men emulated his lifestyle, the liberation of Black people would be very near at hand."

—Herman Ferguson, friend and comrade of Malcolm X in the Organization for
Afro-American Unity

"In describing human traits, it has been said that they come in two types: one, a thermostat, the other, a thermometer. These two objects look identical, and oftentimes confuse people. They can be identical in size and shape: equipped with mercury, allowing both to reflect temperatures, thus making it even harder to distinguish between them. The one big difference, however, is that the thermostat is equipped with a mechanism that not only allows it to reflect temperatures but also allows it to control temperatures. If I had to describe Russell 'Maroon' Shoatz (besides giving him his props for being a man of substance, courage, and principles) he—without doubt—would be a thermostat: Possessing the ability to not only reflect but control temperatures as well. This book, *Maroon the Implacable*, enforces and gives credence to this concept . . . a compelling read!"

—Robert Hillary King, prison justice activist, author of *From the Bottom of the Heap*,
and former prisoner in solitary confinement in the Angola prison in Louisiana

"Many people will be astonished to discover the perspective of Russell Maroon Shoatz when they finally read his work. Though he's been inside for forty of his sixty-nine years on earth, the problems he raises about the justice movement are amazingly up to date; for example, what to do about the organizations that claim to represent the movement but work overtime to control it? And he writes without jargon and even without rancor, though there is plenty to be bitter about. He asks not why we struggle—we should know that by now!—but how we organize to struggle. He is dedicated without being dogmatic and I know from experience that his mind is open and very keen for the views of others. Above all, he thinks organizationally, rather than in mangled, arrogant, academic rhetoric. He is always trying to work out what to do. Where he looks for answers is the only sensible place: not in ideas but in the historical experience of the grassroots. His 'Dragon and the Hydra' provokes and invites a dialogue with activists—a pleasure I for one look forward to."

—Selma James, author of *Sex, Race, and Class: The Perspective of Winning*, and coordinator of Global Women's Strike

"For twenty-seven years I visited four prisoners, one of whom was Russell Shoatz, who we called Maroon. From him I always got a lesson in politics that fortified me and made me understand just what was happening in our country and what I should be doing about it. Just before Mumia was moved out of SCI Greene, he was able to talk with Maroon for two whole days. He told me that those two glorious days were more important to him than all the years he was unable to communicate with Maroon. Maroon never lost his faith in the people, nor his ability to cut through the lies fed to us by the media. He trusted the truth of 'power to the people,' and it kept him focused and hopeful. His body was incarcerated but his mind soared. My mentor!"

—Frances Goldin, publisher of Mumia Abu-Jamal, Barbara Kingsolver, and Adrienne Rich

"Wow! I have been an organizer during the Great Slave Rebellion of the 1960s, to the urban bus riders of today, to the prison rebellions of tomorrow. Shoatz, combining George Jackson and W.E.B. Du Bois, is a fine historian behind bars who writes like a novelist. Whether the maroons were real (which they were) or superheroes (which they also were), the tale of free Blacks, runaway slaves, Amerindians, and working-class whites building a revolutionary army in the swamps is exciting stuff—and just the level of imagery and imagination we need to rebuild the revolution today."

—Eric Mann, author of *Comrade George: An Investigation into the Life, Political Thought, and Assassination of George Jackson*

"More than ever, I am convinced that the answers to human society's dilemmas will come from the margins of our society, from those people who have been excluded or who have chosen the path of exodus, and who are building alternatives in whatever isolated place they can make a stand. As Russell Maroon Shoatz shows us, even someone locked away in solitary confinement for decades, can utilize his imagination to show us 'ordinary citizens' the way forward. This exciting collection of writings explores paths of action for all of us: feminists, revolutionaries, community activists, ecosocialists, human rights campaigners. Extraordinary hidden histories of resistance combine with a vision of the future and a strategic challenge to every one of us to take action to change the world, wherever we are situated. To have your freedom denied to you is a terrible thing. To be held in solitary confinement is torture. No government should be allowed to abuse its citizens in this way, whatever their actions or beliefs. But not only should we support the call to Free Russell Maroon Shoatz—we should be proud to associate with his ideals and his activism, and we should take up the challenge he is setting us from his prison cell, to establish a unifying 'mosaic' movement based on the principle of intercommunal self-determination."

—Janet Cherry, South African activist and historian, former political detainee, and researcher for the South African Truth and Reconciliation Commission.

"With the little that I understand of English, I have been impressed to read of the life of Maroon and what he has written. I was also in prison, when the military tribunal that judged me didn't dare to sentence me to death, which some were calling for. In the various prisons where I was held, in Peru and Argentina, I was treated worse than ordinary prisoners, even though from afar, much better than what Maroon suffers. I respect his fortitude and am grateful for his historical teachings.

"In Latin America, the slaves that escaped were called 'cimarrones' and their organizations 'palenques,' 'quilombos,' 'cumbes,' 'rochelas,' 'ladeiras,' etc. Among the most famous was the 'Quilombo de Palmares' in Brazil. With a population of 15,000 rebel slaves, it lasted for almost the entire seventeenth century. The Portuguese intervened with 6,000 soldiers and it took two years to conquer it. The communitarian democratic organization that it had is not strange; after all this characteristic is maintained by indigenous people all over the world. Where there are indigenous people, the indigenous community exists. Another common characteristic of these peoples is their great love and respect for Mother Earth. There is also a characteristic that has been called 'Buen Vivir,' which consists in a happiness that does not come from a quantity of money, but from a satisfied life. A great solidarity exists, together with a respect for differences.

"These characteristics in their strongest form exist in the most 'savage' people, those who are least domesticated by civilization.

"Now that the ruling capitalist system, in its most ferocious form ever, attacks nature (and thus the human species), 'civilized' people are beginning to take note of the 'ecosocialist' consciousness of these populations, because they emerge with strength in defense of nature, and because (among these peoples) it is the society that makes decisions. This universality of indigenous consciousness shows us that it is not an ethnic characteristic, but that it was the form of human existence since the beginning.

"We have arrived at a crucial conjuncture: Either humanity recovers its primitive ethics or it extinguishes itself, crushed by the egotistical voracity of the great transnational corporations.

"To return to primitive ethics does not mean to disdain all of the positive contributions of civilization. It will be societies themselves that determine which contributions of civilization we can continue enjoying and in what form, without putting the subsistence of the species in danger.

"In terms of matriarchy I am in complete agreement; it will not mean the oppression of men. Also in this we will return to the original ethic, which fortunately we can still see in the Mosuo of the Chinese provinces of Yunnan and Sichuan, a society free of machismo.

"In the common struggle for 'a world where many worlds fit' (which is not only necessary but urgent, before the system exterminates the species), one of our fundamental tasks is to struggle in ever more widespread ways for the freedom of Maroon. We will bring together ever more voices to get him out of prison. *We can do it.*"

—Hugo Blanco, former political prisoner, leader of the Campesino
Confederation of Peru; editor of the journal *Lucha Indígena*

MAROON THE IMPLACABLE
THE COLLECTED WRITINGS OF RUSSELL MAROON SHOATZ

Edited by Fred Ho
and Quincy Saul

PMPRESS

Editors' Note

The essays in this volume represent the prison writings of Russell Maroon Shoatz up until the year of publication. Prior to this book, these essays were scattered far and wide across pamphlets, zines, and websites. We did our best to collect everything, but it is possible that some slipped through our net. In addition, Maroon is certain to keep writing, and readers are encouraged to follow the continuing evolution of his thought by reading his blog at www.russellmaroonshoats.blogspot.com.

These essays do not appear in exact chronological order but are presented thematically in a way that we hope will demonstrate the breadth and evolution of Maroon's thought.

In some of his writings, following the lead of many feminist activists and scholars, Maroon uses alternative spellings, for example "womyn" (singular) and "wimmin" (plural). These, along with some other alternative spellings ("amerikkka"/"Amerika," etc.) and some slang/colloquialisms which appear throughout the text, have been left unchanged from Maroon's original texts.

Maroon the Implacable: The Collected Writings of Russell Maroon Shoatz
Edited by Fred Ho and Quincy Saul

© PM Press 2013

PO Box 23912
Oakland, CA 94623
www.pmpress.org

Cover design by John Yates
Cover illustration by Carlito Rovira
Layout by Jonathan Rowland

ISBN: 978-1-60486-059-7
Library of Congress Control Number: 2012955003

10 9 8 7 6 5 4 3 2

Printed in the USA.

ACKNOWLEDGMENTS

We would like to express our love and gratitude to the following people and organizations, who all contributed and made possible this very important collection of writings by Russell Maroon Shoatz, which we believe will become an iconic text in the years to come:

Russell Shoatz III, Sharon Shoatz, and Theresa Shoatz; Kanya D'Almeida; Iyanna Jones and the Black Waxx crew; Carlito Rovira (for the beautiful painted cover image); Steve Bloom (for copyediting); Matt Meyer and Nozizwe Madlala-Routledge; Bret Grote; everyone in Scientific Soul Sessions and Ecosocialist Horizons; special gratitude to Lutie Spitzer (whose munificent generosity and matron support is unmatched); our friends at PM Press (Craig O'Hara and Ramsey Kanaan); all of the activists who've been supporting political prisoners in the United States; and to everyone who, over the years, has kept Maroon's writings alive and circulating, without whose efforts this book would not have been possible; but most of all to Maroon himself for his graciousness, inspiration, and leadership to all of us!

Note that a major new book, Maroon's autobiography (cowritten and edited by Kanya D'Almeida with Fred Ho), will be forthcoming in 2013. Everyone, please join the Campaign to Free Russell Maroon Shoatz and all U.S. political prisoners!

Fred Ho and Quincy Saul

CONTENTS

Foreword
To the Outer World from Within: The Ferocity to Be Free
Chuck D

These times we live in are dependent upon propaganda through technology to dumb the masses into them asses. Out of sight equals sadly out of mind. Actual rights and history itself are folded into a blur. Memory is selected by this mass control, and thus the contributions of the black community have been swept under a red, white, and blue rug. The prison industrial complex in the United States has been a millennial scar on the earth itself.

While visiting political prisoner Mumia Abu-Jamal some years back in Greene County, Pennsylvania, I got information and a special hello from Russell Maroon Shoatz, a founding member of the Black Unity Council in Philadelphia and former member of the Black Panther Party. I discovered him serving multiple life sentences for a 1970 charge. Knowing J. Edgar Hoover's COINTELPRO had devastated and destroyed black communities and organizations, I was drawn to figuring how I could use my influence to help, however I could.

Beyond and behind the bars, the words trickle to the outer world from within. Especially when they make sense. We live in a society where the words of rap and hip hop have become a one-stop-shop to step into the portal of prison hell, but the endorsement of big corporate industry is less likely to help America hear the logic of the inside. Thus, Russell Maroon Shoatz is one of the most brilliant thinkers on the subject of Black liberation, as well as freedom, justice, and social transformation for all who want a planet free of abuse, oppression, and exploitation toward humans and Earth itself.

As a writer and activist, Russell Maroon Shoatz has worked for all of us to bear witness. This book, written while being imprisoned for more than forty years, with over twenty consecutive years in solitary confinement in a Pennsylvania prison, makes it a high document of true freedom for the masses. This is the first collection of his writings and it will be studied and referred to in the years to come by all serious activists.

The artists and activists of Scientific Soul Sessions are tuned into his theory and practice: Shoatz takes note and takes the lead from the maroons' fugitive slave-community survivor ways, fighting those cowboy ways of the western days. His boldness is legendary because of his repeated escapes from maximum-security prison, a testament to his determination, discipline, dedication, and ferocity to be free.

The Occupy movement is a sign, as with the Arab Spring movements of last year. These political events show a way for disenfranchised communities to reconnect with the land and each other. Shoatz sees the decentralized structure of early maroon communities as a model for grassroots political organizing today. He is an inspiration to all those who propel themselves toward greater self-transformation—to seek to fortify their spirit and intellect by continuing to develop, to never cling to old formulations when they become outmoded—and is the embodiment of a contemporary maroon: escaping from the captivity of Empire and the Matrix, forever fighting for self-determined independence and self-sufficiency.

His work here in words is drawing the connections to the past and unraveling the madness of this present, for the future of many, in a consciousness of prefigurative examples. This is the kind of transformation we all need to make in order to fundamentally change this society.

Again PEace and resPEct
Chuck D
cofounder of Public Enemy

Chuckd@publicenemy.com
www.publicenemy.com
www.twitter.com/mrchuckd

Introduction
The Revolutionary Maroon
Quincy Saul

These writings are explosive, and that's why you haven't seen them before. They are written in a language anyone can understand, but which many may fear to. They meet you where you're at, but they won't leave you there. They point toward an escape from our society, and ultimately toward a revolution against it. They are maroon ideas, maroon histories, and programs for maroon futures.

The life and work of Russell Maroon Shoatz are not widely known, and it is no accident. If the power of ideas can be measured by the energy spent suppressing them, this book is dynamite. Shoatz has been incarcerated for more than half of his life; for over twenty years he has been in solitary confinement in one of the most physically and psychologically brutal manifestations of the prison system yet invented, the "control unit." This prison within a prison, designed specifically to break the resolve of political prisoners, has been successful in confining the man, but has failed to contain his spirit. It has survived the tortures of his captors and surged through their walls into your hands: "I am Maroon!"

Until now, Russell Maroon Shoatz has been known primarily to only a small circle of revolutionaries who have been involved in the Black liberation movement in the United States. A leader in these movements in Philadelphia at their height, he was arrested in the early 1970s. Subsequently, he became known for his dramatic escapes from maximum-security prisons. In 1977, he liberated himself from Huntingdon state prison and evaded a massive national search for twenty-seven days. Three years later, he escaped again for three days. These courageous acts earned him the name "Maroon," after the many thousands of escaped slaves who built autonomous communities of resistance throughout the Americas. By taking on this name, "a badge of pride and constant source of spiritual inspiration," he renews the maroon tradition and lives its evolution into modern times. As Jean-Paul Sartre introduced Frantz Fanon's *The Wretched of the Earth* to Europeans, I am inclined to introduce this book to today's readers on "the outside": "you must open this book and enter into it."[1]

---

1   (New York: Grove Press, 1963), 13.

Behind bars, Maroon has remained implacable. After his second recapture, he continued to organize in prison. In 1982, he was elected president of the Lifers Organization, an informal kind of union demanding basic necessities for inmates. Despite the legality of this organization and its activities, it was following this that the prison authorities moved him to solitary confinement in the control unit, where he has remained to this day. There, despite decades of treatment that is internationally recognized as constituting torture, he has kept his sanity and his resolve for the political vision and struggle that his name represents.[2]

But if he is known somewhat for his actions, he is understood far less as an intellectual, strategist, and theoretician. For decades he has navigated the high frontiers of social theory from the depths of solitary confinement. A uniquely insightful commentator in the realms of history and current events, Maroon is innovative everywhere he goes, from military strategy to matriarchy.

Throughout his writings, he combines a sharp theoretical vision and a close understanding of global history and current events with a popular style of writing, a style "designed to serve imprisoned members of our communities." He writes intensely about big ideas, with the combined sense of urgency and practicality that cannot fail to engage readers and set minds on fire. In translating complex historical and political lessons into immediately accessible language, Maroon's works are a real tool for revolutionaries who seek the way forward.

These writings are sure to ignite the best kind of controversy at many levels. His retelling, from an insider's perspective, of the Black liberation movement in the United States, is without a doubt going to raise eyebrows and challenge a few ("here I'll have to step on a lot of toes," he says in his most recent interview), even as they encourage and inspire many others. His self-critique of the "gangsters" and machismo of the movement to which he gave his life is unparalleled, going far beyond the psychological thriller

---

2   D'Almeida and Grote, "Solitary Confinement: Torture Chambers for Black Revolutionaries," *Al Jazeera*, August 2012. See also appendix 1.

of *Soul on Ice* by Eldridge Cleaver in its implications for a strategic way forward against patriarchy, even as it pays homage and respect to the generation of revolutionaries who sacrificed so much for the freedom struggle. His reflections on strategy and tactics provide fresh insights for aspiring revolutionaries: lessons to learn, errors to avoid, obstacles to overcome.

His analysis of the prison system provides a radical edge to the terrain of literature on this subject that by comparison seems soft. Not only was he writing about the prison industrial complex before it became the popular catch-phrase it is now, but he explains the complexities of the political economy that underlie it. It's not just about racism or Jim Crow; it's about the dynamics of global capitalism, the drug war, and imperialism. He talks about where it's headed, what the terrain of future struggle has to be, and what awaits if we do not heed his warning ("you ain't got nothing coming!").

This is not the plea of a single man. Maroon writes not just about himself but about the millions behind bars, the many tens of thousands in solitary confinement, and all the oppressed communities that have been swept into the "fool's paradise" of the prison industrial complex. Reading Maroon is an antidote to any mistaken notions that mass incarceration can be overthrown by a "new civil rights movement" (comfortable to liberals and retired dissidents), and returns to place revolution front and center as the only practical and ethical alternative to the system which keeps him and millions of others behind bars. Some of the more comfortable in the older generation might bristle, but young revolutionaries will recognize his no-nonsense attitude as the truth that can set us free. Maroon is hardcore.

Maroon excels in particular with his scholarship on the history of maroons and maroon communities. It is no coincidence that this history is not well known. "After all," writes Peter Lamborn Wilson, "history is written by those who believe in History. Yet the [maroons] are attempting to *escape* from History. . . . So, 'the pen is in the hand of the enemy.'"[3] Here,

---

3   James Koehnline, *Gone to Croatan: Origins of North American Dropout Culture* (New York: Autonomedia, 1993), 98.

for one of the very first if not *the* first time, the pen is with the maroons, in the hands of Maroon himself. Has a maroon ever written the history of maroons? His scholarship has huge implications. Not only does he illuminate a history that is unknown and kept hidden, but he draws out its lessons, which range from revolutionary theory and practice generally, to a path-breaking intervention into the debate on the organizational methods of our movements for self-determination. These are not only history lessons but also pose profound challenges for his twenty-first-century readers: "How do you measure up to the generations described here?" he asks in his history of the Underground Railroad. "Look in the mirror and ask yourself where you fit with this historical drama." In another essay, he concludes: "the choice is yours."

Given that Maroon has not had any physical contact with another human being in over twenty years, that he's been in solitary confinement for thirty years cumulatively, that he's approaching seventy years of age, and that he's in a dungeon specifically designed to break the spirit and soul, the fact that he's been able to accomplish everything I've described so far is nothing short of heroic. But this man doesn't rest on his laurels. He is always thinking "straight ahead" (as he signs his letters), beyond the boundaries of established theory and practice. He is always testing and developing ideas, and he is always sharing them, since he knows that "theory takes on a material force as soon as it is gripped by the masses."[4] This is him reaching out beyond bars, through the two thick and thin glass slits that are his only windows in a place where there is no darkness, toward the wide, colorful horizon of a world to be won.

Maroon frequently references *The Matrix*, a movie full of metaphors and allegories for anti-systemic struggles against capitalism and patriarchy. This book is a proverbial "red pill," which you swallow knowing there is no going back. Maroon is a modern-day Morpheus, a visionary captain in a physical and spiritual war, explaining to you how deep the rabbit hole goes, how to free your minds from the Matrix, and how to take on its Agents.

---

4   Karl Marx, *Contribution to the Critique of Hegel's Philosophy of Right* (1844).

On top of his scholarship on the history of maroons, his analysis of the prison system, and his deep understanding of the dynamics of the Black liberation movement, his thoughts continue to develop and change. This collection bears witness to the ongoing evolution of his ideas. In recent years, he has moved from being a feminist (already a leap ahead of many male revolutionaries of his generation) to promoting matriarchy, the original communism. Quoting from an armory of sophisticated eco-feminist theory, Maroon targets patriarchy front and center as the primary structure that must be overthrown in any project of human liberation, not as an afterthought but as an immediate imperative for all thought and action, necessary to save the species from the trauma of centuries of patriarchal domination. Beyond gender equality, Maroon points toward an even deeper radicalism of revolutionary motherhood, which he finds embodied in the writings of many radical feminist scholars: "Everyone needs to look into their ideas and programs. . . . Get a hold of their writings and let them show you how deep the rabbit hole goes."

Maroon is also ahead of the game when it comes to understanding the current ecological crisis. Most recently, he has begun to advocate for ecosocialism, the next stage in the evolution of anti-capitalism. But his head isn't in the clouds. He has specific ideas of how to implement these theories—by organizing oppressed communities around food security, and overcoming gangster culture with urban gardening projects to guide youth toward a self-reliant ecological future. In all this, he references everything from popular movies to histories of international liberation struggles, and uses this knowledge to reflect on current events such as the Arab Spring and the Occupy Wall Street movement. Most recently, he has been discoursing with a new group based out of New York City but with national membership called "Scientific Soul Sessions," which he understands as working to embody the future of revolutionary, ecosocialist, matriarchal and prefigurative thought and action in the twenty-first century (see appendix 2).

Is there a theme that connects the immense breadth of thought that this unique historic figure has put together? For decades, these essays have been scattered around the world in zines, pamphlets, and websites. Perhaps now that we can see them all in one place for the first time, we can think of some answers. His thought is very wide ranging, and he quotes from the ancients as well as from his contemporaries. But if his reading is wide and eclectic, his thought as a whole is very coherent. What holds it together?

Without a doubt, the underlying themes will include the struggle for justice and dignity, for self-determination, against oppression and exploitation, and for revolution. But somehow this does not seem specific enough. What kind of revolutionary is Maroon? If we search for a historical tradition into which his revolutionary thought fits, it is less the history of class struggle (though he is certainly no foreigner to this struggle, and indeed has been a leader in it) than the history of another, even more ancient revolutionary tradition: *Exodus*.

If our understanding of exodus as a revolutionary project is confined to the ancient stories of the Bible, this is only because the writers of history have been on the side of the Pharaohs. In fact, the history of exodus pervades Western civilization since its beginnings. The history of the origin of capitalism in Europe is also the history of those who resisted it, who sought to escape and overturn it, and who very often followed the leadership of peoples outside European civilization. From the 1500s through the 1800s, as one scholar has chronicled, thousands of European "renegades" moved to North Africa and converted to Islam. "Not only had they 'betrayed Our Lord,'" Wilson writes, "they had gone even farther and joined the *jihad* itself," by joining three centuries of undefeated piracy—where the pirate "was first and foremost the enemy of his own civilization."[5] In this same period we find multiethnic maroon communities of Africans, Europeans, and native North and South Americans with their own languages, customs, and trades throughout all of the Americas; exiles from four continents uniting across barriers of race and culture in

5   Peter Lamborn Wilson, *Pirate Utopias: Moorish Corsairs and European Renegadoes* (New York: Autonomedia, 2003), 12, 22.

a common exodus from Western civilization. Holding out for hundreds of years against the most highly trained and equipped European armies, "their efforts cannot be matched in world history," Maroon writes.

These maroons were not just escaping—this was a global revolutionary movement! The maroon communities throughout the Americas were striking at the heart of the growing imperialist world-system. "The slavery of the Blacks," wrote Karl Marx, "in Suriname, in Brazil, in the southern regions of North America . . . is as much the pivot around which our present-day industrialism turns as are machinery, credit, etc."[6] By uniting elements of the European working classes—female and male—with Africans and the indigenous populations of the Americas, the maroon communities were a planetary vanguard, centuries ahead of any organization of the industrial proletariat in making a real international revolution. Even if this movement was not always conscious of itself as such, its powerful, sustained, and widespread trajectory cannot be argued.

That this is not more widely recognized may be in part because white supremacy is still undefeated even on the left. But it is also because of ignorance—this history is simply not known. And this is no accident: the network of maroon communities in the Americas was arguably the most profound existential threat that the protocapitalist world system ever faced. The maroon communities not only offered the possibility of freedom and self-determination to enslaved Africans, but also a basis on which to unite with indigenous peoples against the invaders. Most threatening of all, they presented a living and welcoming alternative to the exploited and oppressed underclass of European colonial societies. Settlers and slavers knew this and were merciless in their endless attempts to destroy them. Hunted over centuries, the maroons have also been hunted out of history. Here again, Maroon is the antidote. Read this book and pass it on!

But he does not understand the maroons uncritically. In his writings, Maroon distinguishes between the "treaty maroons" and the "fighting

---

6   Karl Marx, "Letter to Pavel Vasilyevich Annenkov," December 28, 1846.

maroons"—between those maroons who made shameful treaties with colonizers and slave-traders, and those maroons who refused all compromise to actively fight for their autonomy and self-determination. In her book *The Maroons of Jamaica*, which Maroon cites in this volume, Mavis Campbell writes that, due to the maroons' complex history of not only resistance but also collaboration and betrayal, "we cannot see them as true revolutionaries or even as reformers."[7] The Marxist writer Eugene Genovese writes in his book *From Rebellion to Revolution* that the maroons should be understood in a "restorationist or isolationist, rather than a revolutionary context."[8] While the actions of the maroons may have had revolutionary potential, Campbell argues that they "did not provide an agenda, any sustained organizational structure, a program, and, perhaps, most important, an ideology."[9]

Here, Maroon upholds and carries on the maroon tradition, with a crucial, qualitative twist: he is not a treaty maroon content with only his personal freedom, nor only a fighting maroon content with self-determination, but a *revolutionary maroon*: determined to overturn this patriarchal capitalist system once and for all. He provides what was previously missing: a clear vision of an agenda, an organizational structure, a program, and an ideology; the means by which an international maroon movement can organize and become conscious of itself as revolutionary. His is a project of exodus that intends to topple pyramids.

The maroons of earlier centuries sought to challenge and escape from capitalism when it was first consolidating itself as a global system. At the dawn of the twenty-first century we find ourselves now at the other end of this history. With the triumph of "globalization," there are no longer any mountains or swamps to escape to, as every corner of the world falls prey to the laws of market values and surveillance states. As Subcomandante Marcos of the Zapatista Army of National Liberation has said, "there

---

7   (Trenton, NJ: Africa World Press, 1990), 13.
8   (New York: Vintage Books, 1981), 52–53.
9   Campbell, *Maroons*, 250.

are no seats outside the ring." This system is now pushing its absolute limits, and the breaking of these limits can be seen and felt in economic crises, in mass extinctions, in brutal wars for scarce resources, and in the destabilization of the global climate. What, then, is the relevance of the maroon vision in this day and age? "Rest easy, fighting maroons," he writes. "There are many now and who will come in the future who will derive inspiration from your valorous examples—inspiration that will arm their spirits to fight the good fight . . . *till victory or death!*"

In these end times, the maroon program is more relevant than ever! More than ever, we must study maroon ideas and maroon histories, as the keys to the deadlock holding revolution hostage in the twenty-first century. Many generations of revolutionaries believed that a better world would emerge naturally from this system—that capitalism would produce its own gravediggers, and that we would all be better off than before, with the fruits of Babylon now in revolutionary hands. Now it is becoming clearer than ever that the only future for humanity and the planet is in a revolutionary *exodus* from the capitalist system. As Bob Marley had the courage to say, "Babylon ain't got no fruits."

We are waking up. In the conclusion to their blockbuster trilogy on political theory, radical intellectuals Antonio Negri and Michael Hardt write that "this project of exodus is the primary form class struggle takes today" and that "exodus is more powerful than frontal assault."[10] While these academics are beginning to comprehend the full implications, Maroon is on the front lines. He is living it and sharing it, outlining the theoretical, historical, and practical possibilities for the world to follow. He inherits an ancient tradition, lives it, evolves it, and shows you why and how. This is one of those few books that, if read seriously, followed through to its conclusions, and put into practice, could help save us all, bodies and souls. Time's a-wasting! *Straight ahead!*

Colombo-Harlem, 2012

---

10   Commonwealth (Cambridge, MA: Harvard University Press, 2009), 164 and 368.

Prelude
Fire in the Hole!
Why Russell Maroon Shoatz Is Important to Creative Revolutionaries!
Fred Ho

n the early 1990s, while I was doing support work for the now-renowned U.S. political prisoner Mumia Abu-Jamal, at a time when it was very challenging work to get Mumia's name and case as widely known as it is today, I made contact and did support work for many other U.S. political prisoners, most of whom remain virtually anonymous to the wider public and to most of the "social change" activists of then and now.

One of those prisoners really made an impact upon me: Russell Maroon Shoatz. At first, it was the sheer brilliance of his writings (the classic "Black Fighting Formations," for example, included in this collection) along with the legendary fact of his *two* incredible jailbreaks from maximum-security prisons that earned him the moniker of "Maroon." One could say that the latter fact—of his escaping and avoidance of capture—exemplified the kind of appeal to "macho men" (what U.S. military special forces are trained to do in SERE programs—Survive, Escape, Resist, and Evade). In the early 1990s, I still had this inside of me, though the theory and practice of matriarchy had just started to enter my consciousness and I had begun a personal/political transformation.

But as Maroon and I began our now more-than-two-decades of epistolary exchanges, what most impressed me was that we both were transforming each other, in a mutual symbiotic parallel transformation, toward many of the ideas that are taking root in the theoretical and practical work of an embryonic revolutionary organization called Scientific Soul Sessions (SSS: www.scientificsoulsessions.com).

What were these changes?

First, the theory and practice of matriarchy. While locked in prison, Maroon had begun an extensive self-critical examination of both himself and his movement. More than anyone from the "roaring Sixties," Maroon has not only endeavored to sum up the mistakes and flaws of the revolutionary movement of the 1960s and early 1970s, specifically the Black liberation movement of which he was a part, but made a deep self-criticism of his role in these errors and flaws, both theoretical and behavioral. At first, revolutionary feminism (whether it be labeled "radical feminism" or "socialist feminism") ignited the spark as the entire theory of social change had to be interrogated beyond simply improvements to "the woman question." Ironically, Engels's classic work *The Origin of the Family, Private Property, and the State* provided the foundational premises. But so much of the subsequent movements—as amply demonstrated in the subsequent interpretation of Marxism, Marxism-Leninism, Trotskyism, Maoism, and whatever "ism-version" you want to cite—have overlooked, ignored, or discarded the fact that the first and longest class struggle has been the overthrow of women.

Though the Marxist classics never discussed "patriarchy" (a concept that the women's movement and feminist theory has considerably advanced and propagated), clearly "the woman question" could not be mechanically "solved" by a socialist revolution that continued to be patriarchal, as has been the case everywhere (albeit in most cases with considerable strides made in the advancement of rights afforded to women by the socialist cause).

Maroon was looking at the internal causes of why the movement could not attain its revolutionary promise, and how his own sexism and machismo, and that of so many others, harmed and poisoned the revolutionary cause—no matter how dedicated, well-intentioned, committed, and militant.

I, on the other hand, was since my early childhood continually confronted with the experience of domestic violence. Two major forms of violence, experienced at my youngest age, politicized me. Initially, it was racist violence, which set the direction for my development since age three (a story told elsewhere in my various writings). But growing up with patriarchal domestic violence was "avoided" and "put on the back burner" until the early 1990s, when the revolutionary movement I was a part of—namely, the League of Revolutionary Struggle (Marxist-Leninist)—imploded, turned reformist, and quickly dissolved due to its reformist irrelevance. After the end of the League (and good riddance, as now I believe all the movements, no matter what glory we want to confer upon them or they deservingly achieved, had to go because they were fraught with an incorrect and insufficient revolutionary theory, which inevitably results in a problematic practice and collapse), I was free and unshackled from the doctrinaire hegemony exercised by the League's leadership (willingly accepted by its membership as part of the reciprocity of cult of personality and its attendant lemming syndrome). I was also wondering if I should seek heterosexual marriage and the nuclear family as personal goals, which never seemed to be my nature.

So as sons are not to reproduce their fathers, I was introduced to the theory of matriarchy. Much of this newly arrived freedom allowed me to engage with political tendencies that we in the former League had written off (such as anarchists), and I joined a motley collection of individuals that would become ORSSASM (the Organization of Revolutionary Socialist Sisters and Some Men).

ORSSASM included members of the then-recently-collapsed Love and Rage Collective in NYC, and individuals from Barbara Smith's valiant effort to organize RSOC (Revolutionary Sisters of Color). It also included a loose assortment of Marxist-Leninists, some from previous organizations (like myself) and some who had self-developed, admirably so, from the City University of New York campus struggles of the early 1990s; many were young independent communists, mostly of Black, Dominican, Puerto Rican, and Asian backgrounds.

One of our best projects was the Sheroes/Womyn Warriors calendar, which was first published in 1998 (developed from 1995 to 1997) by Autonomedia, an anarchist press. I sent Maroon the calendars and regularly shared with him all of my thinking on matriarchy during this time.

I was personally driven to answer a question deeply and profoundly rooted to my personal background: how can violence against women end? The answer: only when women defend themselves by any means necessary. With that starting premise, the investigation, study, theorizing, and practical transformation to realize matriarchy began.

For Maroon, the struggle to exorcize his machismo has included tenacious struggle with his fellow inmates (a very macho lot indeed!) and with other male political prisoners (you can surmise the names) and with the movement as a whole (much of which remains clueless about the importance of matriarchy).

Matriarchy goes beyond any form of feminism because it doesn't accept gender (and therefore any social assignation of value or power or status differential accorded to sex). It is the ultimate redistributive social justice and it demands the resocialization of men to become matriarchal mothers! (Go the SSS website for the study on revolutionary matriarchy.)

Maroon is a matriarchal revolutionary man. What does this mean? Since he's been in solitary confinement and has little contact with other human beings, the main focus for his transformation has been to eliminate his machismo. But more than that, he has striven to center his political vision on matriarchy as the ultimate revolutionary goal, marking the end of patriarchy, the state as an instrument of male violence, rejection of macho militancy, and the development of a matriarchal political strategy for revolution that is mother-centric. These ideas are discussed in this watershed collection. In a soon-to-be-completed autobiography (edited by Kanya D'Almeida), the details of his internal struggle to eliminate machismo, to right the wrongs he has committed, will be both graphic and poignant.

Second, Maroon has shifted from the classic "seizure of state power" revolutionary endgame to a clear and marked emphasis on *prefiguration*. This is the process of commoning, of both resisting the enclosures of capitalism and patriarchy as well as creating immediate forms and relations in which revolutionary processes are actualized. He discusses food security and sovereignty, not from the conventional activist orientations toward policy changes, protest, and forcing governmental and corporate concessions à la the pressure campaigns of nongovernmental organizations (nonprofits), but rather with an emphasis upon organizing on-the-ground liberation of space, innovating new, transformative processes, and recommoning people's souls.

Third, he offers us a condemnatory and scathing rebuke of authoritarian and hierarchal vanguardism—though Maroon makes a distinction between leadership and discipline, both critically necessary, and the centralized, top-down commandist structures and culture in which a self-righteous (and self-proclaimed) vanguard substitutes itself as the be-all and end-all.

Lastly, we have Maroon's latent indigenous-centrism. The very histori-cal examples of maroon communities (or liberated base-areas) that he has extensively studied and advocates for present-day application (from community food gardens to decentralized revolutionary organization-building) are all drawn from the first hybridized maroon societies in the Americas, mostly of native peoples and escaped Africans. These communities were examples of subsistence-based economies instead of the ecocidal and empire-building capitalist economies dominated by relations of exchange (or the market). They featured genuine equality without gender divisions and differentials of power and authority, and were self-sustaining and regenerative. They were strongest when in alli-ance with other such communities without becoming centralized, weakest when they adopted and mimicked their enemy's structure (centralism as putatively more powerful).

In 2010, I, along with about ten others, formed the new revolutionary group called Scientific Soul Sessions (see appendix 2). As I near the end of my life from advanced metastatic cancer, Maroon asked me, "Fred, how will SSS continue after your death?" I did not have an answer for him at the time. But now, I have: when you are free, Maroon, you'll make sure SSS continues its creativity and develops new revolutionary leaders!

August 2012

About These Writings
Author's Note
Russell Maroon Shoatz
(2012)

All prisons are harsh, demeaning, and brutal institutions. There are no privileges allowed to their captives that can make that reality go away. To lose one's freedom is a fate second only to losing one's life. That's why all contemporary societies use prison as the ultimate punishment—short of death. But history records the stories of multitudes who risked their lives to obtain or regain their freedom.

Since being imprisoned over forty years ago, I have been forced to spend over thirty of those years in "the hole," which is a separate part of each prison designed to either punish prisoners for breaking rules, or to further incapacitate them—even if that means to kill them by one means or another. Thus, these prison holes are the worst punishment the state can dish out—short of death. "Message from a Death Camp" and "Death by Regulation" included in these writings speak to that.

Among the main survival mechanisms we prisoners developed in the holes we've been forced to occupy have been our efforts to share our thoughts, ideas, and experiences. This served to mitigate our isolation, provide a measure of social contact, self-education, and rehabilitation (where needed)—all of which served to defeat our captors' efforts to punish, torture, and/or destroy us by placing us in a *prison within a prison*.

The primary tools we developed were rigorous and challenging seminars, agreed upon by the participants and constructed from available knowledge, or that acquired from painstaking research and hard-to-come-by reading material. These seminars were generally held six or seven days per week, with either the direct participation or cooperation of the overwhelming majority of the prisoners in the holes I was in up until 1994–1995.

We had no access to either typewriters or computers so we had to do it "the old-fashioned way," namely by reading, note-taking, debating, and finally sharing our theses with the other prisoners (and more than a few prison guards—once they got over the idea that we prisoners could not intelligently interact with them). Unfortunately, most of that effort has not been recorded, due mainly to our captors' strategy designed to periodically strip us of most of our reading and of written material—leaving us to the ravages of commercial TV and radio, if that!

Nor did we have much outside support from the street community or organizations. They were either exhausted from their years of aiding prisoners' struggles, or were up to their necks in battles with the state trying to save the lives of prisoners who were sentenced to die.

Over time, the prisons received a huge amount of funding to build newer high-tech isolation and torture holes they dubbed "control units." These *hellholes* made it almost impossible for us to continue holding our seminars!

Thankfully, around the same time, we were able to gain the aid of a few small collectives of younger activists, and a still-fighting old-timer or two, who took on the task of transcribing our writings, putting them in pamphlets (zines), and making them available—free of charge—through the mail.

Alas, even that method became extremely hard to maintain once our captors learned about it. Our captors were bent on torturing us into submitting to their reactionary regime (sort of like a modern-day inquisition), or, failing that, either keeping us "out of circulation" or killing us—one way or another. Nowadays they go as far as to deny us access *to our own published writings.*

Nonetheless, Scientific Soul Sessions (SSS) has been able to locate a number of my own essays. These were originally written in an effort to continue with those prison seminars, along with other related writings from that period and subsequent to it. They are here being offered to a wider readership.

Keep in mind that the bulk of this writing was designed to serve imprisoned members of our communities. If you feel that there is something worthwhile expressed in this collection, then you should also recognize that the state is determined to repress these ideas and this education with your tax dollars!

My comrades in SSS who have taken the initiative to have these writings published suggested they be called *Revolutionary Maroon: The*

Collected Prison Writings of Russell Maroon Shoatz. This title would have opened the door for my prison torturers to increase their decades-long effort to muzzle or destroy me altogether.

By all international standards and laws, my over forty years of captivity in the prisons and jails of the United States, and the charges that were leveled to effect this incarceration, will confirm the fact that I am a *political prisoner.* Yet, as a warden of the first U.S. prison control unit, set up by the government at Marion, Illinois, stated in open court, "control units are designed to control [and suppress] revolutionary tendencies in the country." And for those who are not familiar with what control units are, just let me say they are prisons within prisons, an archipelago from one end of the United States to the other. These *torture camps* have been condemned by the United Nations representative on torture, but remain in place because they are said to hold "the worst of the worst!" They are places every bit as brutal and dehumanizing as the U.S.-run prison at Abu Ghraib, Iraq, was shown to be.

In fact, the U.S. soldier, Charles Granier—who was convicted and imprisoned after the infamous photos showing him torturing prisoners in Iraq were made public—practiced such barbarities prior to being deployed in Iraq as a prison guard in the same control unit where I am now held captive.

These control units are not the Mel Gibson *Braveheart* movie–type set-ups. The "technicians" who run these places have developed "clean torture" techniques that are primarily designed to break your mind, to break your will to resist, to co-opt you as a willing pawn in their war to pacify and exploit you for the service of capital. They are designed to keep you controlled for your entire sentence, or until you are dead.

In my over forty years as a political prisoner, I've been forced to spend over thirty of those years in control units in numerous prisons. I have been in such units for the last twenty-one years of this stretch. I'm serving two "natural" life sentences and twenty-five more years "after that" (???). Still, I have *no intention* of ever allowing myself to be "domesticated" (read: co-opted). The originally suggested title, "Revolutionary Maroon" would only serve to further alert my captors that they must "double-down" (as the reactionaries are fond of saying) in their efforts to destroy my resistance.

To get a little breathing room, and a chance to share some of my thoughts and ideas in my writings, I suggesting instead that SSS call this book *Maroon the Implacable: The Collected Writings of Russell Maroon Shoatz*. I'm indebted to the original Black Panther Party and Sanyika Shakur, a.k.a. Cody Scott (Monster Cody), for inspiring me to suggest that title.

The Black Panther Party early on taught that in the struggle against racism, domestic colonialism, capital, and imperialism, "the Implacables would remain true to the cause." The Implacables were those who proved incapable of being appeased, significantly changed or mitigated in their struggle for liberation from oppression and exploitation—though positive changes are accepted and encouraged!

Indeed, I'm sure the prison captors place me in that category, although they strive to hide their crimes and fears by reversing the reality and labeling me as the "worst of the worst."

Regarding Sanyika Shakur: in the 1990s, a publication called *This Just In* tried to keep political prisoners in the United States informed of each other's struggles. I was a subscriber and read about Sanyika being placed in a notorious control unit at Pelican Bay, California. Sanyika is a victim of this dysfunctional socioeconomic system engendered by centuries of capitalist exploitation and racial discrimination, which produced the gang culture in which he grew up. Born Cody Scott, his misguided efforts to find a way forward led him to evolve into a gang member so ruthless and brutal that his peers named him "Monster Cody." All too predictably, by the 1990s he had landed in one of the most dehumanizing control units ever built.

Although at that time I had not yet corresponded with him, the younger prisoners in my control unit swore by the book Sanyika had penned while at Pelican Bay. It was called *Monster: The Autobiography of an L.A. Gang Member*. In addition to prisoners, the book had also been well received by the wider public. Having an earlier background in gang culture, I was curious to learn how his book compared to all of my misguided steps as a youth.

As I was requesting information on how to order this book, coincidentally, an update on my situation was published in *This Just In* and, to my surprise, I was addressed as "Maroon the Implacable" by Sanyika Shakur himself! He inquired about my health and general well-being, then provided me with a way to obtain a free copy of his book.

Only after receiving and reading his book did I understand that Sanyika had entered prison as Monster Cody, but while there, like Malcolm X and many others, he painstakingly began the process of reforming himself, dropping the Monster Cody moniker and adopting Sanyika Shakur. And to my utter surprise, he had been helped along by some of my Black Panther Party–inspired writings!

So here we are. This title, *Maroon the Implacable*, does not raise as many red flags. The word "implacable" will not be logged into the databases of the technicians like the word "revolutionary," not yet anyway.

During the period I've been active in the politics of social change, I have changed in my ways, something the writings in this collection will show. I'll leave it to the reader to determine how to label me, and, more importantly, discover whether these writings can be useful in the struggle to better our existence.

Straight Ahead!

Russell Maroon Shoatz
AF-3855
175 Progress Drive
Waynesburg, PA 15370 U.S.A.

I Am Maroon!
(1995)

The wild Maroons, impregnable and free,
Among the mountain-holds of liberty,
Sudden as lightning darted on their foe,
Seen like the flash, remembered like the blow.[1]

Many have asked me why I call myself "Maroon." Most have never heard of a name like this but suspect that it has some meaning outside of a color associated with the dark reds. I had adopted the name Harun Abdul Ra'uf in 1972. In 1977, I escaped from the State Prison in Huntingdon, Pennsylvania. I lived off the land for twenty-seven days while trying to evade scores of state police, prison personnel, FBI agents, and local police and volunteers. I had cause to reflect on and gain courage from all of the freedom fighters I'd read about and this did much to guide and reinforce my determination to succeed.

However, I was recaptured and on my return to prison, a friend mentioned that he had kept up with the search through the press. After a while he said, "They were chasing you like a maroon!" "Harun" (Ha-roon) sounds like "maroon" and he started calling me "Maroon." From that time on the nickname stuck.

I knew very little about the maroons at that time. I certainly did not know that their hundreds of years of struggle totally annihilate the commonly held view that our Afrikan ancestors (by and large) did not fight tenaciously, heroically, and brilliantly against their slave owners!

Historically, "maroon" came to be used as a generic term for slaves who became fugitives from their owners in North and South America and the Caribbean Islands. You have (what I consider) two types of maroons: "treaty maroons" and "fighting maroons." Treaty maroons are those who, after militarily defeating the Spanish in Mexico, the Dutch in Suriname (South America), and the British in Jamaica, succumbed to collaborating with their former enemies—similar to the way many later North American "reservation" Indian tribes did, such as those who helped kill

---

1   Campbell, *Maroons*, 44.

Chief Sitting Bull and Crazy Horse, or subsequently ran Geronimo to ground, who had fought against other Native Americans for either the French or British in their ongoing struggle to control the Americas.

The treaty maroons fell victim to their own lack of a comprehensive "pan-African" world-view, which caused them to settle for their own freedom from slavery, not recognizing that until all Africans were free, all remained in peril from those bent on subjugating them.

The "fighting maroons" were fugitive slaves "of iron will, nurtured in survival tactics; cruel, courageous, resourceful and scornful of danger."[2] Fighting maroons began their struggles from the first years of landing in the Americas. They had established the "Republic of the Palmares" in northern Brazil as early as 1595. For two hundred or more years, fighting maroons used and perfected guerrilla warfare to defeat the best armies that the European powers could field against them.

Theirs was a struggle that was no less than heroic! They broke their shackles; took to the woods or swamps or mountains; found, took, or grew their own provisions while simultaneously fighting and defeating their former slave masters. The efforts of these men, women and children cannot be matched in world history. Their struggle was only eclipsed by that of revolutionary Haiti (1791–1804). There, the revolutionary slaves and their maroon allies had a clearer idea of how to consolidate and extend the gains they had won on the battlefield.

Among this group of illustrious fighters, a few names stand out for honorable mention:

The legendary "Granny Nanny" of eighteenth-century Jamaica is variously recognized as a female guerrilla leader, guerrilla spiritual leader (*Obia* or *Obeah*), a freedom fighter who has a town named in her honor in the maroons' "liberated territory." There may have been more than one Nanny (of note). At this time in Jamaica, Nanny is looked upon as a national hero.

Zumbi dos Palmares and his maroon community of sixteenth- and seventeenth-century Brazil deserve special praise. The republic of the

---

2   Ibid., 94.

Palmares was forged and maintained for over a century by African slaves and their allies among the Indians and anti-colonial whites bent on having their freedom or death! From 1595 to 1659, through twenty-seven major wars with the Dutch and Portuguese colonialists, the maroons maintained their liberty. Against all odds, they never gave in, preferring death in battle or suicide to a life in slavery. To this day, November 20 is commemorated in Brazil to honor Zumbi dos Palmares.

The redoubtable Makandal of prerevolutionary Haiti is recognized as spending ten years of his maroon experience organizing an island-wide conspiracy, designed to free all of the island's slaves. Descending on the slave owners' plantations and towns, he held their lives and property in the balance while he recruited, organized, and trained a secret cadre for the planned uprising. He was betrayed before he could launch the revolt.

His efforts were not in vain. Two of those who followed, Jean-François and Biassou, carried their own, and other maroon communities into the front ranks of the Haitian revolution (1791–1804). Both of these fighters and their comrades were among the first leaders, even before Toussaint L'Ouverture, Dessalines, and Henri Christophe. They provided heroic and invaluable service to the Haitian people's determination to be free.

There were "fighting maroons" throughout South and Central America in countries like Panama, Venezuela, Colombia, Guyana, Suriname, and Brazil. For hundreds of years, they honed their fighting skills to the point where they were unbeatable on the battlefield!

It is certain that maroon communities existed in what is now the United States. However, most scholars either are unaware of them or feel that it's not worth mentioning. Herbert Aptheker is a rare exception with his *American Negro Slave Revolts* and a number of other writings on the subject. The "African-centric" scholars have been aware of this part of history and have produced some work on the subject, but not much has been circulated to date.

I had in the past gained inspiration from reading about the intrepid Native American fighters and their struggles and exploits against the people who were trying to take their land and oppress them in the early centuries of the European arrival. The lives of individuals like Mangas Coloradas, Victorio, Nana, Geronimo and the exploits of the Apache, Sioux, Modoc, and various other tribes gave guidance to my thinking. Their unbending efforts on behalf of their people always inspired me to dig down deeper within myself for strength and courage. I was also greatly encouraged, of course, by the sheer tenacity and bravery of Harriet Tubman while admiring all of those African slaves who revolted against slavery, whether it was Nat Turner, Denmark Vesey, Gabriel Prosser, Will the Executioner, or the lesser-known men and women. I was, however, duped by the Eurocentric-dominated sources of information (books, movies, TV, etc.) into thinking that the most tenacious fighters against early amerikkkan settlers and slave owners were non-Africans.

The maroons' accomplishments are unequaled in the historic annals of "slave" vs. "slave owners" whether among the Greeks, Persians, or even the great Spartacus-led rebellion against the Roman Empire. The maroons are alone in defeating their owners militarily before all parties sat down to sign treaties that allowed them to coexist in the same society as free individuals. Haiti, as mentioned, went a step further by totally suppressing or expelling the former slave owners from the society.

As I gradually began to learn about the maroons, I became inspired by these audacious fighters and the nickname "Maroon" became a badge of pride and a constant source of spiritual inspiration. I would later become sick at heart to learn of the shortcomings of a number of "treaty maroons." Their collaboration with their former owners and downright betrayal of other Africans were disgusting! My study of history also indicated similar betrayals experienced among their "comrades-in-arms"—the Apaches, Nez Percé, Sioux, and other Native American fighters. This does not excuse the "treaty maroons." It does, however, give one pause before dismissing the unbelievable "turnaround" without a thorough analysis, an attempt to learn the causes of this phenomenal turn of events between victorious slaves and beaten slave owners. These "treaties" enabled the enemy to gain through diplomacy far more than they could ever have hoped to gain through warfare. They lost the war, but won the peace. Nonetheless, the history of the maroons still remains glorious and heroic by any standard! It cannot be judged by the faults of those who were "tricked" out of the gains the fighters made over hundreds of years. Those were hundreds of years of liberty from slavery. No matter how painful it was to keep that liberty, it cannot equal the humiliation, degradation, and soul-killing experience of remaining enslaved.

Just as I still have profound respect for Geronimo, Victorio, Nana, Sitting Bull, Crazy Horse, and the other tenacious fighters, and I do not hold against these fighters the short-sighted collaborationist betrayals by Cochise, Chief Joseph, or Little Big Man, I cannot apply any other standard to the maroons!

Rest easy, fighting maroons. There are many now and to come who will derive inspiration from your valorous examples—inspiration that will "arm their spirits" to fight the good fight . . . *till victory or death!!!*

Message from a Death Camp
(1997)

There is a war going on in America.

Normally we can't see it, because our enemies have laid down a heavy smokescreen to maneuver behind. Our enemies have become so skilled at these maneuvers that at times they even tell us about this war. Yet even then their deception is working to put us to sleep—all the better to attack us. They call it a "war on poverty," a "war on crime," a "war on drugs," or a "war on childhood disease," and tomorrow they will make up another deceptive title to maneuver behind. Hide they must, because our enemies fear the day when we wake up to the fact that hidden in all of this rhetoric is an impoverished spirit which is alienated from life, fearful of difference, greedy, and confused.

We are involved in a "cultural war" which has many fronts: political, economic, social, moral, and ethical. However, it's the ideas, behavior, and institutions of America—in their many forms—that are being fought over. If you do not recognize this fact, then your soul will be stolen by our enemy and used to fuel their machine. They are death-dealers and death-merchants, and they destroy anyone who threatens to slow down or expose their mindless accumulation of wealth, power, and control. It makes no difference whether you are the innocent, the young, or the elderly. If you cannot add to their accumulation of power, they will grind you to dust! Still more, they will vilify, mock, and otherwise distort who you are to the end of getting everyone on their side.

They will use their monstrous media apparatus and their agencies of government—soldiers in police uniforms, judges, and prisons—to help do the dirty deed. They will even use you against yourself or some other "target" if you're not constantly vigilant, watching for their maneuvers and tricks.

They are always maneuvering under the cover of a catchy slogan like "welfare to workfare," which really means "take them off our dole and put them in a hole." We were warned that the so-called "war on drugs" was really a nickname for a stepped up war on Black youth. The tens of thousands of young Blacks in the federal and state prisons show this was all too true!

There is virtually no end to the examples of this "real war" if we only just look! But we are bombarded by the enemy so often that most of us have become shell-shocked. For all too many of us, it's just a matter of survival on a day-to-day basis. If our enemy sets off a firecracker, we dive into our bunkers and wait until the "shelling" is over.

I cannot think of a better way to seal our own fate. Those of us who recognize that our enemy is trying to destroy our spirit of resistance, our spirit of life, and most of all our human soul, realize that we must resist, that we must get others to resist, and that we must destroy this culture of death.

I'm writing these words from a prison. Don't get bent out of shape about that, because I'm actually freer than many of you. I am no less community-minded, moral, or ethical. You see, everyone in prison ain't a "bad guy." In fact, you can be put in prison for refusing to be a bad guy— that is, refusing to go along with the real bad guys: the greedy billionaires, lying politicians, and visionless social workers.

I have a warning that I need to relay to you: I have to let you know that you have to get up out of your bunkers and do something about it before it gets worse. I'm being housed in a "death camp." I mean that literally. It's going to be hard for most of you to take that seriously enough, because of who I am and where I'm at and the fact that our enemy has laid down so much smoke about crime and prison that most of you are blinded.

Our enemy calls this place "State Correctional Institution at Greene," or "SCI Greene" for short. It's located in Greene County of Waynesburg, PA. That's so far from Philly that if you ride past it you end up in Morgantown, West Virginia, before you can find a new station on your car radio. I say that SCIG stands for "State Concentration and Internment Ground." That's because there is nothing resembling "correction" that goes on for most of these prisoners. Like the Nazi concentration camps, this is a death camp for sure!

Our Brother Mumia Abu-Jamal and over one hundred other men, who our enemy plans to kill, are locked up here as well. I am not under a court sentence of death. I have, however, been sentenced to "death by regulation." Our enemy calls it a "natural life" sentence. I've spent over twenty-five years in that condition.

The men in this prison are serving the full range of sentences and many of them will be released back into your communities someday, perhaps soon. Yet even they are under a sentence of death. They're under a sentence of "spiritual death."

The mission of the prison overseers is to break the spirits of these men. The point is not to break them of their bad habits and help them reform. No, the only objective here is to terrorize these prisoners so that they will carry the message throughout the prisons in this state: "if you're sent to Greene County, you ain't got nothing coming!"

That's what prisoners tell other prisoners.

I know that most of you are thinking that this sounds like a good "tough love" approach. That's because you're blinded by the smoke again. This prison has what is called a "control unit," and the enemy calls it the "restricted housing unit." It's the largest control unit in the state, with a capacity of 772 although there are about 386 here at present. This is where the breaking takes place. This is also where the court-ordered death sentences take place. I've been in this control unit for close to seven years and I was told that I will never be released.

A young prisoner who used to be a couple of cells away from me would get up every morning singing this song: "This must be hell, well, well, well" and would continue in this manner throughout the day. That's because in his bathroom-sized cell, he had nothing to occupy his twenty-three hour days but two *Reader's Digests* that he was allowed to order from the library once a week. He was further allowed to exercise in a "dog cage" for an hour five days per week and allowed to take three five-minute showers. The rest of the time was spent in that cell. Except for being outside of the cell for three plain meals, this is the daily, weekly, monthly, and yearly routine for the majority of the men in the control unit.

Most of the men sentenced to death by the courts are qualified to watch TV or listen to radios. But, of course, if our enemies have their way this will only be "temporary." It is a good way to keep them from thinking about their fate and, for some, from working to beat the hangman.

But most others here are trapped in the twilight zone, in a life-and-death torture of nothingness that kills one's spirit and soul. The prisoners have twenty-three hours which they can in theory use to read, study and develop themselves—from a *Reader's Digest* or the other mindless books in the prison library. If you order or have books sent to you, they are stored away until you're released from the control unit. When your relatives come to visit you, you are separated from them by bulletproof glass and sit handcuffed to a waist belt for one hour.

When one cannot take this grind and refuses to follow one of the ever-changing set of petty rules, that prisoner will either be given more time in the control unit or be beaten by the guards. That is in addition to the "initiation beating" that most prisoners get as soon as they step in the door. Recently a prisoner named Henry Washington was beaten and had a guard's nightstick shoved up his rectum. New York is not the only place that this brutality happens! [Editors' note: This refers to the sodomizing of Abner Louima in 1997.]

Our enemies are making very bitter men out of most of these prisoners. Many of them will be "monsters" when they eventually return to your communities, and most will be returning! But I can read your minds: a lot of you are preparing yourself to accept our enemy's next trick. If many of these men were bad actors before going to prison, and the prison overseers are making them worse, then the "rational" solution is to keep them there forever. (Death by regulation—see how easy it is to fall for their tricks once you're conditioned!)

And what about the prison employees who do return to their communities every evening?! Surely you can see that if an individual torments even a wild animal and makes it vicious, then that individual is as responsible as the animal being vicious, if not more so, and for making the animal probably more dangerous!

It is true that most of the prisoners who come in here need help in reforming their character and behavior. But they are not getting any help in doing that at SCIG. If you don't do something to help these men when they get out . . . you ain't got nothing coming!!!!

Twenty-First-Century
Political Prisoners:
Real and Potential
(2002)

Ever since the mid-1960s there has been a struggle in the United States over whether it holds political prisoners (PPs)—in particular, whether or not Blacks fighting against racism should be looked on as PPs when jailed for offenses related to their political work. That struggle intensified after it was learned that federal, state, and local governments and their agencies conspired to carry out a "counterintelligence program" known as "COINTELPRO." Furthermore, it was discovered that COINTELPRO not only targeted Blacks, but also Native Americans, whites, and many organizations and individuals who had absolutely no idea that this was taking place, even though they suffered from suppression, repression, jailings, and deaths.

In time, nevertheless, it became accepted among a sizable segment of activists that there were, in fact, PPs jailed in this country: former Black Panthers, white anti-imperialists, American Indian Movement members, MOVE members, Black Liberation Army fighters, Puerto Rican nationalists, and Chicano/Mexican fighters, as well as many of their offshoots and supporters.

Furthermore, the struggles engaged in by these groups and the fight against racism, along with this country's aggression in Vietnam, caused many otherwise politically "unconscious" prisoners to join the fight. This created a new segment of PPs who, after going to prison for committing social crimes, became politically active there. George Jackson remains a model for that type of PP.

By and large, however, struggles by these PPs have been kept on the margins for over thirty years, although they still remain strongly supported by those aware of them.

Ironically, it is the ongoing government suppression that is causing many to examine the whole subject of PPs and how it should be viewed and dealt with. In that regard, what's becoming clearer every day is that in addition to the "real political prisoners," there are literally hundreds of thousands of other "potential political prisoners" being held in prisons in this country! They fall into the following categories:

1. death row convicts

2. those with three strike and mandatory sentences
3. those serving life without parole
4. juveniles sentenced as adults
5. immigrants
6. environmental/ecological defenders
7. Muslims and "suspected" foreign terrorists
8. gang members
9. right-wingers
10. Mariel Cuban migrants (boat people) from the 1980s

Note: Some of the real political prisoners are also prisoners of war (POWs): namely those jailed for fighting to gain independence and self-determination for their peoples.

Since the catastrophic events on September 11, 2001, it's generally agreed that this country jails and holds PPs suspected of being terrorists, or being in league with them. Indeed, the government goes out of its way to "terrorize" the general public with warnings of what the (other) Muslim terrorist will do if the state is not given more power to imprison and ruthlessly suppress anyone it chooses.

On the other hand, hardly a day goes by without the public being bombarded with images of migrants from Mexico, Central America, or Haiti being rounded up and jailed. Joining them, moreover, are sensational shots of police with guns drawn trying to identify, catalog, and arrest (so-called) dangerous gang members. And, of course, the ongoing battles over the death penalty, three strikes, and mandatory sentencing laws cannot escape the consciousness of the majority of this country's citizens.

In fact, the only categories within the aforementioned ten that are not widely known and debated are inmates serving life without parole, juveniles sentenced as adults, and environmental/ecological defenders, along with right-wingers (though the Oklahoma City bombing is an exception).

Regrettably, we cannot reach a consensus on a definition of just what makes one a PP, which leaves this author to adamantly insist that we view all in the ten categories as potential political prisoners! Clear political realities overshadow the alleged criminal acts that landed these individuals in prison. Let's examine them:

1. **Death penalty prisoners**: against the law in 90 percent of the world, these prisoners face this penalty so that U.S. politicians can appear "tough on crime."

2. **Three strikes and mandatory sentences**: a political ploy instituted by "tough-on-crime politicians" after their failure to address the underlying causes of crime.

3. **Life without parole**: while only practiced in a few states, it should be outlawed because it violates the equal protection clause of the Constitution, but "tough-on-crime politicians" protect it.

4. **Juveniles sentenced as adults**: this only applies to certain states and is against international law altogether! Again, "tough-on-crime politicians" protect this violation of the Constitution and international law.

5. **Immigration law violators**: migrants commit no crime in crossing artificial borders seeking to better their lives! The government recognizes this fact when it allows certain migrants (like "regular" Cubans) to stay in the country.

6. **Environmental/ecological defenders**: they almost never harm any people but instead concentrate on disrupting the work of those who are attacking everyone by destroying the environment and ecology that sustain us. They too must be suppressed by our "tough-on-crime," clueless politicians.

7. **Muslims and suspected foreign terrorists**: since 9-11, thousands of Muslims and "suspected" foreign terrorists have been jailed, but less then a handful have actually been convicted of anything! The overwhelming majority are victims of a ruthless bunch of status-climbing public bureaucrats, politicians, conflict profiteers, and plain old racists!

8. **Gang members**: this group is very, very rarely offered any comprehensive programs designed to channel their energies into anything

productive! Why? Because most of our educators and politicians, having already failed them before they joined gangs, abandon them to the police, courts, and prison system.

9. **Right-wingers:** they're usually close to the government (as far as immediate aims go) and are allowed to do pretty much as they choose. They are, however targeted for suppression whenever their political and law enforcement allies think they're becoming too independent.

10. **Mariel Cuban migrants (boat people):** in the past the government tried to return them to Cuba, with no success. So to cover the politicians' total lack of ideas about what to do with them, they're just kept locked up.

Finally, there's another little-understood or accepted factor that, although not touching all ten categories, still accounts for more of the hundreds of thousands of twenty-first-century potential political prisoners than any other: the so-called "War on Drugs." I will not go into this in depth, except to state that this war accounts for four of our categories, containing astronomical numbers due to the conscious illegal, immoral, racist, shortsighted, and (ultimately) genocidal decisions taken by this country's top former and present politicians, its major bankers, foreign government political and military allies, the domestic police, courts, and prison administrators.

On the other hand, all of those jailed as a result of the parts they played in "the drug game," although conscious actors, never realized that they were truly pawns in an international, high-stakes game of drugs, money, racism, political corruption, and prisons, equaling *genocide*!

The real criminals all got away!!! Clearly then, when the "players" wake up to the fact that they were played like pawns—that they're no more guilty than those who continue to make, enforce, and get rich off of their misery—then maybe they will join the drug war "victims" and the real political prisoners in fighting for justice!

Taxpayers and Prison:
A Fool's Paradise
(2011)

The state-administered correctional system includes 26 correctional institutions, 54 state-operated or contracted community corrections centers and a motivational boot camp. . . . Approximately 18 percent of the inmate population requires mental health treatment. . . . Given that 90 percent of offenders incarcerated in the commonwealth's state prisons will eventually be released into the community, the Department of Correction emphasizes programs that prepare inmates for responsible crime-free community living.[1]

As Granny Hawkins told Josey Wales in the 1976 movie *The Outlaw Josey Wales,* "That big talk's worth doodly-squat!"

Across this entire country the lovely taxpayers have been bamboozled into believing that their hard-earned tax dollars are helping keep them safe because the state and federal governments are each year spending tens of billions to imprison individuals for years on end. Meanwhile, every statistic shows that those policies of mass imprisonment are a complete failure when it comes to their stated objective: to "prepare inmates for responsible crime-free community living." Creating a revolving-door system that does nothing to make communities safer, they instead cause the lovely taxpayers to hemorrhage money and keep an unworkable boondoggle in play. Nonetheless, every year politicians fight with each other over whether billions should be plowed back into their dysfunctional prison system, or go to other needy projects like education or to repair infrastructure. All the while the taxpayers stand on the sidelines, mesmerized by sensational TV coverage of crime, sports, and celebrity scandals—trusting that the local police, courts, jails, prisons, and politicians are serious about doing everything possible to keep "the criminals" from their "safe and secure" doorways. Even if the budgets of all these entities continued to grow, it is without any real difference being made in terms of solving the problem. These taxpayers are living in a fool's paradise.

---

1   Governor of Pennsylvania Tom Corbett, Executive Budget (2011–2012).

Outside of the total failure of the criminal justice system (police, courts, jails, and prisons) to show that they know how to do anything but lock people up, there's another cancer eating away at the taxpayers' future, to which they remain totally oblivious. Taxpayers are being purposely kept in the dark by a select group of cynical politicians and prison profiteers about the workings and failures of the criminal justice system. Politicians receive benefits by allowing and helping private prison operators and services to function and profit from the prison system. Politicians use the fact that there are prisons in their voting district and claim to be bringing prison jobs into their districts, at the expense of the other taxpayers who don't have prisons in their areas. But it's a cancer: the criminal justice system cannot be financially sustained. Thus the taxpayers must one day choose between trying to continue with the folly of supporting a bankrupt system until it saps all of the potential from their communities, or invest in something that works. Billions of dollars are being poured into the criminal justice/prison "hustle," risking our children's education and neglecting the crumbling roads of our neighborhoods, bridges, libraries, and water and sewage systems. Our open areas, parks, and housing options continue to deteriorate. We must refuse to continue allowing tax dollars to be poured down that sinkhole, while searching for an alternative to the failed ways that the state and federal government have been mishandling the situation.

As a prisoner who has been incarcerated for over forty years, many may be put off by my background and feel uncomfortable about considering my suggestions for ways to get out of this fool's paradise. But consider this: I've been around this sorry state of affairs far longer than those who the taxpayers are trusting to handle the problem. That means I must have learned something about its workings. Therefore, I ask you to set aside your reservations about me, and first read and ponder my ideas before you judge whether they are self-serving or otherwise.

Right now I'm sorry to inform you that you are living in a fool's paradise.

Wake Up, Taxpayers!

[An addendum to the original essay.]

Congressional hearings in Washington were recently held about solitary confinement and the abuses in these places. Now Pennsylvania lawmakers are also holding hearings about our state's prisons. That's something I, too, could relay some horror stories about, but the root of the problem rests with the taxpayers, who are asleep to the fact that their tax dollars are being held and used in a giant, statewide racket called "the Department of Corrections."

The millions taken from the budget for education, public transportation, the fixing of bridges and roads, and the scores of other pressing problems, are blinding you to the fact that the state is still shoveling billions of your tax dollars into a prison system that would be a joke if it were not so brutal and costly. This is a racket that has been steadily growing for forty years, while the state's population has not.

On top of that, some of the state's cities are on the verge of bankruptcy, and they're still building more prisons! Instead of providing jobs and education to keep our youth out of prison, they're building multi-million-dollar warehouses for them—places where youth are kept without learning anything to help them rehabilitate.

That's how the racket works. Billions of tax dollars go to warehouse people in a revolving-door con game.

I have a suggestion: Send some of those hard-pressed college students into the prisons to prepare *both* the prisoners *and* guards to permanently leave these places and become productive assets in a twenty-first-century sustainable workforce. Then there won't be any need for so many prisons, with no solitary confinement and brutality for idle young people. When the prisoners leave, they will be educated enough to not want to return to prisons in order to be tortured in isolation cells. And the taxpayers can direct their hard-earned dollars into more useful projects.

But first you'll have to wake up, taxpayers! You're being played for fools.

Death by Regulation
Pennsylvania Control
Unit Abuses
(1995)

A control unit is a special section within a prison that is designed to house prisoners who administrators have determined should be locked up for twenty-three hours a day for an indefinite period. Other names for this type of facility include: "Restricted Housing Unit" (RHU), "Secure Management Facility" (SMU), "Super Max," "Maxi-Maxi Prison," and "Administrative Maximum Facility" (ADX).

Pennsylvania Gets a Control Unit Facility

In 1994 the Pennsylvania Department of Corrections (DOC) opened its flagship "control unit" at its brand new State Correctional Institute at Greene (SCIG) located near Waynesburg, Pennsylvania. Until that time, the PA DOC had a number of mini control units scattered throughout other prisons in the state. Many of these are still in operation, but SCIG is officially their premier institution for the implementation of control units.

Control units differ from all other forms of restrictions within a prison (the "hole," or solitary confinement) because of their "indefinite" nature. These other prison restriction methods are governed by clearly defined rules which dictate how long a prisoner will be subjected to the confinement and what a prisoner can and should do to have the restriction removed. In control unit facilities, however, prisoners can be kept in confinement for the duration of their sentence, or until death.

Alcatraz: A Brave New World of Torture Is Born

Between 1933 and 1963 the federal government operated the most notorious control unit in U.S history: Alcatraz, or "the rock," as it was known. Alcatraz, which sits on an island in the San Francisco Bay, was used to house what were termed "incorrigible" prisoners. Daily life at this control unit was so severe that being sentenced there was known as "death by regulation." Prisoners could be kept on "the rock" indefinitely. During its existence, Alcatraz was the site of some of the nation's most violent uprisings. It has since been exposed as a place of both official and unofficial torture and human depravity on the part of prisoners and officials.

Officially, the idea behind Alcatraz was that if all of the "incorrigible" prisoners were lumped together in one place, both the prison system and society would benefit. Unofficially, however, the facility was designed to make life so brutal that most of its inhabitants would suffer a complete breakdown and therefore be pacified. Alcatraz proved to be a dismal failure. Instead of breaking down the will of the prisoners (unofficially of course) the harsh regime only embittered them. It thus engendered a fierce determination to survive and take vengeance against their real and perceived enemies. By separating out "incorrigibles" from other prisoners, the penal system may have benefited. However, the communities to which the inhabitants of Alcatraz were released did not. Prisoners who did time in Alcatraz were, in large part, far more dangerous after they left.

Scientists Make Advances in the Field of Human Rights Abuses

The "technicians" who helped engineer and operate this diabolical new methodology began their work roughly around 1962. They were influenced and inspired by new advances in the field of "behavior therapy" and sought to introduce aspects of this field into the penal system. Impressed with the argument that foreign enemies (namely the Chinese, Russians, and North Koreans) had used these new methods of control on American prisoners of war during the Korean conflict, the technicians reasoned that if such techniques could work on trained and hardened soldiers, then surely they would work on criminals! Also exciting to the technicians was the possibility that these methods could seemingly be implemented without obvious signs of physical abuse, as the methodology did not rely on bodily force or a dungeon-style environment to impart its effects. Rather, it centered on the manipulation of the mind. The objective was to cause the prisoner to suffer a mental breakdown rather than trying to "break the prisoner down" physically. It was believed that this could be accomplished while still adhering to the "evolving standards of decency" that federal courts had mandated the prisons to implement, particularly in response to the struggles of prisoners and to community awareness of such struggles.

Sensory Deprivation 101

The brain and nervous system, the mind, cannot function normally without stimulation. Neither can it function normally when given too much stimulation. The brain and nervous system must be maintained in a "steady state."[1] The primary tools used in this new method of mind control and torture were sensory and perceptual isolation.

> The new style control units were clean, well lighted and outwardly "clinical" and appeared comfortable. Prisoners were fed a well-balanced diet and the typical prison regimen of physical punishment was not introduced. [However] . . . the evidence appears overwhelming that solitary confinement alone, even in the absence of physical brutality or unhygienic conditions, can produce emotional damage, declines in mental functioning, and even the most extreme forms of psychopathology such as depersonalization, hallucination, and delusions.[2]

Control unit facilities are designed to be devoid of adequate levels of external stimulations. There is very little if any activity that provides educational instruction, shop training, physical exercise, or contact with the outside world.

"Life" at State Correctional Institute Greene

At SCIG the control unit facility is completely separated from the rest of the prison by eighteen-foot walls. Each building is compartmentalized into four "pods" of twenty-four cells each. Each pod functions independently of the others. Within each 12 x 6 cell there is a steel bed, steel

---

1 Thomas B. Benjamin and Kenneth Lux, "Solitary Confinement as Psychological Punishment," *California Western Law Review* 13 (1977): 265–96.

2 Ibid.

eating surface, stool, steel toilet, sink, mirror, and bedding. All meals are taken in the cell. A prisoner is only allowed out of his cell for five hours of outdoor exercise per week and allowed three ten-minute showers. The exercise is taken alone in a space enclosed by a razor wire–topped fence, and no exercise equipment is ever provided.

Each prisoner is issued a jumpsuit, tennis shoes, and work shoes for winter, two pairs of socks, two T-shirts, two sets of underwear, two sheets, a mattress, one blanket, one pillow, one towel, and one washcloth. Soap, shaving gear, toothpaste, toothbrushes, combs, and toilet paper are issued periodically. Besides the daily meals these items are all that a control unit prisoner has contact with. Furthermore, these articles are strictly regulated and it is forbidden to possess an extra ration of any item. Each article is exchanged on a one-for-one basis. With the exception of a ration of fruit, no food can be saved.

The control unit is governed by the Department of Corrections Administrative Directive 802 (DC-ADM 802). It reads (in part) as follows:

A. Administrative Custody is a status of confinement for maximum custody level of inmates which provides the highest level of security and control. Inmates confined in this status shall not have the privileges accorded to inmates in lower security levels. The following conditions apply:

1. Smoking will be limited to 2 packs of cigarettes or their equivalent per week.

2. There will be no radios, televisions, telephone calls (exception: emergency or legal), personal property or commissary except writing materials.

3. Non-legal visits of one per week (one hour) will be allowed. They will be allowed legal material that may be contained in one Records Center box . . .

4. They will be allowed incoming mail. . . . However no books other than legal materials and a personal Bible, Holy Koran, or other religious equivalent will be permitted. Leisure reading material (2 books per week) may be requested on a weekly basis from the library.

B. PRC (Program Review Committee) or Security Level 5 Unit Teams may add to the above *privileges* based on an individual need, on safety and security and on behavioral *progress* of the inmate [emphasis added].

As if this spartan environment was not severe enough, control unit prisoners are forbidden to hold conversations with other prisoners in other cells as it is considered "loud talking." Given conditions at control unit facilities and their indefinite nature, one can easily see that they are far from country clubs or even warehouses. There are men in SCIG who have seventeen, twenty-three, even twenty-six years in control units with no prospects of ever being released!

If prison personnel severed the nerve cells in prisoners' hands, we would easily recognize that they were intentionally destroying their ability to function and feel normally. Such a conclusion would be obvious. Although these methods of control are based on psychological torture rather than physical abuse, and the side effects of this torture are somewhat less apparent to the average observer, control unit facilities are equally cruel and barbaric, if not more so.[3]

United States Violates UN Declaration on Human Rights and Own Constitution

Again: SCIG's control unit is being operated in violation of the accepted standards of the United Nations, the United States Constitution, state law, Department of Education and Welfare policies on human experiments, and the "evolving standards of decency" in our society.

After witnessing the results of solitary confinement, we believe that it is criminality at one of its highest levels. We are drawn to this conclusion when we ponder the International Covenant on Civil and Political Rights. This Covenant is in accord with and expands upon the rights that have been established by the Universal Declaration of Human Rights (UDHR). The United States and all of its federal and state agencies are bound by this

---

3   Paraphrased from Benjamin and Lux, "Solitary Confinement."

declaration since its adoption by the United Nations General Assembly on December 10, 1948. The United States ratified it in June of 1992. The Covenant states in part: "No one shall be subjected to torture or cruel, inhumane, or degrading treatment or punishment." Article 7 of the UDHR imposes an affirmative duty on each state and country government to afford protection against the acts prohibited, whether inflicted by people acting in their official capacity or in private capacity.[4]

Our government, its agencies, the media, and general public recoil in horror upon hearing of atrocities committed by foreign powers such as the former Soviet Bloc, China, and various countries in Asia, Africa, and South America. The same concern and outrage should be directed to the U.S. government which sanctions the same sorts of torture—social torture paid for with tax dollars. Our taxes help support polices of "social suicide" by returning former control unit prisoners—whose time in such facilities has only worsened their emotional and mental condition—to their communities. (Remember Alcatraz?!)

Of course such vampirish prison policies do exist in full view of the public. Several years ago the federal government was forced to close a control unit facility for women in Lexington, Kentucky, after various organizations, concerned individuals, and relatives made conditions there known to a broader section of the public. Other control unit facilities would surely meet the same fate were they subject to the same level of public scrutiny. Such treatment has been universally condemned: Article 10 of the Covenant prohibits convicted prisoners from being subjected to any hardship or constraint other than that resulting from the deprivation of liberty. The UN Human Rights Committee has commented that treating prisoners with respect for their human dignity "is a fundamental and universally applicable rule."[5]

Control unit facilities cannot be allowed to exist. They serve no purpose other than to dehumanize their occupants. Our collective welfare demands that we do everything within our power to bring about an end to this form of imprisonment and torture.

---

4   *International Human Rights Instruments*, HRI/GEN/1, September 4, 1992, General Comment 20, Article 7, 44th Session, 1992: No 1

5   General Comment 21, Article 10, 44th Session, 1992: No 4

The Black Liberation
Struggle in Philadelphia
(2006)

Interview conducted by Comrade Sobukwe and Marcus Schell, both supporters of the Russell Maroon Shoatz Defense Committee. Marcus Schell is the son of the late Reggie Schell, a founding member of Philadelphia's Black Panther Party.

How did you get involved in the Black movement of the 1960s and 1970s?

As a Black male who was born in Philadelphia in 1943, I can honestly say that until the age of twenty I was "dumb-as-do-do" so far as political and broad social issues go. Moreover, my father was a long-distance truck driver and he made pretty good money. So outside of eating some "surplus cheese" here and there, my family and my "working/middle-class" neighborhood was not a place of economic hardship. Thus, there was no incentive there.

In fact, my parents, and the adults in this neighborhood in general, were all on the "go to school," "go to church," and "be home at a respectable time" kick. Social and political issues were never discussed or hinted at in the homes, churches, or schools!

All these "Negroes" (what we were all then known as) were busy tying to get ahead as best a Negro could, even though in Philly just about everything was dominated and controlled by whites: city hall, police stations, firehouses, all the schools, neighborhoods, downtown businesses, and transportation. A Negro couldn't even become a Boy or Girl Scout!

So, although there was no out-front segregation, like in the South, Philly's Blacks were segregated in neighborhoods and allowed to leave only in order to work, shop, pay bills, and travel—sort of like apartheid South Africa.

Until I was twenty, that was my life, with the addition of being deeply involved in gang activities.

Although by 1960 I could see some of the southern civil rights struggle being played out on TV, I couldn't relate to the nonviolence that they practiced. Everybody I knew believed in "an eye for an eye and a tooth for tooth," except when it came to the police. We were uniformly scared of them.

Consequently, I can put my finger on the exact instant, the exact circumstance that began my awakening and journey into political life: going to a rally in Harlem, New York, and listening to Malcolm X speak!

In 1963, I was twenty and had moved to Harlem to live with an aunt, get away from my Philly gang and find a job. I was also running from an arrest warrant for a rape, which is a whole other story. Anyway, my aunt warned me not to go around to 116th Street and Lenox Avenue (now Malcolm X Boulevard) because "the nationalists are having a rally, and there might be some trouble." Now I had no idea what a nationalist was, but trouble was my thing. I was still steeped in the gang culture's way of viewing things.

Malcolm, flanked by Nation of Islam security, talked on an outdoor stage for hours. The street was shut off and throngs of people were on the sidewalks, in the street, in the adjoining park, and hanging out of buildings and high-rise projects—all alternately deeply engrossed in his words, then shouting, clapping, and screaming at the top of their voices!

But not me. I was, instead, oscillating between being mesmerized by his "A to Z" explanation of things, and a nagging fear. I was like Neo (in *The Matrix*) when Morpheus told him he had "been living in a dream world." My whole world was being blown away and reshaped as I listened. What put the icing on the cake was the actions of the police, who were dispersed throughout the crowd. They were "smoking and joking" like they were not listening to Malcolm take apart everything they and the entire American system commonly indulged in!

And although I couldn't understand everything, I still knew he was challenging them to either come up there and prove him wrong, or come up there and shut him up. Never had I seen anyone handle the police like that.

And although nobody could tell me that I wasn't a tough guy, that was some deliciously scary shit that won me over to begin following politics and important social issues.

But, like Neo, I wasn't ready just then to become actively involved. In fact, it wasn't until after a squashing of the rape allegations, a return to Philly, a failed marriage (that produced four offspring), and a horrible stint as a drug-dealing hustler that I finally ran out of places to hide. In order for me to begin living like a whole human being, I had to cast all fear to the wind and start following Malcolm's example.

What was the Black Unity Council and why did you help found it?

1967–68 found me completely fed up with being a modem-day slave—a conclusion I had come to since Malcolm had begun my awakening. It was doubly maddening because damn near all of my friends, family, and neighbors seemed content to continue to go along with the bullshit that (by then) was being exposed and attacked in Black communities, on college campuses, and elsewhere—from one side of the globe to the other. They were still trapped in the Matrix.

A former gang buddy named Points, however, had reached the same conclusions that I had, so we decided to put out the word that we were gonna have an open meeting and form an organization to address some of our concerns. Of course, by that time there were other organizations in Philly that we felt good about, but none in our immediate neighborhood.

So, one weekend, we held the meeting at the house of another gang buddy named Brick and, surprisingly, about fifteen to twenty people showed up, male and female, including my blood sister Gloria, who I had no idea shared my concerns and ideas. Indeed, we all were experiencing feelings of frustration and isolation.

So, right there the name Black Unity Council (BUC) was chosen and the group was formed, although no officers were selected, nor would the BUC ever choose any officers. We always worked by consensus—at least up until we got deeply involved with paramilitary activity about two years later.

In fact, outside of current events and local concerns, the BUC never discussed political theories, ideologies, or much about Black history. Most of us were nevertheless very impressed with the "cultural nationalist" Blacks. We admired their knowledge of Black/African history and their choice to dress in African garb (especially how beautiful and graceful it made women look).

We especially liked their emphasis on armed self-defense! At that time, the Revolutionary Action Movement (RAM) was very active in Philly. Their cultural workers, and semiclandestine paramilitary arm called the Black Guard (BG), had a center close to our neighborhood, and we would always hang out there. They had regular seminars, history/cultural classes, karate classes (for women and men with some very sharp sistas along the *Crouching Tiger, Hidden Dragon* vibe!). In addition, they had a "liberation school" that the BUC planned to emulate.

At that time, the BUC had about thirty regulars—mainly in southwest Philly and Germantown. We were able to assemble enough people to fill a gym or large church when we would jump on hot-button issues like police killings.

Otherwise, we met regularly in a local church and in each other's homes. Eventually, we rented a large house and furnished it with the necessaries for our own liberation school. We charged a can of food to attend our affairs, which we would give to needy families.

Since a number of us had a gang background we also became involved in citywide efforts to get gangs to sign a truce.

Yet all of that was brand new to everyone in the BUC. We didn't have any experienced political/social workers to work with us on a regular basis. As a consequence, I know now, our emulation of RAM's emphasis on armed self-defense—not balanced with other considerations—caused many in the BUC to push it to become a strictly paramilitary group. On the other hand, the extremely brutal and terrorist Philly police, coupled with our newfound consciousness that freed us from our fear of them, also played a major role!

We had listened to Malcolm chide Blacks for being ready, willing, and able to kill each other, and even hundreds of millions of Chinese (while in the U.S. Army), but being (essentially) cold cowards when it came to defending themselves right here at home. And RAM hammered that same message home by preaching that Blacks had to stop believing that the police were "bulletproof"!

Regrettably, although many in the BUC were no longer afraid of the police, most of the community members that they sought to serve still were—sort of like Morpheus telling Neo that he must remember that those they were trying to free from the Matrix were not ready for that. On the other hand, the police (no doubt) couldn't imagine that we had lost our fear of them!

Anyway, within two years the BUC had turned into a paramilitary group with about fifteen male and female members—fully armed with shoulder-fired weapons, side arms, and even hand grenades. We belonged to shooting/hunting clubs, practiced karate, went on outdoor maneuvers, and fortified all of our homes. In fact, think about today's "survivalists" and you'll really see where the BUC was at: food, water, first aid stocks, and all.

Undoubtedly, today's readers may also have a hard time understanding the BUC's zeal, unless they view a documentary like the acclaimed *Eyes on the Prize*. Only then will they get a proper feel for the type of social, political, and psychological ferment that surrounded the BUC.

Thus, when the paramilitary BUC first learned about the Black Panther Party (BPP), we had already been established for close to two years. Indeed, we liked what we were learning, but on the other hand we grieved for their comrades being killed off in the streets and in their offices like sitting ducks. So, we decided to contact them in order to see if we could assist them in their work, and in staying alive!

Hold up! I need to backtrack for a minute in order to elaborate on the BUC's decision to become a paramilitary-style group. Otherwise the reader may be left with the impression that the BUC was some kind of nutball formation.

The fact of the matter is, by 1968, Philly had similar Black paramilitary-style formations all around the city. Essentially, all of them were motivated by a heightened consciousness, a need to make more sophisticated their neighborhood's defenses against adjoining white neighborhoods—which had always displayed aggression but were now more fearful due to the rising Black pride on display. We also wanted to prepare for the inevitable showdown with either the police or National Guard in the event of another rebellion (so-called "riot") as happened in North Philly in 1964.

Certainly, most of these groups could easily be identified by their military-style clothing, which (unlike today) signaled to everyone that the wearers were paramilitary elements of the movement. In that regard, RAM was the largest and best-known local practitioner of this approach. Around that time, moreover, RAM had a very large youth group of Black males and females called "the Liberators." They always wore black berets, jackets, pants, and combat boots. This is before most people in Philly knew that the West Coast–based BPP also dressed in the same way. And the police didn't wear black back then!

The BUC, in fact, was in negotiations with the Liberators' leadership about merging forces, with the more mature BUC members being asked to serve as officers for the younger Liberators.

Obviously, the police were always aware of this paramilitary-style activity, especially due to RAM's open agitation and spray-painting of "Join the Black Guard" all over the city. Another formation threw hand grenades into a police parking lot, damaging patrol cars and provoking heavily armed police to raid Black neighborhoods all over the city.

By the time the BUC decided to contact the local Black Panther Party, many of RAM's leaders and many of the other paramilitary formation leaders had been jailed, forced underground, or decided to become less militant. As Malcolm said, a lot of people were not clear on what they were doing. He told us that once they found out, they would "get back in the alley, they would change their names."

Anyway, in mid-1969, the BUC contacted the local Panthers, headquartered in North Philly. Although by then we had read a lot about the national organization, our talks left us disappointed. In a nutshell, it was apparent to us that the BUC cadre was much more advanced than the local Panthers—militarily anyway. Since that was where they were the weakest, and we were the strongest, we felt that we could "negotiate" a relationship as we had done with RAM (the BUC was still governed by consensus).

We found out, however, that the local Panthers couldn't do that, since the Black Panther Party was a tightly controlled, top-down organization. Our disappointment arose from the fact that they were getting killed all over the country and their leaders couldn't come up with a strategy to combat that, in addition to being too rigid to allow local leaders the flexibility needed to do so. So the talks broke off, more or less. I say more or less because the BUC never gave up supporting the local Panthers, and around that time some things occurred that cannot be revealed here, because that would endanger the freedom of others. If this was not the case, I could give up some raw, hardcore rap that is usually hidden from this generation. Like Malcolm used to say, "Those who know don't tell; those who tell don't know." As a result, a lot of cockeyed urban legends have sprouted up and become accepted as historical fact. I will attempt to set the record straight as much as possible.

First off, people must understand that in dealing with the history of the Black Panther Party, nobody—not the Panthers, not the police/FBI or other repressive arms of the state—knows it all! This is because a whole lot of activities happened on a need-to-know basis. In other words, a lot of stuff was so delicate that it was known and handled only by those who needed to know about it, the downside to this being that if things didn't go right, or if you got caught, you were on your own. That's how it worked in the real world. Cadre who went on those types of missions accepted that up front.

So, why did the BUC merge with the Black Panther Party?

In December of 1969, the Chicago police led a deadly raid that resulted in the death of Panthers Fred Hampton and Mark Clark and the wounding of others. When members of the BUC heard this on the news, we were furious, sad, and disgusted all at the same time. Certainly our fury was directed toward the killers, and our sadness for the dead, wounded, and terrorized Panthers. Our disgust was reserved for the Panther leadership that persisted in an unimaginative strategy that was getting some of the best and most sincere youth in the urban areas killed and jailed. We were not experts, but even we had reached the conclusion that Panthers "shooting it out" with more heavily armed police from fixed positions was downright ludicrous! Even if they survived, it still left them in jail or hospitalized, causing everybody else to have to drop important work to bail them out and raise money for their legal defense.

Consequently, after some discussion, we essentially decided to again get in touch with the local Panthers. But this time we planned to stick to them closely, no matter what. We just wanted to be around when their turn to get "vamped on" (raided by police) came. Of course, they had already been subjected to home raids, but nothing deadly. We planned to be in a position to upgrade their defenses and react to the expected attacks.

Rightly or wrongly, the BUC had reached the conclusion that in order for Blacks in the United States to be truly free, we would have to wage armed struggle. We believed that our oppression had many facets—social, political, economic, cultural, and psychological. We did not have a handle on the intricacies surrounding these aspects, but we did know that, in general, Blacks did not have any substantial political power. Economically, we were "last hired and first fired," and culturally we had been stripped of everything that would anchor us to our African past. We knew that it was up to us to prove we were as much man or woman as anyone else!

Can you describe your experience working within the Black movement's armed underground?

In a nutshell, it taught me the absolute necessity of all armed actions having broad, deep, multidimensional support. Otherwise they are open to isolation and destruction, which was the fate of the Black Liberation Army.

This has nothing to do with whether armed actions fall into the so-called "terrorism" category. That accusation is made on purely self-serving and hypocritical grounds. The need for multidimensional support has to do with the simple fact that we must have the resources, energy, creativity, and enthusiasm of the people on the side of the armed struggle. Otherwise, armed movement forces have very little chance of winning against the oppressive forces that do have broad and deep support.

Calculations concerning pulling together this support, and constantly increasing it must be very well thought out. In a multiracial, multicultural, sexist, and class-ridden country (and world!) this is a tough task!

That said, I think that we do not learn enough from the successes of the past. We have a goldmine of tried and tested successful approaches if we study how our ancestors used the Underground Railroad (UR). It's well known that the UR is a shining example of a broad and deep multidimensional movement that set the stage for the destruction of slavery. Check out my essay [included in this book] called "The *Real* Resistance to Slavery in North America."

Quite frankly, I'm fed up with so much narrow-minded, paranoid crap masquerading as ideology being dished out to young people who are hungry for direction by a lot of cowardly veteran activists who don't want to step out of their comfort zones. Building conscious support is the absolute first step toward militantly challenging our oppressor. These old cowards know that! Nothing is more important than putting in work to stop this global, genocidal oppression!

How did the split in the Black Panther Party affect the local organization?

In my opinion, the "split" in the BPP is of secondary importance. We must instead look deeper into the BPP, the movement in general, and toward those forces opposing us for a better understanding of what occurred and what should have been done.

Certainly, splits in organizations during every historical period are more common than not. Splits serve good ends just as often as bad. The 1971 split in the BPP helped destroy it as a revolutionary organization.

From the ashes of the split, the Huey Newton–led West Coast faction showed its true intentions: to gut as much of the old BPP as possible and guide the remainder along clearly reformist and less threatening lines in exchange for some breathing room from the government repression and the campaign of terror that COINTELPRO was leveling against the party.

Perhaps this was a necessary "strategic retreat."

On the other hand, the East Coast faction never got on its feet, essentially due to the sheer lack of experience of its youthful cadre in attempting to do the following:

1. Reorganize itself separately from the West Coast—which had control of their main organizing tool: *The Black Panther* newspaper
2. Continue along the revolutionary path by fielding a semiautonomous armed wing
3. Continue to expand its political base
4. Survive the intensified government repression

True, they did begin publishing their own paper called *Right On!* But nobody ever heard of it, and it was shortly plagued with all types of problems hindering its organizing utility.

Their role in fielding the armed wing, however, served as a double-edged sword. On the one hand, the escalating terror leveled against the entire BPP hit the East Coast faction hard. Another batch of bogus arrests was planned to decimate their ranks, like the earlier "New York 21" (when twenty-one New York BPP members were jailed, tortured for two years, and finally found not guilty by a jury). But this time the arrests would be connected to a COINTELPRO-provoked "shooting split" in the BPP.

On the other hand, many BPP cadre decided to take the courageous decision of joining the fledgling armed wing that came to be called the Black Liberation Army (BLA)—instead of chancing arrests and trials in this (by then) well-known "conspiracy"-to-commit-a-grocery-list-of-crimes dance.

Thus, they chose to continue down the revolutionary path, but as armed members of the movement. (Although the BPP started off in an "armed self-defense" mode, by 1971 it had essentially gotten rid of that tactic, on Huey Newton's orders, except in a ceremonial mode—mainly for funerals.)

So that was a positive decision under the circumstances. The separate armed wing would take away the government's ability to justify its ongoing oppression of those BPP members who didn't go "underground" with the BLA. And the BLA could still use armed members to help protect the movement and the community from rampant police terror and murders, as well as provide the oppressed with a sense of hope that one day they might build up a counterweight to the armed might that they had always been crushed by—an evolution of the BPP's original mission.

Still, so many BPP members going underground, coupled with the ongoing repression and all-around lack of experience in handling such a complex maneuver, all but brought the expansion of the political base to a halt. This was because most of the veteran organizers were either in the BLA or providing them with support.

Finally, the handful of East Coast BPP members not fully occupied with the above were easily intimidated, and subsequently demoralized by the repression. They opted to either give up or try to join the underground.

Plus, and I hate to say this, it's hard for me to see how such an inexperienced group of young people could have surmounted all of those obstacles, except with the charismatic and visionary leadership of a few key BBP members. This would have at least given them (us) enough time to adapt to such a task! We did, however, prove Malcolm and others right: the oppressors ain't bulletproof!

What can we learn from the strengths and weaknesses of the armed underground?

For my part, I've written an essay on that entitled "Black Fighting Formations: Their Strengths, Weaknesses, and Potentials" [included in this book]. In that piece, I generally critique Black armed groups in this country from 1960 to 1994.

How were you treated by the prison authorities after you were initially captured, given that you were charged with a "crime" that was highly publicized and political but was a direct assault upon the system?

Well, of course the jailers at Philly's Detention Center locked me and my comrades who had been captured with me in our cells all day. But for some reason, in a few days, they sent a high officer to let us into the general prison population—after threatening us sufficiently, of course.

Actually, it might have been due to the presence in lock-up of Shamsuddin Au, Philly's Nation of Islam power, who was known as "Captain Clarence" back in 1972. The so-called "Black Muslims" had hundreds of members in that and other local jails. I believe they wanted him in the general population in order to keep them under control. So we were also let out so it wouldn't be obvious that the jailers were using him in that manner.

In places such as California, New York, and New Jersey, the BPP/ BLA had a tremendous presence and influence in the prisons. To what extent did the BPP/BLA have a presence inside the Pennsylvania prison system?

Regrettably, by 1972, the local Black Panthers in the streets had all either been ordered to move to Oakland, California, been expelled on bogus allegations connected to Huey Newton's attempts to distance the BPP from its militants, had left to form other organizations, had just retreated altogether, or gone underground to form BLA units.

And connected to that was an aggressive recruitment strategy under-taken by the Nation of Islam and orthodox Muslim groups that essentially swallowed up most of those in the Philly jails, and later in Pennsylvania state prisons, who were most susceptible to revolutionary-sounding ideas and organizing.

Moreover, just about all of my own comrades from the BUC/BPP merger, as well as other local BPP/BLA soldiers who had been captured in armed activities, along with those political-minded prisoners under their sway, also became Muslims. Indeed, the feeling was that joining these religious groups was simply the next step in our collective evolution toward true self-determination. This, however, proved not to be true. But that's a story best left for later.

Nevertheless, BLA recruitment and activity still grew in the midst of this situation, and was only eradicated after a protracted struggle within the state jails and prisons.

What are your ideas about prison organizing and what should forces on the outside be doing?

It would help to first give a few reasons why we must see this as a crucial strategic task for our times. Quite frankly, it's hard for me to imagine anyone living in this country who is not simply terrified by the thought of falling victim to any combination of circumstances that would lead them into the clutches of America's jails or prisons! And the gatekeepers, the paramilitary police, and paparazzi-style prosecutors will come down on you whether you're eight or eighty, blind, crippled, rich, or crazy!

So, if for no other reason, we must not allow ourselves to be held hostage by those in power through the use of the police, prosecutors, jails, and prisons.

Yet that's still too abstract, especially since most people just think that they can stay out of the way. On a real level, the Black and Brown communities of this country, in particular, are the victims of an extremely callous set of political and economic calculations—in which the jails and prisons play a controlling role—invariably leading to the "normalization" of a reality in which a huge segment of its population is simply fuel for the prison-industrial/depressed-communities hustle.

Furthermore, we have to do our homework so that we'll see beyond the obvious racial aspects of all this. In truth, it's not race that's the determining factor as to why Black and Brown people populate the jails, detention centers, and prisons in such overwhelming proportions. No! It's a matrix of foreign policy concerns, immigration control, government/CIA-controlled drugs, money, political corruption, racism, and prisons.

To be sure, this is not an easy thing to fully come to grips with. Of course, most of us have our strong suspicions about how it fits together, but I know it's still murky in the minds of most people. The matrix of drugs, money, political corruption, racism, and prisons equals genocide! Go research for yourself and see if I'm right or not! We have to start educating people about this, about the fact that the overwhelming majority of today's prisoners—Black, Brown, and otherwise—are pawns in a giant domestic and international con game. This is the exact thing that I and other political prisoners were fighting against in the 1960s, '70s and '80s.

We must also refine our ideas about how many political prisoners this country holds and just who they are. Then we can actively move to integrate efforts to free the ones already recognized, as well as those who have not yet been recognized.

Check out my essay "Twenty-First-Century Political Prisoners: Real and Potential" [included in this book]. No doubt, such an analysis and its recommendations will not sit comfortably with some, who may think it's too broad or too diverse to include those imprisoned for distributing drugs, for example, as political prisoners. To these individuals, I can only shake my head and wonder: where do they think we'll amass the counterweight to overcome those powerful and self-serving elements controlling this hustle, if not from other "self-interested" elements? And this says nothing of one's moral and ethical responsibility to struggle and fight against the real gangsters in the White House, State Department, banks, police agencies, U.S. military, along with all the other bloodsuckers.

So unless you have an analysis and plan that can convince me that my own eyes are lying to me . . . let's get started!

Black Fighting Formations
Their Strengths, Weaknesses, and Potentials
(1994–1995)

A study of the various Black political organizations in the United States between the years of 1960–1994 will reveal a number of "fighting formations." These formations were usually subdivisions or offshoots of larger organizations, which were not primarily envisioned as combat groups. This lack of original dedication to a "fighting mission" will go a long way in helping to explain their strengths, weaknesses, and potentials.

Not included in this study are the nonpolitical Black fighting formations found among the street gangs or those dedicated to criminal activity. However, mention will be made of them in regard to the loss of potential that Black political fighting formations originally had.

We must look to Sun Tzu (ca. fifth century BC) and Karl Von Clausewitz (nineteenth century AD) for the most concise writings on the philosophy of warfare, the ultimate reasons for engaging in it and the main dynamics controlling its many variables. *The Art of War* (Sun Tzu) and *On War* (Von Clausewitz), are mentioned by military practitioners around the world as two of the best, tried and true, volumes available on the subject. There have been many outstanding military practitioners of African descent as well: Thutmose III (the first imperial conqueror), Ramses II and Ramses III (consistent subduers of the barbarian and savage hordes of Europe and Asia), Queens Nzinga and (the) Candace(s) of Angola and Ethiopia, Shaka Zulu (warrior par-excellence), and Toussaint L'Ouverture and Antonio Maceo (who out-led and out-fought vastly superior European armies in Haiti and Cuba). Finally, we must add the outstanding guerrilla leaders among the maroons and the African anti-colonial fighters. Although guerrilla warfare is often sufficient, it must be kept in mind that "guerrilla warfare" is only a subdivision of and sometimes a forerunner to "total war." Despite the successes of these African warriors there is very little written work available about them and thus we must rely on the work of Sun Tzu and Karl Von Clausewitz.

Sun Tzu, in his *The Art of War*, instructs: "War is a matter of vital importance to the state. [It is] the province of life and death, [and] the road to survival or ruin. It is mandatory that it be thoroughly studied."[1] In *On War*, Karl Von Clausewitz states: "War is an extension of politics, politics by different means."[2] Both of these authors demonstrate the connection between politics and warfare and the relative importance of both. ("Politics" here is simply the science and art of governing people.) It follows that those who are involved in shaping political affairs must recognize that they will, at some point, be required to pursue their political objectives "by different means" (Von Clausewitz) as "the road to survival or ruin" (Sun Tzu): warfare!

For the revolutionary, warfare cannot be a haphazard or belated consideration, as ignoring these principles (nonviolent pacifism) will ultimately lead to total destruction.

Therefore, all of our Black political organizations should have had a military component right from the beginning. From their inception it would have been the mission of these military components to study and prepare for war. This presupposes that the political and military leadership is sagacious enough to discern both the long-range interests of their people and the potential conflicts that they will invariably encounter by pursuing these interests. In other words, our Black political organizations should have known, right from the beginning, that they had to build a military component capable of defending our people from the attacks they were undergoing as a result of working to free themselves from oppression. Sadly, this was not the case.

In order to understand better what must be done now we need to learn from the mistakes of the past. When 1960 dawned, there were no Black fighting formations with the exception of the Nation of Islam's paramilitary wing known as the Fruit of Islam. This was formed largely in response to Malcolm X's tireless efforts. However, the Fruit of Islam was completely dedicated to internal security and static defense of the Nation of Islam's leadership and property. It was further hobbled (in

1   (New York: Oxford University Press, 1984).

2   (New York: Viking Press, 1983).

qualitative development) by the group's unwillingness to become actively involved in the civil rights struggle, where most of the action was taking place. Members of the Fruit of Islam were not much better than department-store security guards, far removed from the reality of "total war." Subsequent events would expose its weaknesses.

To its credit, however, the Fruit of Islam had perfected a method of recruiting, organizing, and training (to the extent that training was done) that is unparalleled to this day. The secret of its success rested on the fact that it concentrated its main recruiting efforts among the most downtrodden segments of the Black community: the drug addicts, prison inmates, prostitutes, and destitute poor. It took a great effort to recruit and organize these people, but once they were fully brought into the organization they became steadfast and loyal members of their new (psychological) family. By the time the Nation of Islam had "fished" them out of the mud, they had no other family that would stand by them, as they had burnt their bridges well. These recruits were kept under extremely close supervision and were always provided with the means to acquire food, clothing, shelter, security, and entertainment (which was usually social fellowship in religious trappings). The Fruit of Islam provided everything that a functioning family would provide its members.

The organization itself had a nationalist-sounding program but no grand strategy to achieve any of its ends. The first dictum of war, "war is a matter of vital importance to the state ... and it is mandatory that it be thoroughly studied" (Sun Tzu) was not observed. This statement is not just a matter of opinion—events have proven this to be true. It does not take long to build military capability. Of course, the organization has not had a free ride, as it continues to fight the government's infiltration and manipulation in addition to the petty jealousies and rivalries that exist among leaders. Nevertheless, it is clear that with a few exceptions, the Fruit of Islam has thus far missed the boat when it comes to being an important Black fighting formation.

The civil rights movement was launched in 1955 with the Montgomery bus boycott and quickly spread throughout the South. In addition to many local groupings, which in some cases had already been active in their communities, a number of other organizations began to emerge on the national scene by 1960: the Southern Christian Leadership Conference (SCLC), the Congress of Racial Equality (CORE), the Urban League, and the Student Nonviolent Coordinating Committee (SNCC). The National Association for the Advancement of Colored People (NAACP) had been around since the early 1900s. From 1955 to 1965, all of the major actions taking place in the Black freedom struggle occurred in the South, and the aforementioned organization led these struggles. Each of these organizations professed nonviolence as their strategy, but ultimately relied on someone else's armed force to protect them, usually that of the U.S. government (with disastrous results). These groups would call ahead to the FBI and alert them to their plans, requesting protection. The FBI, in turn, would contact members of the local police force, who were often card-carrying Ku Klux Klansmen, or it would contact their undercover agents/operatives in the Klan who would subsequently organize a shooting, burning, bombing, or killing. These organizations were violating every rule in the "art of war." Instead of observing the rule "destroy your enemy and preserve yourself," they were actually aiding their enemy in their own destruction. This exact pattern was repeated, to one degree or another, when the government provided U.S. Marshals or federal troops. Despite this short-sighted, cowardly, and disastrous strategy, because of the heroic sacrifices made by the rank-and-file (largely Black men, women, and children) a number of changes were forced through during this period of time. And these groups did, albeit belatedly, give rise to a few armed fighting subdivisions and offshoots.

The Monroe County, North Carolina NAACP branch was headed by a Black man named Robert F. Williams who saw early on that his chapter of the NAACP would suffer countless casualties and could not survive unless they got rid of the nonviolent approach and adopted an armed self-defense strategy. This brother strongly advocated that all Blacks in the United States should adopt armed self-defense.

Williams walked his talk as his Monroe Country NAACP branch was both armed and trained. Because of this, its members survived a number of shootouts with the local KKK (citizens and police). Unfortunately, he could not affect any widespread acceptance of his methods and his chapter was therefore isolated. After a so-called kidnapping of some white people, he was forced to leave the country.[3] He continued his work while in exile by traveling throughout Africa and visiting China in an attempt to raise support for the struggle in the United States. He became a nationalist and published a paper called *The Liberator* in which he advocated the overthrow of the United States through guerrilla warfare. After a number of years, he was able to return to the United States as head of the revolutionary group, Republic of New Africa (RNA). He avoided prison, as RNA was able to expose and squash the trumped-up kidnapping charge.

At the same time, an organization called "Deacons for Defense and Justice" was formed in both rural Alabama and Mississippi. Unlike Williams's Monroe County chapter, the Deacons for Defense and Justice was not a subdivision of the NAACP. Rather, it was an offshoot, and therefore autonomous, from the national nonviolent leadership. The Deacons recruited, organized, and trained solely from this perspective. Because of this, they were more sophisticated than any other part-time militant Black organization during the civil rights struggle. For instance, the Deacons provided a tightly organized security and communications net around some of the most important civil rights marches. While the civil rights groups provided their posted marshals with armbands, the Deacons had roving patrols armed with automatic rifles. After a few skirmishes and firefights with Klan and Night Riders (part-time Klan who were afraid to show their faces during the day), they gave the Deacons a wide berth. Ultimately, however, the Deacons had a circumscribed potential for growth due to the civil rights movement's overall strategy of reliance on the U.S. government for protection.

---

3   Editors' note: The details about this complex and unfortunate frame-up cannot be detailed in full here. Readers are encouraged to investigate this further in the *Robert and Mabel Williams Resource Guide* (San Francisco: Freedom Archives, 2005) and in *Radio Free Dixie: Robert F. Williams and the Roots of Black Power* by Timothy B. Tyson (Chapel Hill: University of North Carolina Press, 1999).

Rural Mississippi had also made believers out of the young SNCC cadre. SNCC had started its "Mississippi Freedom Summer" campaign in 1964 as nonviolent activists. After experiencing the death of several of their comrades and supporters and the raw terror that the police and Klan/ Night Riders inspired, all of the SNCC cadre had armed themselves by the time they left Mississippi. SNCC leader H. Rap Brown was arrested when a rifle and banana clips were found in his luggage after a flight from Mississippi. SNCC eventually changed its name to the "Student National Coordinating Committee," dropping the "Nonviolent" description. Yet it was too little, too late, as the momentum was already shifting to the cities of the North and the West. SNCC's last effort in 1965 was to organize the Lowndes County Freedom Organization, whose emblem was a black panther (with no direct association to the Black Panther Party founded in October 1966). The Lowndes Country Freedom Organization adopted armed self-defense from the beginning. Although they experimented with the slogan "Black Power," they did not make any far-reaching progress, as their political goal was still "civil rights."

The 1965 Watts rebellion in California was the signal that the momentum in the Black struggle was shifting to the cities. Within two years, a number of rebellions occurred in other major cities and small towns. This was a qualitatively different situation. Rather than peaceful demonstrators seeking to acquire "civil rights," these events were massive and widespread rebellions (Watts: thirty-four dead; New York, Philadelphia, Birmingham, and Newark: twenty-six dead; Detroit: forty-three dead. And in each case there were hundreds wounded, with massive property damage). The keen political observer could not miss the parallels between these rebellions and those that had preceded revolutions and armed struggles in other countries. But guess what was missing from this equation? No urban-based Black political groups had armed components.[4] There were no Black fighting formations to organize, control, and direct these rebellions. The

---

4   National Advisory Commission on Civil Disorders, Report of the NACCD, Washington, DC: U.S. Government Printing Office, 1968, 19–21.

Fruit of Islam was clearly not up to the job because they had not been able to properly respond to the killings and shootings of their members by the local police. Nor could the rural-based groups lend any support, as they were still involved in life-and-death struggles with the Klan and southern police. SNCC made a half-hearted attempt to transfer their operations to urban areas. However, besides H. Rap Brown and a few others, it seemed that after their southern experience SNCC was scared off.

The urban rebellions brought forth scores of new political formations and these formations generally adhered theoretically to the idea of armed self-defense. Along with this shift in tactics came the new nationalist (sounding) politics, which were usually of a separatist bent—although the rediscovery of pan-Africanism began to occur as well. Unfortunately these new formations adopted the "high profile" strategy of the civil rights movement, which brought excessive media coverage. In reality, these organizations were no longer part of the civil rights movement and were now involved in the "Black liberation struggle." The civil rights people needed this type of exposure to get their message across and to help protect them against the most flagrant abuses. The Black liberation struggle, however, demanded a more clandestine way of handling affairs. It had to prepare for a guerrilla war and to take on this preparation in secret.

This fact was lost on the new, younger organizations. They were impressed by Malcolm X and the fiery orators but did not realize that Malcolm X had served as a motivator and educator. They did not understand that they were embarking on a new phase that demanded quiet, patient organizing and training. The tens of thousands of potential recruits were already showing, through the massive rebellions, that they were already sufficiently stimulated and were waiting for someone to show them how to get the job done. ("Rattling a sword makes a lot of noise . . . drawing one is silent.") There was still a good deal of agitation, propaganda, and education that needed to be done, but not by those who saw their mission as forming Black fighting formations. This mistake was usually made because these groups tried to combine the activities of the military and political workers in the same cadre. They did not realize that the situation demanded specialization: both political workers (motivators, educators, marchers, etc.) and military workers (armed self-defense and assault units). The Deacons had had it right!

An outstanding practitioner of this new form of resistance was the Revolutionary Action Movement (RAM) which began an intensive organizing campaign in the Northeastern states in 1966 and 1967. Much of its activity was centered in Philadelphia. RAM was militant, nationalist, and high profile. Its cadre spray-painted "Join the Black Guard" slogan on walls in the communities. (The Black Guard was their public military arm). RAM's leaders were in front of the cameras on all the important issues and the Black Guard cadre could often be seen at their "cultural centers," wearing fatigues and black berets. The sisters and brothers in RAM's youth group, "The Liberators," dressed in black with black berets. These activities helped members of the Black community feel good and believe that revolution was right around the corner. (Ironically, no one in Philadelphia had heard of the similar group, which began in California, known as the Black Panther Party for Defense and Justice.) RAM's activity scared white folks, especially because some members of RAM went out of their way to ensure this. They reasoned that they had been kept down long enough and it was time to strike back!

Unfortunately in 1967 the white establishment struck back too, and over a period of months H. Rap Brown and other leaders and key cadre were arrested. While RAM advocated self-defense and owned weapons, its members did not carry them in public. Consequently, they were arrested for everything from jaywalking to conspiring to put cyanide in police department rations at a major holiday celebration.[5] RAM had not fired a shot, however some alleged members and supporters were arrested bringing dynamite back from Canada (allegedly to blow up the Statue of Liberty!).

---

5   Maxwell C. Stanford/Akbar Muhammad Ahmed, "Revolutionary Action Movement (RAM): A Case Study of an Urban Revolutionary Movement," Master's Thesis, Atlanta: Atlanta University, 1986.

These arrests crippled RAM and the organization never regained its former vitality. Its leaders and cadres were forced to deal with the trumped-up charges for years afterward. RAM was not the only group facing this scenario, as it was also played out in Black communities around the country. In fact, the FBI—the original coordinators of this attack on RAM—transmitted its results to police forces throughout the country. The government's success in carrying out this campaign resulted from the fact that all of these groups were inexperienced. They were never given the time to get grounded after they publicly demonstrated their militancy. These Black fighting formations never had the chance to fight and many of their members became discouraged after such experiences, turning to crime and/or drugs.

The situation with the Black Panther Party for Defense and Justice (BPP) was somewhat different. This group, founded 1966 in Oakland, followed the same pattern as RAM, but it had an advantage. There was a clause in the California State law that allowed citizens to carry arms in public as long as they were not loaded. The BPP took full advantage of this clause in order to brandish weapons wherever they went. At that time, this seemed to be the height of militancy and they received more attention than any other group from the community, media, and police. Despite this attention, they could not be dealt with as easily as RAM because RAM always carried loaded weapons. After a few confrontations with the police it became apparent that the police could not bluff or intimidate these young Blacks. Because of this, BPP members were provoked into gun battles with the police and, within a year, cofounder Huey Newton had been shot and was imprisoned for killing the cop who shot him. "Little" Bobby Hutton was the first BPP member to be killed after two carloads of Panthers were ambushed by the police. Others were wounded and jailed. Bobby Seale, the other cofounder, had been jailed for marching into the state capital with other Panthers to protest a new law which prohibited carrying guns in public. The top three leaders, Newton, Seale, and Eldridge Cleaver (who was captured after the shootout with the police in which Hutton was killed) were all in prison, along with other key leaders and cadre.

There was a positive side to all of this, however—membership in the BPP skyrocketed! Chapters were formed up and down the West Coast, in the Midwest, Northeast, and South. The BPP became a magnet that attracted most of the smaller local organizations which were of a similar mindset. Additionally, the assassination of Martin Luther King in 1968 inspired even greater numbers to join. At this time the BPP was not carrying guns in public and yet the police onslaught continued. BPP offices and homes of Panthers were raided from coast to coast. Police agents infiltrated their ranks, provoked deadly confrontations with local police, and instigated rivalries with other Black organizations. BPP members were actually hunting and killing each other because of these agent-provocateurs. The Panthers were a potentially strong Black fighting formation but they were forced to take to the streets before they were ready. ("The field of battle is a land of standing corpses.") Panthers were dying in the streets, in raids, and in prison (Soledad, San Quentin, Attica, and Atmore-Holman to name but a few). It was a "war to the knife!"[6]

The Panthers were not the only Black fighting formation. There were other revolutionaries and "free shooters" who were every bit as committed, armed, and involved in the Black liberation struggle. Examples of these others include:

Fred Ahmad Evans and his squad of Black guerrillas who were able to trap the Cleveland, Ohio, police in a deadly ambush in which a number of police were wounded and killed. Some guerrillas were unfortunately killed as well and others were wounded, while Evans was imprisoned. He later died in prison. In response to the ambush the police demanded more men and guns and displayed a .50 caliber heavy machine gun that had raked their squad cars.

Mark Essex, a "free shooter," held off an army of police atop a high-rise hotel in Louisiana and inflicted many casualties. A helicopter gunship had to be called in to kill him.

---

6   George Jackson, *Blood in My Eye* (Baltimore: Black Classic Press, 1990).

Jonathan Jackson, who walked into a courtroom in San Rafael, CA, and pulled out a submachine gun from his duffel bag, disarmed all of the sheriffs (and gave pistols and shotguns to James McClain, William Christmas, and Ruchell Cinque Magee, who were comrades of his brother George Jackson). They rounded up the white judge, district attorney, and a number of jurors as hostages. After forcing their way past the rest of the sheriffs and other police, their get-away van was riddled with bullets, killing Jackson, McClain, and Christmas. Magee was wounded but survived. Before they died, they shot the judge in the head with the shotgun they had taped under his chin. The DA and a juror were also shot, but survived. Jonathan Jackson's brother George was a field marshal in the BPP and was killed the following year in San Quentin, although not before he was able to kill three prison guards and two inmate snitches. As it turned out, all of these brothers were set up by agent-provocateur Louis Tackwood, who had married one of their sisters![7]

The revolutionary Republic of New Africa (RNA) that Robert F. Williams once headed, gunned down a number of Detroit police after they tried to storm a meeting RNA's leaders were holding out in a church. A few years later they killed a sheriff after their headquarters was raided in Jackson, Mississippi. That raid sent their entire leadership to prison.[8]

"Free shooters" killed police in sniper attacks in projects in Philadelphia, Chicago, St. Louis, and New Orleans.

H. Rap Brown became a fugitive after a bomb in his comrade's car went off outside of a court building. A year or so later he was wounded and captured after a gun battle between his "liberators" from East St. Louis and the police in New York City. A number of the liberators were captured.

---

7   See Gregory Armstrong, *The Dragon Has Come* (New York: Harper and Row, 1974), and Paul Liberator, *The Road to Hell* (New York: Atlantic Monthly Press, 1996).
8   See: Imari Abubakari Ohadele/Milton Henry, *Free the Land!* (Washington, DC: House of Songhay, 1984.)

Police were being attacked while they sat in their cars or directed traffic. It was war: There were sisters and brothers hijacking passenger jets to Cuba and Algeria, where the BPP had a branch of fugitives headed by Cleaver. (Cleaver had left the country to avoid going back to prison for the Little Bobby Hutton shootout.) All of this was very sobering for BPP members. The early flash and profile was giving way to a desperate search to find a way to regain the initiative and plug the security gaps. Finally, it was decided that what was needed was an autonomous strike force that could handle all of the armed actions while the rest of the BPP would keep up and expand the community programs, such as free breakfast, education, sickle-cell testing, clothing drives, and so forth. In reality, it was again too little, too late.

Most of the mistrust had been instigated by the actions of the agents and their handlers (FBI, police). This was only possible because the youthful leadership had no firm understanding of intelligence and counterintelligence activities or how to combat them. More importantly, they did not have a firm grip on *The Art of War*, which included instructions on how to deal with all that troubled them. Unfortunately there was no turning back. Orders went out to the field marshals to begin organizing a separate guerrilla group known as the "Black Liberation Army."

A very important piece was missed at this point and that was the recruitment of the street gangs. The BPP had only made a half-hearted attempt to reach them and a lack of experience hindered that effort. The fact of the matter is that the street gangs were only susceptible to a program that included fighting as its main component. The street gangs told the old BPP, who wanted cadres who were both political and military workers, "Come back when you're ready to fight." Now the time for fighting had come, but in its haste to begin this new phase, the BPP ignored the gangs again. It must be recognized that events were happening at such a rapid and desperate pace that it was hard to do anything but proceed full steam ahead. Nevertheless, a little foresight would have indicated that there were benefits to thinking a strategy through in a more developed manner.

A major stumbling block in the launching of this new phase was the growing unrest among the rank-and-file because of the leadership's belated effort to deal with these problems. Despite this, the "new phase" was launched with the BPP cadres studying texts on guerrilla warfare, refusing to be arrested for any reason, and launching planned attacks on various targets. In New York City, a gun battle broke out between the police and BPP members after an attempted arrest for carrying concealed weapons. When the smoke had cleared, a cop was dead along with BPP member Harold Russell. Two other BPP members, Robert Ra'uf Vickers and Anthony Kimu White, were wounded and Kimu was arrested. Ra'uf escaped and went underground where doctors helped him heal his wounds. He was then able to return to the field. In California, Geronimo ji-Jaga Pratt was out on bail in connection with the 1969 gun battle that resulted from a police raid on the Los Angeles BPP headquarters. He went underground and formed a guerrilla group. In Philadelphia, a guerrilla group raided a police station, killing one cop and wounding another. BPP guerrilla groups were raiding banks for funds, hijacking food to give to the community, and acquiring sophisticated military weapons.

This intensified activity was bringing the pressure down on the BPP political workers and, after the raid on the Philadelphia police station, the police raided every BPP office in the city. The BPP, however, was ready for them.

After gun battles at two of the offices, the Panthers were forced to surrender. This activity also provoked gun battles between the police and other Blacks. In a forty-eight-hour period the score was: six cops in the hospital with gunshot wounds and one cop in the morgue, Panthers and guerrillas in prison, and other guerrillas on the run. They were learning! All of the Panthers were released because the police could not officially justify the raids in the face of a massive protest from the Black community.

It is unfortunate that groups in the Black liberation struggle did not operate this way from the beginning. The growing awareness on how to attack their problems had not being digested at all by the larger movement, and a split developed between those who advocated the new phase of resistance and other leaders who advocated taking armed struggle out of the movement altogether. The latter group was moving backward and did not recognize that the lessons learned from Philadelphia were crystal clear: police were killed and wounded while the Panthers were released from prison and there were no Panther casualties. There was also heightened community support and participation. A few weeks after the Philadelphia incident, BPP members held a major convention in the city without any police interference. The convention was also held despite police intelligence sources within the BPP correctly informing their superiors that the guerrillas accused of the raids had been regularly seen at BPP offices and that one of them, Robert Saeed Joyner, was there every day. The Black community could clearly see a tenuous separation between those who were participating in planned assaults (the guerrillas) and the BPP political workers. It was also clear that there was no reason to suspend armed action and it was probably too late to do so.

Beyond the disagreements and splits over the issue of arms in the struggle, there were numerous complaints about the new "opulent" lifestyle that various leaders of the BPP had adopted. After his release from prison in 1970, Huey Newton hung out with Hollywood stars and rented expensive apartments. Despite disgust and anger over these developments, the real beef was with the poor strategy that continued to get members killed and imprisoned. Newton, who was still the top leader, advocated no guns. For those who wanted to fight or who were underground, he sent an open communiqué to the North Vietnamese government that he would make one thousand BPP members available to fight in Vietnam against U.S. forces. This was very odd to say the least. Of course the Panthers were highly supportive of the Viet Cong's fight, but very few could see any reason why they should not show their support by stepping up armed action within the United States rather than offer to fight on foreign ground. The Vietnamese government was of a similar opinion. It openly declined the offer and suggested that the BPP could better help by supporting them from within the United States.

At this point, other Panther leaders started speaking against Newton more strongly. Eldridge Cleaver (who had been feuding with Newton from Algeria) stated emphatically that it was time to stop bullshitting and that the armed struggle needed to be fully supported. He made arrangements with the Algerian government for Panthers and others to come to Algeria for military training. Similarly, Field Marshall George Jackson continued to advocate and write about the necessity for a similar shift in the struggle and how it needed to be carried out. He unquestionably would have been the most effective leader to implement this new strategy because of his superior theories, his desire to implement them, his desperation (at the time he was preparing to go to trial for the killing of a prison guard), and most importantly because of the widespread respect and admiration he received from others.

It would not have been difficult to "liberate" him from prison, provided that the BPP put its full resources behind the effort. There was no lack of BPP members, female and male, who would have volunteered for such an honored mission. Sadly, the West Coast leadership of Newton and company, along with the police and prison establishments, had cut him off from direct contact with those who were ready, willing, and able to carry it out. Consequently, he was set up by these establishments and was assassinated—though not before Jackson and his prison "Black Guerrilla Family" killed five of the enemy. Magee had recovered from his court-house wounds and was in the battle as well.[9] August 21, 1971, the date of Jackson's death, was a sad day. After his memorial, Attica exploded and the battle ended with forty-three deaths. Black guerrillas walked into a California police station, killed a sergeant and shot up the station. The George L. Jackson Assault Team of the BLA took credit for that act.

The question of the "split" on policy and strategy was solved after a force dispatched by Newton shot and killed Robert Webb when he revealed unfavorable details about the inner workings of the West Coast

---

9   Eric Mann, *Comrade George: An Investigation into the Official Story of His Assassination* (Cambridge, MA: Hovey Street Press, 1972.)

leadership clique. Robert Webb was a top Panther leader and bodyguard of Newton. It was his words at a New York meeting, attended by disgruntled Panthers from all over the country, that were the most damaging to the West Coast leadership. Allegations of opulence (penthouses, limousines, etc.), pimping BPP female members, and cocaine addiction were raised. The following day, the main West Coast representative, central committee member Samuel Napier, was found dead in a burned-out office. He had been tied to a chair and riddled with bullets. Shortly thereafter, the West Coast delegation placed themselves under police protection until they could make arrangements to return to California! The word went out that the police were looking for a number of people in connection with the shooting and the previously held meeting and this forced many to go underground. Although the Panthers should have been prepared for a situation like this, sadly they were not. Once again, the dictums of *The Art of War* were ignored. While some tried to adhere to them, too many others were still running their operations and actions in a haphazard and shortsighted manner.

This unfortunate situation did swell the ranks of the guerrillas considerably, however. Intensive training was undertaken by these new guerrillas. They raided banks for funds and gun stores for arms and ammunition. Once again, this should have been a new beginning, but because the situation was forced on them as a result of the actions of older BPP members, aboveground political work and activity was all but destroyed. The same mistake that the civil rights movement had made was revisited upon the BPP: Both had put too much stock in one facet of the resistance. With the civil rights movement there was too much focus on political work and not nearly enough on military components, and with the guerrilla groups it was just the opposite. It was not clear to either of these groups that professionals must lead revolutions if destruction is to be avoided.

One may not be professional from the start, but it's imperative that professionalism be acquired as soon as is possible. The hallmark of the professional is the ability to proceed from point A to point B without wasting energy, learning from the mistakes of others and one's own, not repeating them, and emulating the successes of others whenever possible.

This new phase had not been solidly launched—rather it was launched in an unprofessional manner. Adequate time was not taken to evaluate where the movement had been, where it was at, and where it was going. After finally adopting the right style, it lost contact with the substance of what the struggle was all about. "War is an extension of politics"; it is "politics by different means." It follows that the military wing had to take its cue from whatever was happening in the political arena, as the Deacons had done. But it was not to be. The BLA groups were busy acquiring and consolidating their logistical base (raiding banks, gun stores, acquiring transportation, safe houses, etc.) and this was understandable and proper. At the same time they were launching deadly attacks on the police, and since these were planned assaults they were much more successful than the old BPP shootouts. Usually these attacks were carried out so swiftly that when the smoke had cleared the cops were either dead or wounded and the guerrillas had disappeared. They had learned how to reverse the killed and wounded ratio. Once again, they should have been operating this way from the beginning. They still suffered casualties from the rare operations that resulted in a running gunfight, when they were subjected to car stops, and when they were forced into confrontations. The casualties in these situations were devastating because the BLA did not have an adequate political apparatus to replenish their forces, nor did they understand the necessity to integrate local street gangs into their activities.

The BLA became the top priority of the special FBI/local police task forces. To a great degree, BLA guerrilla groups did not fall victim to being infiltrated by agents. If they had not been caught off balance, they would have had to make some other mistake to give these task forces an advantage, such as increased surveillance. The BLA fielded the most effective Black assault units since the maroons! Their primary weakness, and the situation which caused them the most harm, was their failure to properly integrate themselves with the Black masses and their inability to interact with aboveground revolutionary political groups. The BLA did attempt to reintegrate political workers who had left or been expelled from the BPP. Since most of these workers were located on the East Coast, they were known as the East Coast Panthers. This group did not have any of the same vitality, stature, resources, or connections that they had previously enjoyed, but they did have the know-how to put together a new political organization that could eclipse even the BPP by using aboveground recruiting from former Panthers and other political Blacks. In order to do this, they would have had to channel their energies and resources away from their armed activities while taking time to rebuild a political apparatus. Before the BLA guerrillas would come to this conclusion, however, they were imprisoned, killed, and exiled.

BLA members continued their revolutionary commitment after being imprisoned and several were able to escape or attempt escape:

BLA member John Andalewa Clark was killed in 1976 at Trenton State Prison in New Jersey, after he and other BLA members fought a battle against armed guards. Clark and his allies were armed with homemade weapons and bombs. The State Police discovered a van parked a few blocks from the prison that was loaded with weapons and camping supplies.

A BLA member was killed in a fall from a high-rise prison in New York, after another prisoner had descended on the same rope.

BLA member Herman Bell was overpowered after holding a guard hostage while attempting to escape from Rikers Island prison in New York. A rubber raft and other gear were discovered outside of his building.

Russell Maroon Shoatz and three other BLA members escaped in 1977 from the State Prison at Huntingdon, PA. Two of these brothers were recaptured and BLA member Wayne Musa Henderson was killed. Maroon was recaptured after a twenty-seven-day hunt.

BLA member Assata Shakur was liberated in 1979 by a BLA task force which walked into the Clinton Prison in New Jersey and commandeered the visiting area. She later resurfaced in Cuba.

BLA member Kuwasi Balagoon escaped from a New Jersey state prison. He was part of the BLA task force that liberated Assata Shakur.

Arthur Cetawayo Johnson and Robert Saeed Joyner, two BLA members, took over a cellblock in the State Prison at Pittsburgh, PA, in 1979 in an attempt to escape. They and a few of the brothers, who had helped, were overpowered.

Russell Maroon Shoatz and Cliff Lumumba Futch escaped from a state mental hospital in PA in 1980. They and Phyllis Oshun Hill, who had smuggled them the escape weapons, were captured three days later after a gun battle with the police and FBI.

BLA member Sundiata Acoli and a number of other prisoners were almost killed in 1980–1981 when guards at the federal prison at Marion, IL, opened fire after they learned that they were trying to cut through the security fence.

BLA member Joseph Joe-Joe Bowen and three other brothers held guards at gunpoint for six days in 1981 after a failed escape at the State Prison at Graterford, PA. Joe-Joe and the BLA member Fred Muhammad Kafi Burton had assassinated the warden and deputy warden at the Holmesburg prison in Philadelphia in 1973.

There were many more incidents and the prison authorities dealt with them by keeping BLA members in the hole for five, ten, even fifteen years. BLA member Ruchell Cinque Magee (courthouse shootout and the San Quentin rebellion in which Jackson was killed) has spent most of his thirty years in the hole. The prison authorities cut them off from the general population, just like they had done to Field Marshal George Jackson. Most of them have sentences that make it unlikely that they will ever be released back into society. A campaign for their deportation to a foreign (African) country holds real possibilities that can serve as an organizing tool. There is much more that needs to be said about the lessons these Black fighting formations learned on a tactical level. However, that is another paper.

The Dragon and the Hydra
A Historical Study of
Organizational Methods
(2006)

You have fifteen, twenty, years of civil wars and people's struggles to go through, not only to change the conditions but in order to change yourselves and make yourselves fit for political rule.
—Karl Marx, addressing the International Working Men's Association, the body that would later become the First International.

Marx's words hit close to home. I've been involved in such struggles for forty years, a product—originally—of the Black liberation movement of the 1960s, and subsequently of being held as a political prisoner in the United States since 1972. Over that period, I've participated in a number of mass and party formations. It never fails to amaze me how much energy and time is dedicated toward establishing the claims of various groups to be the so-called vanguard of some struggle for justice, when in the end most of these exercises turn out to be sterile—when they don't degenerate into fratricidal conflicts.

Furthermore, I'd hazard to say, that the entire history of Marxist-Leninist social change has known few other methods, leading me to say further that a sober analysis of that history points to a struggle for supremacy—not only over the bourgeois ruling class, but also against the working class and all other oppressed people; against any and all formations that escape the control of these so-called vanguard groups. Thus, their mantra of doing everything to seize power for the working class and oppressed is a farce.

If there has ever been a Marxist-Leninist vanguard party that has found itself in power and did not subsequently follow this script, I'm not aware of it. While arguments can always be found to rationalize why it was/is necessary to resort to such measures, and many such arguments do make sense—initially—a closer look always seems to force adherents to fall back on the mantra of the flawed individual(s) who did not hold true to the principles of Democratic Centralism (DC). These are wide open to interpretation and manipulation, in order to seize the initiative in a struggle for domination—as opposed to trying to make a "concrete analysis of concrete conditions," as V.I. Lenin instructed.

I had reached these conclusions on my own. Later, I was astounded to learn that the Marxist giant C.L.R. James (the author of the theory that explains state capitalism, and the mentor of the African revolutionaries Jomo Kenyatta and Kwame Nkrumah—who brought both Kenya and Ghana out of colonialism) as early as 1963 had said:

> We have repudiated the conception of the vanguard party. That conception ruined the socialist movement, and the movement of the proletariat, for a generation. . . . The vanguard party conception ruined all attempts to form a Marxist party in the U.S. and contributed substantially to the catastrophes which have befallen it. . . . What has happened is that their whole outlook and mentality have been dominated by the concept of a vanguard party which had to teach the people about Marxism and other such matters which would make the people understand that they, the preachers, were the ones who should be followed as they were the leaders of the socialist revolution. . . . The whole Stalinist experiment, the whole Nazi regime, are not the result of evil men. They are the result of the drive towards the unification of the executive and political organization of all aspects of the State [democratic centralism's historical modus operandi, which is supervised and enforced by the vanguard party].[1]

At the same time, history has shown that such ruthless methods are effective: if the objective of those who used the DC methods was simply to seize power, then their record during the twentieth century is impressive. It has proved itself as brutally efficient and capable of outdoing anything bourgeois forces are capable of.

---

1   C.L.R. James, *Marxism for Our Times*, ed. Martin Glaberman (Jackson: University Press of Mississippi, 1999), 104–5, 110–12

Nevertheless in the end, those who gained power using DC have always ended up using it to defeat the aspirations of the workers and oppressed, and to subsequently install themselves as a new oppressive ruling class.

How could it be expected to produce any other outcome? DC concentrates more power in the hands of a relative few than any mechanisms that the masses themselves—who practitioners of DC purport to be serving—can muster. It is a recipe that's bound to create conflict given the vagaries of flawed humans.

Stan Goff, in his masterful *Full Spectrum Disorder* (2004), believes that DC as practiced by Lenin and his Bolsheviks did have a democratic basis, whereby an open and intense democratic struggle was carried out in order to arrive at positions and policies. Then all the party workers would move in a decentralized, free-wheeling manner to make possible the implementation of those decisions (in the teeth of czarist repression), which ultimately had the effect of centralizing their combined efforts. Only later did these methods change, leading to an all around centralization and very little democracy, if any. Without a doubt, any number of other Marxist/Leninist/Maoist (style) groups have had similar experiences.

Yet, if the clear historical tendency is to always gravitate toward less democratic and more oppressive forms of control, then, quite frankly, for one to suggest that we can use historical materialism to formulate correct ideas, theories, and plans for liberation by using DC is ludicrous!

The Contemporary Situation

Here we are, at the beginning of the twenty-first century, facing a global crisis unknown heretofore in the entire history of humankind. The threats to our collective existence are so multidimensional that it would take many pages to detail them all. Consequently, I'll limit myself to those that I believe are paramount in helping us to break out of self-imposed mental roadblocks that hinder our efforts to move forward.

The main threat to humankind, to the flora and fauna and to our entire biosphere, is capitalist imperialism: a totally out-of-control, predatory, global system of accumulation and oppression that's on a collision course with the limitations of our planet: daily devouring children, women, people of color, the poor, workers of all stripes, wildlife, and the environment in pursuit of profits.

All of our problems rest primarily on artificial divisions that have been engendered between different oppressed groups for hundreds of years: divisions based on gender, race, ethnicity, culture, geography, sexual preferences, age, and similar factors. These divisions have been fostered, historically, by those who have sought to use them in their pursuit of power and material gain.

Under imperialism, the overwhelming majority of our planet's humans are, ultimately, workers. Thus, Marx's address to the IWMA still holds true today—although he underestimated the degree of opposition the workers would face, and the length of time it would take for them to overcome all of the obstacles in their path.

Marx, superb analyst that he was, remained trapped by Eurocentric predilections. He overlooked or dismissed important workers' struggles that fell outside of Europe. At the very least he failed to study them with the same intensity that he devoted to those in Europe, upon which he (primarily) based his otherwise well-grounded analysis. That set in motion a process by which others willfully neglected to formulate a proper evaluation of these other struggles, even to today. A thorough study, evaluation, adaptation (wherever applicable) and understanding of some of these workers' struggles will help us move forward in our struggle against imperialism. There, we'll find proven, workable alternatives to the flawed DC forms of organizing: ones that mirror Stan Goff's analysis of the strengths of the early Bolsheviks.

Back to the Future

First off, let me state that I'm not an anarchist. Yet, a lot of what you'll read here is going to look a whole lot like anarchism! To that end, I will only quote an unknown ancient, who, after racking his brain to formulate answers to vexing problems, later discovered that those who came before him had already expounded on what he thought were his intellectual inventions. He is supposed to have blurted: "Confound those ancients, they've stolen all of our best ideas."

Therefore, to the anarchist reader, let me say that what follows cannot properly be termed anarchism, simply because the practitioners themselves never knew that word, nor were they in contact with people of that view, as anarchism is a European ideology. These parties—for the most part—were Africans and Amerindians with very limited input from a small number of outcast Europeans. Further, all of the struggles written about here had pretty much taken off and gained success prior to the spread of this concept—under its classical anarchist thinkers and practitioners.

Still, the affinity between anarchism and the analysis which follows is not rejected. On the contrary, it's welcomed as a sister set of ideas, beliefs, and concepts—so long as the anarchists understand that they stand on equal footing, in a spirit of intercommunal self-determination.

Historical Overview

The following is a short outline of various workers' struggles against early European imperialism, as practiced in Suriname, Jamaica, a number of southern areas of what is today the United States, and finally Haiti. I'll outline how workers who had been enslaved fought longer than Marx's "fifteen, twenty, fifty years of civil wars and peoples struggles" in order to ultimately exercise their own forms of self-determination and political rule. And although all of these struggles were as stratified as we are today, they were still able to democratically derive methods and policies that were collectively pursued by decentralized formations of their own making. And once they won freedom from the various imperialist powers, unlike the later states ruled by Marxist vanguard formations, their worker-based autonomy was never again relinquished, until the present day, with one exception (Haiti) that deserves special attention.

Afterward, I hope that you will do your own in-depth research and study, because to most people the bulk of this history will be unfamiliar. Then you can decide whether such organizational forms and methods would be useful to us in our struggle to save ourselves and the planet.

Suriname

"We must slay the Hydra." That was the Dutch imperialists' main concern in Suriname from their earliest days there. (Hydra: In Greek mythology, a many-headed monster whose heads regrew when struck off. It was finally killed by Hercules. It is also the largest and longest constellation in the sky, but with no particular bright star.)

On the northern coast of South America, this tropical country borders Guyana and French Guyana and fronts the Caribbean Sea, with Brazil to its south. In total landmass it is more than one-third as large as Cuba.

The first European interlopers to visit the area were the British, who were followed by the Dutch. The territory frequently changed hands between them, but the Dutch were the main imperial power to occupy the country, from the mid-1600s up until the 1970s. Throughout this period, the overwhelming majority of the indigenous Amerindian populations were either suppressed, forced to flee to less hospitable areas, or exterminated.

The Dutch were one of the world's major imperial powers at that time, vying alongside of the British, Spanish, Danish, Portuguese, and the French for control of North and South America, the Caribbean, and other parts of the world.

The Dutch West Indies Company was one of the first corporations in the world. In Suriname, it launched plantation-based production of cash crops on a large scale, using enslaved workers imported from different parts of Africa. Added to that were a number of other plantations run by other European "entrepreneurs," along with their overseers, shopkeepers, militias, artisans, administrators, bureaucrats, sailors, and a small percentage of (mostly) poor white women who had been exiled from Europe.

Compared to the enslaved Africans and the suppressed Amerindians, one could compare everyone else—except the small number of plantation-operating entrepreneurs and administrators—with what we today recognize as the labor aristocracy and petty bourgeoisie of the technologically advanced countries. Those elements were fully dependent for their livelihood and for the protection of their persons and property from the enslaved workers and remaining indigenous people, on the Dutch military, militias, the imperial court, and the big mercantilists.

I make this comparison because we all-too-often fail to point out that the enslaved Africans were transported across the Atlantic to assume the role of workers, and just about everyone else associated with their plight were also—first and foremost—other workers, similar to our plight today. And the issue of race did not—could not—change this basic fact! So keep that in mind as we develop this analysis.

Among the Africans were many different ethnic groups from different areas of the continent, all speaking different languages and with many varied religious and cultural practices. To get an idea of the stratification of these Africans, consider the fact that they all had dark skins meant next to nothing to them in terms of solidarity. Where they originally came from everybody had dark skin, friends and enemies alike! Further, it was the practice of the plantation owners to try to purchase workers from different backgrounds in order to keep them divided as much as possible. And because the work was so brutal and the food so inadequate, most plantations were really death camps, where the African workers were literally worked to death in a few years—only to be replaced with newly imported enslaved workers who would also go on to make handsome profits for the owners. Thus, the turnover itself was a powerful check on the formation of any solidarity between the enslaved workers.

Be that as it may, almost from the first importation of enslaved Africans there developed a tradition of flight from slavery: Africans ran away to the forests, swamps, and highlands. These fugitives came to be known as "Bosch Creoles" (Dutch for "Bush Creoles") or "born in the forest" and later "bush negroes." We'll call them "maroons" throughout our study, as a generic name that has come to be an accepted way to describe fugitive, enslaved people throughout the Western Hemisphere.

Everywhere we look in that part of the world, we witness these collective maroons developing and using a very effective form of decentralized organizing that not only served to help them defeat their former enslavers, but has also to remain autonomous from all unwanted overseers for hundreds of years—until our time.

It must be recalled that the Suriname Africans were from many different backgrounds, so when they would come together as maroons that reality would have to be factored in. They had to organize using democratic methods, and the glue that held them together was their collective focus on defeating their enslavers' attempts to control them. *This* is what centralized their efforts.

There remained, however, one class within these communities which was different: those Africans who did not flee, but were forced by maroon raiders to leave the plantations. These individuals did not enjoy a say in community affairs until they had proven themselves.

But as a general rule, individuals and small groups would flee the plantations to join the maroons. On some occasions large conspiracies were organized that saw the enslaved workers prepare the groundwork for maroon guerrillas to raid plantations and liberate scores at a time.

This example shows how decisions could be arrived at by truly democratic means, and then carried out in a centralized manner by otherwise decentralized groups—long before our Bolsheviks!

Over a 150-year period, the various maroon communities of Suriname would wage a guerrilla war with the Dutch and English slavers to remain free. Today in Suriname their direct descendants still occupy the land on which their ancestors fought, and most of them have never been enslaved—dating from a time even before the United States signed its own Declaration of Independence in 1776.

Even as this is written they remain autonomous from the government of Suriname, which gained its independence from the Netherlands (whose Dutch ancestors we're discussing) in 1975. In fact, the descendants of the early maroons were again forced to fight another guerrilla war against the newly independent government in 1980—a successful effort on the part of the maroons to maintain their autonomy and control over the lands they've historically occupied.

Their decentralized methods had their drawbacks. Their enemies in the imperialist camp were able to manipulate various maroon communities into signing treaties that gave them their freedom from enslavement and land to use—in exchange for cooperation in hunting down and capturing other fugitives. In this way, the enslavers could avoid the all-but-useless wars designed to capture or kill the skillful maroon guerrillas. Everyone in the maroon guerrilla communities, including the women and children, could and would—at the drop of a hat—pack their belongings and escape to prearranged and fortified alternative settlements, while the men (and some women) busied themselves in fighting rearguard actions against the pursuing colonial soldiers.

It turns out, however, that although the treaties did solve some of the imperialists' problems, the Suriname maroons never really fulfilled their obligations to help the imperialists hunt and capture other maroons. A narrative of the Dutch forces' generations-long wars designed to either capture or kill the Boni Maroons is instructive in that regard.

By the mid-eighteenth century, the Dutch had been forced by over one hundred years of maroon guerrilla warfare to sign treaties with three of the most powerful maroon communities: the Ndjuka, the Saramaka, and the Matawai. All of these maroon communities had evolved over generations from fugitive Africans of many ethnicities into new ethnicities that adopted these names. Most importantly, they had soundly defeated all of the imperialist forces sent to capture or kill them, while continuing to expand their numbers and offer an ever-growing threat to the Dutch colony.

The treaties came with yearly "gifts" of all kinds that the Dutch would deliver to the maroons: textiles, pots and pans, guns, powder, axes, knives, mirrors, nails, liquor, and just about anything agreed upon during the periodic sit-downs between the parties. The underlying objectives of the imperialists were to rid themselves of a dangerous enemy and turn them into valuable allies.

Yet once it became known to the still-enslaved African workers that they could no longer rely on the Njuka, Saramaka, and Matawai for refuge and protection, they began to seek out smaller maroon communities. In the early 1700s, one of those small groups was headed by an African named Asikan Silvester. Born into this group was a child called Boni. His mother was a fugitive African and his father either African or Amerindian. Subsequently, the group chose Boni to be its new head, after Asikan became too old. This group of maroons would eventually become known to the Dutch as a new center of resistance, and for the next two generations Boni would lead them. They would become known to history as the "Boni Maroons," transforming themselves into an ethnicity. Thus, the Boni Maroons became a new contentious force, while the imperialists thought they were suppressing resistance by the signing of treaties with the other maroons. Consequently, the imperialists would not sign any more treaties with either the Bonis or any other maroons, which lasted to the end of the slave period.

Boni, for his part, would lead his group to aggressively wage war on the imperialists until his death in his mid-sixties.

Yet even while the Bonis became the main fighting force among all of those maroons who were still at war with the Dutch, they still observed and respected the democratic wishes of any fugitives or maroon groups they dealt with, never trying to centralize all control in their hands. Although the Bonis were masters in the use of coordinated guerrilla campaigns among all of the decentralized groups—during which a unified command was essential—they still never demanded that everyone integrate themselves into the Boni community. Nor did the other maroons put themselves directly under the Boni's leadership outside of agreed-upon guerrilla campaigns and raids. While leaders such as Kormantin Kodjo, Chief Puja, Boni, and Baron often united for large campaigns, their respective maroon communities remained decentralized and autonomous.

Unlike the "treaty maroons," the Bonis never became dependent upon the imperialists for anything, instead relying on their raiding capabilities to capture guns, powder, cannons, and other useful items. Moreover, they had perfected methods of large-scale open field agriculture that allowed them to raise, harvest, and store more food than they could consume—along with more farm animals than they could use to supplement their diets.

Dutch soldiers recorded discovering Boni and related maroon fields that took them an hour in one direction and thirty minutes in the other to mark off for destruction, along with so many domesticated chickens they had to slaughter the excess after feasting on them for days. The Dutch and other European colonizers always noted how much better the maroons were fed, and how much better physical specimens the maroons showed themselves to be. It became a prime goal for the Dutch-led troops to hunt and locate maroon food stores and farm animals in order to supplement their own poor diets.

During the final major Dutch campaign in the second Boni war, an expeditionary force of 1,600 Dutch regulars and European mercenaries, accompanied by thousands more colonial soldiers and enslaved African workers and "free negro rangers," were also unsuccessful, causing the commander to return to Europe with less than a dozen remaining from the force he'd led to Suriname. The commander himself died within a year.

From then until the ending of slavery, the Dutch relied on treachery—trying to manipulate the various treaty and (still) fighting maroons against each other. Although they did succeed in getting a younger, less-experienced generation of treaty maroons to assassinate Boni, Chief Puja, and Kormantin Kodjo (who were old men, and who had turned over their leadership to younger maroons), the other fighting maroons continued to exercise their autonomy until slavery was abolished. And today the Boni maroons still live autonomously in Suriname proper, where there are more than seventy thousand direct descendants of the "bush negroes."

The Dutch imperialists tried their best to slay the Hydra! They failed. Was it because the maroons' decentralized formations prevented the Dutch from concentrating their superior resources against any one centralized leadership—any bright star? I think so.

Have the various "bush negro" ethnicities been able to maintain their autonomy over hundreds of years, against all oppressive forces, through their refusal to allow themselves to be subjected by any broad centralizing forces? I think so again.

Jamaica

Across the Caribbean from Suriname—in Jamaica—from as early as the 1650s there developed similar decentralized maroon communities, only here they were fighting against the local enslavers of the British Empire. After generations of unsuccessful campaigns by the British against the maroon guerrillas, they too hit upon the necessity of trying to divide the fighting maroons from their main source of new recruits: the enslaved African workers. So the British offered the maroons "treaties" similar to those in Suriname.

Fighting tenaciously, skillfully and bravely for over a hundred years, the Dutch were forced to adopt nonmilitary trickery. And even though these methods were used, we also witness a number of new decentralized groups arising, who came to be recognized generally as the "windward" and "leeward" Maroons: the former located in the eastern (windward) end of Jamaica, and the latter on the westward (leeward) side. History records the most noted maroon of the windwards as an African womyn named Granny Nanny—who even had a town named after her in the maroons' liberated territory. Indeed, Nanny Town became the center of the resistance to British plantation imperialism in Jamaica, the headquarters from which the maroon bands almost succeeded in driving all of the imperialists from the island altogether—even though British soldiers captured and burned Nanny Town on a number of occasions.

The dominant personality among the leewards was an African man named Kodjo. History records Kodjo as leading a tightly controlled and centralized operation. But when the windwards had to make a trek across the island during one fierce effort to suppress them, seeking help from the leewards, even Kodjo could not force them to abandon their autonomy.

Tellingly, it was Granny Nanny who led a segment of decentralized windwards to resist signing treaties for the longest time. She went so far as to have the British envoys killed on more than one occasion, and only submitted after Kodjo and all of the male maroon leaders had capitulated.

After that, these maroons were used to help the British hunt and capture new runaways, as well as to suppress revolts among the still-enslaved African workers—although they fiercely clung to the freedom and autonomy they and their ancestors had fought for!

In fact, more than a generation later their descendants would again engage the British in the Trelawny War during the middle of the 1790s, in which a mere 267 maroon guerrillas fought thousands of British soldiers, local militia, and enslaved Africans to a complete standstill. However, they were then tricked and placed on boats to be deported to Canada, and later to Africa—after accepting a truce.

Even so, from then until now, the descendants of these remaining maroon communities in Jamaica still continue to occupy the lands they fought on. And they've never recognized any overlords, neither the later British nor Black governments!

The United States

It's ironic that those of us who live in the United States continue to neglect a thorough study and critique of the well-documented history of the anti-imperialist and anti-expansionist struggles that have occurred here since the start of European colonization, other than the well-known Native American suppression and genocide.

Like the volumes of works written about the civil rights and Black liberation struggles of the 1960s and 1970s, the early labor movement, womyn's suffrage movement, abolitionist movement, and reconstruction period, there's a mountain of other revolutionary material we can learn from. And, not surprisingly, that information concerns the struggles of enslaved workers on these shores prior to the abolition of chattel slavery. In fact, it mirrors the already-mentioned struggles in Suriname and Jamaica, with the important distinction that it encompasses multiracial aspects—more so than either of the former cases. Specifically, in the United States—until the abolition of slavery—Africans, Amerindians, and Europeans (in some areas) allied themselves to fight against the imperialist and expansionist powers. That phenomenon was also evident in the Caribbean and South America, but due to the large percentages of enslaved Africans compared to enslaved Amerindians and Europeans, most of those struggles were primarily between the enslaved Africans and the European imperialists.

Thus today in the United States, such emotionally charged epithets as "hillbilly" and "poor white trash" are totally divorced from their historical roots. The first people to be labeled as such were the descendants of the indentured European workers who had escaped that status and allied themselves with both the Amerindians and Africans—who had also escaped from slavery or servitude. All of them combined into maroon communities in areas that are now a part of the United States.

Initially, the derogatory "poor white trash" label was reserved for the rebellious, unexploitable, and nonconformist early Europeans who the colonial and imperial elites could neither control nor use to increase their power—thus the "trash" label. Later the "hillbilly" label and imagery were used to similarly isolate those runaways who moved into the southern Appalachian mountains, to escape their former indentured status. Both segments were staunch enemies of the imperialists and colonists. They often allied with Africans and Amerindians, who were also fugitives from enslavement. At times these three groups formed tri-racial maroon communities. At other times they were firmly allied though living separately—except in the case of the Amerindians and Africans who mixed freely.

Consequently, from the seventeenth century until the abolition of slavery in the United States, there were also maroon communities in areas stretching from the pine barrens of New Jersey, down the East Coast to

Florida, also in the Appalachian mountains and later in Mexico's northern border regions. The best known (but little studied) was a group that occupied the dismal swamp of Virginia and North Carolina, and the Seminoles of Florida, who contrary to popular belief have never been an Amerindian tribe but—from their beginnings—a group made up of Africans and Amerindians who came together to form a new ethnicity, just like the Boni Maroons did in Suriname.

All of this replicated the decentralized organizing forms of the maroons in Suriname and Jamaica. And although their political histories fall short of winning and maintaining the degree of autonomy achieved in Suriname or Jamaica, the descendants of the Seminoles in Mexico and the United States still fiercely guard their communities against the Mexican and U.S. governments. In Florida they're recognized as a semiautonomous tribe, and the Africans (Seminole negroes) in Oklahoma, Texas, and Mexico also distinguish themselves from their neighbors—while calling Blacks in the U.S. "state negroes." According to New Afrikan nationalist cadre from the United States who have worked with them, the African Seminoles never considered themselves citizens of the United States the way African Americans do.

Finally, the legendary history and present posture of the people of the southern Appalachians—in still refusing to fully integrate into the fabric of the United States—rests more on a forgotten history of their ancestors' struggle to remain free from all servitude and domination than they or we understand. Instead, we've adopted the bourgeois myth about a group which is hopelessly backward and ultraracist, although in reality true hillbilly culture and practice is isolationist and independent, reflecting the autonomist spirit of their ancestors.

Haiti

The history of Haiti provides an excellent laboratory in which to test my thesis. What became the country of Haiti was once known as San Domingo or Saint Domingo, the western part of the island of Hispaniola in the Caribbean. Today the country of the Dominican Republic occupies the larger, eastern part of the island.

There, between 1791 and 1804, we witness one of the most titanic struggles ever engaged between (enslaved) workers and their overlords. Through an examination of the events surrounding that struggle, we can clearly measure the strengths and weaknesses of our dragon and hydra: centralized and decentralized forces of change. Here is a much-neglected goldmine in our search for historical lessons—on a par with the great French Revolution of 1789.

For generations prior to the French Revolution—which set the stage for the Haitian revolt two years later—maroon guerrillas and communities had been operating throughout the entire island of Hispaniola. Later, many of their descendants would distinguish themselves among the multitudes of the little-known heroic figures of those times. Most notably, the intrepid Mackandal, in the prerevolutionary period (circa 1750s), organized and led a select group of African maroons and enslaved plantation workers in a conspiracy designed to overthrow the French and colonial powers through the massive and bewildering use of poisons—against individuals, livestock, supplies, water, and any African workers who were believed to be sympathetic to, or in league with, the French.

After years of terrorizing the colonialists of the island, Mackandal slipped up. He was betrayed and subsequently burned at the stake—fatally crippling his tightly organized, centralized movement.

By that time, in just about all of this territory, original Amerindians had been exterminated. They were replaced by an endless supply of enslaved Africans. The latter produced so much sugar and other agricultural produce that San Domingo became the crown jewel of the French empire and the backbone of the French economy. So Mackandal's terror campaigns were quickly pushed to the back of the exploiters' minds.

But within two years of the outbreak of the French Revolution and the subsequent turmoil caused by it in that colonial territory, a new generation stepped into Mackandal's shoes. One dark night, a large assembly of the colony's Africans met at a secret ceremony on a mountain, including both enslaved workers and maroon guerrillas. They represented thousands of other Africans—both on the many plantations and in the fugitive communities in the mountains. The ceremony and last-minute plans were being overseen by Boukman and an enslaved female—both Vodun (Voodoo) spiritual leaders. There was no need to haggle over any last-minute plans. They knew better than Karl Marx's (later) "wage slaves" that they "had nothing to lose but their chains." And the horrible treatment that their "masters" heaped on them added a sense of desperation to kill, or be killed, once they began the revolt!

Yet, Boukman and the female offered more inspiration than centralized leadership. And when the revolt was launched shortly thereafter, it was led by scores of decentralized bands of African workers and maroon guerrilla groups—who were all joined shortly thereafter by separate mulatto-led groups.

Before the well-known Toussaint L'Ouverture appeared on the stage, the Haitian revolution was being led by figures that the decentralized groups propelled forward: the maroons Jean Francois, Bissou and Lamour Derance; and the rebel-enslaved workers Romaine the Prophetess and Hyacinthe, the fearless leader of the battle of Croix des Bouquets. The mulattos had a number of their own independent groups and distinguished leaders. In addition, there was also a small segment of whites who were in league with the anti-slavery wing of the French Jacobins, and who loosely allied themselves with one rebel group or another.

Within two years of the beginning of the French Revolution, and continuing for twelve harrowing years, the Haitian revolutionaries would go on to militarily engage and defeat first their colonial enslavers, then a succession of armies fielded by Spain and England—as well as a traitorous Mulatto army and finally tens of thousands of Napoleon Bonaparte's veteran French "revolutionary" troops.

The victorious Africans would go on to found the country of Haiti in 1803–1804, the only country in world history established by formerly enslaved workers.

What better example could we use to weigh Marx's words about the "workers" engaging in "fifteen, twenty, fifty years of civil wars and peoples struggles . . . in order to change yourselves and make yourselves fit for political rule"?

The Marxist giant C.L.R. James, who penned the classic *Black Jacobins* (1963), dissects that struggle. In it, James compares the Haitian revolutionary army led by Toussaint and later Jean-Jacques Dessalines and Henry Christophe with the later Russian Bolshevik party: "[Toussaint and] his Black army and generals [filled] the political role of the Bolshevik party."[2] This brilliantly led, tightly organized and courageous army represents my dragon here. And James's book does much to rescue them from the shadows of history so that we may study them. They are the ones who surface as the most notable elements, while scores of the decentralized fighters receded to the background.

So on first reading about these events, you might think that this centralized dragon (L'Ouverture and his army) was the best weapon. But, the European empire-builders of France, England, Spain—and the U.S. wannabes—were not going to give up easily, even though they had all been defeated, or were afraid to directly intervene (in the case of the United States).

As it turned out, however, when Toussaint—backed by the "revolutionary" army—assumed governance of the island, the imperialists were able to pressure and maneuver him into a position where he and his (dragon) army began to impose intolerable conditions on the revolutionary masses of workers. "In the north around Plaisance, Limbe, Dondon, the vanguard [masses] of the revolution was not satisfied with the new regime."[3] Astonishingly, in the teeth of Napoleon's renewed threats and the hostile machinations of the British and Americans, Toussaint submitted, along with his generals.

Thus, at one fell swoop, these leaders had been maneuvered into playing the role of neocolonial compradors. Our dragon had been corralled,

---

2   James, *Black Jacobins*, 283.

3   Ibid., 275.

handcuffed, and chained. They subsequently set out to use the "revolutionary army" to deliver the masses back into slavery! Simply because Napoleon feared them, his secret plan was to place all of Haiti's Africans into chattel slavery and he sent his brother in law and (eventually) sixty thousand more French troops to accomplish his aims.

Recognizing the weaknesses of the dragon forces and the true intentions of the French, "[Lamour] Derance and the petty chieftains, North, South and West, each in his own district summoned Blacks to revolt."[4]

So, here we see the hydra doing battle with the (now) traitorous dragon and the French imperialists. It is a recurrent tale, this (Dessalines and his generals hunt down these "brigands"). "Once more, the masses had shown greater political understanding than their leaders."[5] Our formerly heroic revolutionary army had been reduced to suppressing the revolutionary masses and forcing the latter into, "fighting Black generals [who were] trying to crush the 'brigands' for the French"—propelling our hydra back to center stage. "The little local leaders . . . beat off [their and the French] attacks . . . causing the French to be more open to yellow fever."[6]

Consequently, we witness the decentralized hydra elements launching the revolution, being displaced by Toussaint's army—the dragon—only to resume their leadership roles during a crisis that saw the dragon capitulate to the French, thus showing the hydra to be the most indispensable weapon that the revolutionaries developed.

Later, as is well known, Toussaint was kidnapped and taken to France where he later died in prison, opening the way for his chief lieutenant, Jean-Jacques Dessalines, to (again) switch back to the rebels' side, rally the revolutionary army to also switch back to the masses' cause, and (along with the hydra forces), go on to totally annihilate the remaining French forces on the island and declare independence, appointing himself the new country's emperor.

---

4   Ibid., 327.

5   Ibid., 338–39, n.39.

6   Ibid., 346–47.

An excellent soldier, Dessalines showed himself to be a cruel tyrant over the Haitian people. Thus, he was assassinated by them within a few years of assuming power. He was replaced by another general from the dragon forces: Henry Christophe, who was appointed president in 1807. But in 1811, Christophe declared himself king. He, too, was be killed by his own people in 1829.

Thus, we can clearly see how Haiti's dragon forces played a very ambivalent role in the rebel fight for independence. They started out as tenacious and brilliant fighters against all of the European imperial and colonial elements and against the traitors among the mulattos, who were bent on keeping the enslaved Africans underfoot. During the course of the revolutionary struggle, they opportunistically switched to the French imperialist side and attempted to drown the still-revolutionary masses and their decentralized groups in blood—hoping the French would allow them to serve as a new elite class of African policemen against a reenslaved African working class.

Failing to suppress the rebels, the dragon forces rejoined the hydra elements and lent their weight to totally defeating the French, only to once again turn against the revolutionary masses by establishing themselves as a dictatorial and exploitative African elite.

For its part, the decentralized hydra forces never veered from their objective of winning as much freedom from servitude and oppression as possible. From the prerevolutionary times of Mackandal, up through the 1791–1804 Haitian revolutionary war, and even down to our time, they've continued to struggle toward that end. And it's highly instructive to know that in addition to fighting the French during their revolution, they were also under attack by Toussaint's dragon forces, who displayed hatred and fear of everything—from their refusal to relinquish their maroon/decentralized organizational formations to their practice of traditional Vodun (Voodoo) spiritual systems, which did a great deal to inspire their fighters to martyr themselves for the cause of freedom. And the treacherous attacks carried out on them by Christophe and Dessalines—even while both sides were allied against the imperialists—were early signs that the dragon forces were ultimately concerned with power for themselves.

After being pushed to the side after the French were driven out, the decentralized hydra elements were forced to again go underground and eventually morph into semisecret Vodun societies that remain a little-recognized or understood autonomous element among the oppressed of Haiti until today. Wade Davis's classic *The Serpent and the Rainbow* and *Voodoo in Haiti*, by Alfred Metraux, paint a fascinating picture of how these decentralized elements went from centuries of being maroon guerrillas and revolutionary fighters, to being forced underground, only to surface as today's Bizango, Zobop, Bossu, Macandal, Voltigeurs, and other semi-secret Vodun societies. This is a major segment of Haitian culture that no domestic or foreign oppressor has ever been able to eradicate—although the dictator "Papa Doc" Duvalier was able to manipulate some of them by integrating them into his dreaded "Ton Ton Macoute" secret police.

In another book by Stan Goff, *Sex and War*, he tells us, "There are maroons in Haiti again, with the wave of repression sweeping the country in the wake of the last U.S.-crafted coup d'état (February 29, 2004). . . . Twice in 2004 I visited one of these maroon communities in the Central Plateau."[7]

We have looked here at four case studies to examine the strengths and weaknesses of centralized and decentralized groups. But we could also explore the history of how decentralized forces defeated Napoleon's army in Spain, how decentralized forces have defeated every known invader in the border regions of what is today Afghanistan and Pakistan, and how decentralized insurgents are today defeating the United States and its allies in Iraq.

Some Parting Words from a Farsighted Marxist

C.L.R. James penned *The Black Jacobins* many years before he would later crystallize his theories. Yet in the introduction to *Marxism for Our Times: C.L.R. James on Revolutionary Organization*, we learn that

---

7   Goff, *Sex and War*, 8.

in 1948 James wrote what was eventually published as "Notes on Dialectics." This was a study of working class organization in light of dialectics and marked the ultimate break with Trotskyism, the rejection of the vanguard party. The importance of this break and the theoretical validation of James's viewpoint was demonstrated eight years later in the Hungarian Revolution of 1956 and later the French revolt of 1968, the Czech spring of 1968, and the *Solidarność* movement in Poland in 1980.... On the one hand, no group of the left or of the right was in any way prepared to accept the possibility of proletarian revolution in the totalitarian dictatorships of Eastern Europe or in a democratic country such as France. All of their assumptions proved false: that the working class needed a party to lead it in revolution; that the working class needed a press and a network of communication; that what was needed was some crisis in the society such as a depression or a war. With none of these factors in place, the workers of Hungary in forty-eight hours took over all of the means of production in that society, created a form of dual power, forced the Communist Party to reorganize under another name, and was crushed by nothing in Hungarian society but by an invasion of Soviet tanks.[8]

And in his own words, James wrote:

Now if the party is the knowing of the proletariat, then the coming of age of the proletariat means the abolition of the party. That is our universal, stated in its boldest and most abstract form.... The party as we know it must

---

8   Edited by Martin Glaberman (Jackson: University Press of Mississippi, 1999), xvii.

disappear. It is disappearing. It will disappear as the state will disappear. The whole laboring population becomes the state. That is the disappearance of the state. It can have no other meaning. It withers away by expanding to such a degree that it is transformed into its opposite. And the party does the same . . . for if the party does not wither away, the state never will.[9]

"On the other hand, even after the fact, the left could not deal with events that demolished their theories of the necessity of a vanguard party, and proceeded to ignore the movements in Hungary, in France, and in Poland—movements which Marx or Lenin would have pounced on to study and to hone and bring up to date their revolutionary theories."[10]

Conclusion

It's clear that today's center of gravity, the aspect on which all else is dependent and rests, is the shared (global) consciousness of the multitudes of the earth's workers and oppressed peoples, that their lives are daily becoming more and more intolerable, hence solidifying them ideologically around the necessity for revolutionary change (as our earlier maroons were solidified around the need to escape enslavement), along with the ability of these multitudes to communicate with each other and share ideas and methods about the best ways to proceed toward that goal.

Therefore, the global hardships brought about by today's imperialists, by their voracious accumulation of wealth and their destruction of the environment and cultures, will propel the multitudes to use any and all means to bring about the needed changes—or perish. And modern means of communications will provide them with an ability to update or imitate the earlier hydra's strengths, and also avoid its weaknesses—while

---

9   C.L.R. James, *Notes on Dialectics* (London: Allison and Busby, 1980), 175–76.

10   Glaberman, *Marxism*, xvii.

guarding against the tendency of the dragon to concentrate oppressive power in its hands.

Thus, since the shared necessity for change is already present, along with the tools to communicate, our final question is whether or not these masses must centralize their organizing (not to be confused with the obvious need to coordinate their efforts!). To that I answer with an emphatic "No!" Further, I contend that such centralization will only make it easier for our oppressors to identify us and level repression upon us—prolonging the crisis our generation must deal with.

The historical records of our dragon hydra are clear. The choice is yours.

[Editors' Note: The following section, titled "The Mosaic," appears in some of the versions of this essay as it was originally circulated. It represents a strategic conversation between Maroon and a Philadelphia-based activist, about how to realize an organizational form for revolutionary action drawing from the decentralized models and principles discussed in this essay. It represents a work in progress, which the editors decided to include as an example of Maroon's constant interest in realizing concrete prefigurative projects along the lines of his theoretical and historical research.]

The Mosaic

Mosaic: a surface decoration made by inlaying small pieces of variously colored material to form pictures or patterns. (Merriam-Webster Dictionary)

At present, there are many sectarian divisions due to racial, ethnic, gender, sexual orientation, cultural, and geographic differences. These hinder individuals, organizations, and entire communities who already interact, share many of the same concerns, are faced with similar obstacles to their well-being, and already cooperate to various degrees. But we can all come together like a "mosaic" with a goal of creating positive changes in our collective well-being.

The "mosaic" will not be an effort directed toward imposing any type of multiracial, multiethnic, gender-neutral, or conformist utopian universalism. No! The mosaic will allow individuals, organizations, and entire communities to exercise self-determination in deciding what types of social orders they choose to struggle to bring into being, while at the same time learning how to better come together with others to form societies that will be superior to the ones in which we now live.

Thus, the word "mosaic" fits us in many ways. We will add to the dictionary definition by defining ourselves as "the mosaic: the movement of oppressed sectors acting in concert."

The "mosaic" is an ideological jumping-off point that will serve all of our separate and collective interests; it can also be termed "Inter-Communal Self-Determination," which we can understand in the following ways:

Inter: existing between

Communal: 1. Of or relating to a community. 2. Characterized by collective ownership and use of property. 3. Shared, used in common, or participated in by members of a group or community.

Self-Determination: 1. Free choice of one's acts without external compulsion. 2. Determination by the people of a territorial unit of their own future political status.

Our "mosaic" would consist of elements from many diverse individuals, groups and communities—some of whom are already benefiting from interacting and working together—while allowing room for expansion. They include, but are not limited to:

+ women (individuals and groups)
+ new Afrikan and Pan-Afrikan peoples
+ Puerto Ricans
+ anarchists and anti-authoritarians
+ Asians
+ Chicano and Mexican peoples
+ Native Americans
+ gay, lesbian, transgender, bisexual, and genderqueer peoples
+ Euro-Americans

+ ecological activists
+ animal rights activists
+ working-class peoples
+ people with disabilities
+ people who are/have been incarcerated

Our political posture would include, but not be limited to, the following:
+ pro-self-determination for everyone
+ anti-economic, political, and cultural domination
+ pro-gender and sexual choice and freedom
+ anti-racism, gender, caste, and class oppression
+ pro-full human rights for everyone
+ anti-capitalism
+ pro-sustainable economics
+ anti-entropic environmental, species, and technological practices
+ pro-species and environmental projections

The "mosaic" will be built on the principles of seeking to recruit from both the most oppressed segments and from among the most selfless. The former are found primarily within the ranks of the lower class, women, people of color, and LGBTQ peoples, while the selfless are found, to a lesser degree, among all segments.

The "mosaic" must immediately begin to spread its messages by recruiting people who are willing to help, by producing publications of all sorts, as well as utilizing any and all other means that do not transgress its principles to aggressively push its messages. All mosaic people can contribute to this effort autonomously, while always keeping in mind our collective stance, as well as the sensibilities of other mosaics and oppressed peoples. Finally, the mosaic must immediately begin a dialogue toward building a consensus—as soon as possible—about how to best further coordinate our collective efforts.

Recommended Books

Davis, Wade. *The Serpent and the Rainbow*. New York: Simon & Schuster, 1985.

Glaberman, Martin, ed. *Marxism for Our Times: C.L.R. James on Revolutionary Organization*. Jackson: University Press of Mississippi, 1999.

Goff, Stan. *Full Spectrum Disorder*. New York, Soft Skull Press, 2004.

Goff, Stan. *Sex and War*. New York: Soft Skull Press, 2006. www.insurgentamerican.net/download/StanGoff/Sex-n-War.pdf.

Hoogbergen, Wim S.M. *The Boni Maroon Wars in Suriname*. Boston: Brill Academic Publishers, 1997.

James, C.L.R. *The Black Jacobins*. New York: Random House, 1963.

Leaming, Hugo Prosper. *Hidden Americans: Maroons of Virginia and the Carolinas*. New York: Garland Publishing, 1995.

Metraux, Alfred. *Voodoo in Haiti*. New York: Schocken Books, 1972.

The *Real* Resistance to Slavery in North America (2005)

Long before the founding of the country, Africans were transported to what later became known as the United States of America. Some came as free individuals and companions of Europeans from Spain and elsewhere. They were ship guides, sailors, soldiers, explorers, and adventurers. Others, however, were enslaved workers.

The earliest known enslaved Africans were brought by the Spanish to serve in a colony that was set up in what is today the Carolinas. There, within a couple of years (around 1528) the survivors are reported to have "rebelled and escaped to dwell amongst the Indians."

In the mid-1500s, an even-less-known but larger group came as "free colonizers" from South America. They numbered at least three hundred that had been formerly enslaved but were part of a successful rebellion and takeover by enslaved Africans and English, along with "mixed-race" privateers, or pirates.

They, together with a larger group of indigenous South Americans, were recruited by England to help shore up the failing English colony at Roanoke, Virginia/North Carolina. They eventually abandoned Roanoke and melted into the countryside—never to be heard from again.

Between the sixteenth and eighteenth centuries, the Spanish, English, French, Dutch, Portuguese, and Danish vied to control North, Central, and South America as well as the Caribbean Islands. At that time, however, the Amerindians—contrary to popular myth—were still the strongest military power in all of these areas, not discounting the breakup and conquest of the large Aztec and Inca empires. Thus, Europeans were forced to use a strategy of "divide and conquer," forming alliances of convenience with and using the various Amerindian ethnic groups and confederations to fight each other—primarily to enslave the defeated and sell them to Europeans, but also to keep all of them off balance while the European colonies were weak and, finally, to police the enslaved Africans and "indentured" whites.

Outside of a small number of coastal enclaves where the Europeans could concentrate their power with the aid of ships and cannons, the only leverage they had over the militarily strong Amerindians was the use of their "trade goods." Many Amerindians deeply desired these goods and eventually allowed themselves to become "enslavers"—on a massive scale—in order to acquire the metal utensils, tools, jewelry, cloth, blankets, mirrors, guns and gunpowder, alcoholic spirits, knick-knacks, and other items. They wanted these either for use, for status, or—in the case of the guns, powder, hatchets, and knives—for sheer survival!

It is true that the Amerindians practiced a form of enslavement prior to any contact with Europeans. However, this form of slavery had an overall effect that was relatively mild, mainly because, although the Amerindians practiced farming on a broad scale, the plantation farming introduced by the Europeans—which demanded huge numbers of tightly disciplined and overworked enslaved people—was inconceivable and undesired.

Ironically, the Amerindians were successfully manipulated by the European colonialists to become deeply involved in conflicts with neighboring groups, the same way that on the continent of Africa, vast numbers of people and wide expanses of land were simultaneously falling victim to an equally disastrous cycle of wars by Europeans to enslave people for trade goods and weapons, in order for each group to defend themselves against enslavement by others.

During this early period, race—as it's viewed today—made little difference. After all, one could find Africans, Amerindians, and whites all equally enslaved on the same plantations, in the towns, and on ships. History shows clearly that all three cooperated with each other in rebellions, escapes, and other enterprises. Indeed, such cooperation was always dreaded by the slave masters and was one of the primary reasons that the enslavement of whites and Amerindians was eventually phased out all over the Western Hemisphere.

Amerindians and whites found it easier to escape enslavement. The Amerindians knew the land and also had kinfolk to help or seek out. The whites could better blend in with free people, or join others moving to colonize other parts of the land. The Africans, on the other hand, had no such advantage. They either found sympathetic Amerindians to help them, or had to try to find and join with other runaways called "maroons," fugitive enslaved people of North, Central, and South America and the Caribbean Islands who had set up their own communities.

Africans continually escaped enslavement, from as far back as 1502 when they were first brought to this hemisphere. Thus maroons were always active to a greater or lesser degree. The early maroons were Africans, whites, and Amerindians, and were viewed as a major threat to the entire institution of plantation slavery. In certain areas, they threatened the elite colonizers' domination and control of their colonies. In the elites' calculation, any large maroon community stood a good chance of uniting the Amerindians not addicted to their trade goods with both the indentured and "poor whites," and also with the enslaved Africans—all of whom heavily outnumbered the landowning and other upper-class whites.

This writer, contrary to popular practice, will not dwell on or attempt to outline the innumerable ways individuals resisted slavery. Nor will I detail the names of the multitude of known actors—except for a few that cannot go unmentioned. No doubt, one surefire way of miseducating people of all races about the real resistance to slavery has been, and continues to be, the highlighting of the most spectacular instances of resistance, while burying the remainder of the oppressed in the depressing day-to-day inhumanity of the slave system—a method that cannot help but sour most people's desire to learn more about the overall subject.

Instead, I will help you see the more or less "hidden" resistance to slavery in North America by outlining three major, long-running, and ultimately successful efforts to resist and overcome that system. Then, once you see how much crucial historical data has been kept under wraps, I'm confident that you will be stimulated to go beyond what is being conventionally taught in search of further knowledge on the subject, as well as decide what lessons that knowledge holds for us today.

We will consider three case studies: the successful 150-plus years of maroon resistance centered on the Dismal Swamp of Virginia and North Carolina; the equally successful 150-plus-year struggle of the Black Seminole maroons and their Amerindian allies in Florida and throughout all of the areas they were forced to travel; and the Underground Railroad of the United States, Canada, and Mexico.

The Dismal Swamp

The awesome, defiant, and legendary Dismal Swamp straddles the eastern sections of southern Virginia and northern North Carolina. Even today it contains vast expanses of extremely harsh and dangerous wilderness areas, although much of the original swamp has been drained.

From the fifteenth to the nineteenth centuries, however, it stretched at least one hundred miles one way and sixty miles the other, which means it was almost as large as the state of Delaware. It was recorded to contain everything from poisonous snakes and other reptiles to alligators, bears, big cats, and insects unknown to the early colonists. Its swampy marshes and bogs were so treacherous that only the most daring and knowledge-able—or foolhardy—Europeans would venture far into them.

From all accounts, the first known maroons to occupy and use this swamp as a place of concealment, a natural fortress, a liberated territory, and a home were Amerindians. They were, sadly, escaping from the en-slavement that had all but engulfed the eastern and southern sections of the continent. They were joined there by kinfolk and other Amerindians who had suffered defeats in wars with rival groups, acting in league with European colonists.

It's unclear whether the Amerindians were first joined by runaway Africans or whites. One would assume that white runaways would seek out more hospitable surroundings. But below I'll lay out a much-mis-understood social phenomenon that helps explain such a discrepancy. It hardly matters though, as the historical record reflects repeated examples of Amerindians, Africans, and whites all using the swamp as a refuge from as far back as the early 1700s.

These early maroons were able to overcome language barriers, mistrust, and the growing influence of racial doctrines that eventually evolved into the white-supremacist cultural construct outside of the swamp. This is not to say that they didn't have any racial or ethnic prejudices. It's absolutely clear, however, that they overcame them enough to be able to live, support, protect, fight, and die for each other for well over a hundred years.

Obviously, there was also intermixing. Between the Amerindians and Africans it proceeded to the point where it became virtually impossible to distinguish between them. The whites on the other hand, though also mixing with the Africans and Amerindians, still by and large remained phenotypically "Caucasoid." That, however, worked to everyone's advantage because the white maroons and their descendants could still interact with the surrounding white society.

Indeed, white maroons largely came to occupy areas of the swamp that bordered on the surrounding white-dominated society, while the other maroons stayed in the interior. Such an arrangement helped to establish and sustain lively trade that was carried on by those in the interior who would hunt, fish, and trap wild game for sale through their white maroon allies. Also, wood products were produced in abundance in the interior—so much so that it began to affect the local economy. This caused George Washington—who would later become president—to find himself in hot water after he was accused of using Dismal Swamp maroons to provide his private company with wooden house shingles.

Interestingly, the white maroons were probably the first to be labeled with the "poor white trash" derogatory epithet. When reflecting on the social evolution of reality, consider the following: after escaping indentured servitude, one had to remain ever-wary of being found out and returned. Over time, therefore, those who did not melt into the broader white society took on a self-protective, insular, standoffish, hostile to strangers, semi-outlaw mentality. Assuredly, they would trade with the broader white society. But they occupied (if they could be said to be "occupiers" of any permanent places at all) their own hardscrabble areas—land so inhospitable that they attracted only scorn. Generally, they wouldn't dedicate themselves to being reliable employees of any landowner, mill owner, ship captain, or even slave catcher! Plus, they were known by all as being under none of white society's other social restraints. So the elites labeled them not "poor whites," but "trash," since they were seen as unable to be restrained, unreliable and useless! It is only much later that the epithet would be used to shame and discipline poor whites in general.

In fact this same phenomenon came to play itself out a little differently further west in the Appalachian mountains and foothills, except there the many descendants of runaway indentured whites came to be called "hillbillies." Unquestionably, the latter's legendary clannishness, hostility to all outsiders, secretiveness, and fierce protectiveness of their kin and tiny communities—as well as the disdain, economic isolation, and poverty that has systematically been imposed on them—leaves very little doubt as to their history!

Although they are generally viewed as being ultraracists, placing their racism in the context of their hostility to and vision of outsiders as enemies puts their "racism" in a different category altogether. Furthermore, real hillbilly culture does not see itself as being in league with the dominant culture or system. Their loyalty is ultimately to their own small clans and communities. And all law enforcement authorities know it!

In addition, such elements bring a historically ultramilitant and violent posture to labor disputes—between coalminers and mine owners, supported by police and the National Guard, in Appalachia. They have always been diehard operators of illegal liquor stills and nowadays are major marijuana growers. Yet, the primary difference between today's hillbillies and the white maroons of the Dismal Swamp (up until the end of the Civil War) is that the latter were the close and trusted allies of the African and Amerindian maroons.

So, up until 1776 the Dismal Swamp maroons lived as free people, protected by the harshness of the swamp and by well-organized and capable defenders from among their collective ranks. Each maroon settlement had its own armed members who were responsible for patrolling its surroundings, warning of intruders, decoying or attacking any hostiles—while giving the other maroons enough time to escape to other preplanned and fortified settlements. In the event of sustained, heavy searches by outside militia, posses, or bounty hunters, the maroons had gradually evolved a system of coordinating their defenses and a unified command structure—which was known to have been headed by individuals from all of the various racial and ethnic groups—and which saw its mission as one of driving the hostiles out of the swamp and outlasting any intrusion. An attack of that nature was dealt with as an attack on all!

Moreover, within the swamp, the maroons were unbeatable! The swamp itself was so treacherous that it could not be traveled without fear of being swallowed up at every turn. There were fast moving rivers concealed by thick vegetation, quicksand, heavy undergrowth-encased mud, deadly sharp thickets and concealed protuberances, poisonous insects, snakes, reptiles, alligators, and big cats. Then, there were the maroon-laid snares and traps, along with the possibility of being ambushed by the maroon guerrillas, who would lead pursuers into even more treacherous terrain that only they knew how to traverse. In fact, the maroons developed and passed down effective ways to cross otherwise uncrossable terrain by using methods employed by certain animals.

Remember, we're talking about a swamp that was one hundred miles one way, and sixty miles the other. The bottom line is: at no point in recorded history did outsiders succeed in capturing or killing all or even substantial numbers of the Dismal Swamp maroons, nor could they be forced out of their lair. The outsiders tried to drain sections of the swamp for commercial and travel reasons, but even that left an area almost the size of a small state.

Therefore, when the colonists' efforts to shake off England in their so-called War of Independence reached the swamp, both sides found fully trained and tested militias among the maroons. Only one side, however, offered anything of value. England, through its loyalists in Virginia and the Carolinas, let it be known that anyone fighting for the British would be guaranteed freedom from slavery and indentured servitude, and could also look forward to dividing up some of the estates of any plantation owners who were participating in the rebellion. So once word got around, tens of thousands answered England's call: maroons, enslaved individuals from the plantations and towns, and poor whites who wanted to help break the stranglehold that the plantation elites had on the South.

The Dismal Swamp was not the only place that maroons could be found. There were, astonishingly enough, thousands upon thousands of other maroons throughout the backwoods and foothills of all states from Delaware to Georgia. (Florida is a special case that we will discuss later.) All characteristically lived in fiercely independent and semi-outlaw conditions. Some were the forefathers and mothers of the Appalachian hillbillies. Huge numbers of them answered England's call and they eventually received arms and went on to fight the entire war on England's side.

Although most of today's "teachers" of history are fond of reminding everyone that Blacks provided over five thousand fighters to the colonists' cause during that struggle, they hardly ever highlight that at least ten times this number fought for England. Or, more accurately, they fought to get the plantation ruling elite and their followers off of their backs and out of power. So saying fifty thousand–plus Blacks fought for England is not historically correct. However, it can be said that the aspirations of those fifty thousand–plus Africans, Amerindians, whites, and mixed-race individuals were closer to those of the overwhelming majority of the enslaved and oppressed Blacks of their time than to the rest of colonial society.

Even so, England was forced to grant the colonists independence—not due to losing the war in most of the areas that saw massive maroon participation (southern Virginia to Georgia), but because George Washington and his army held on in the northern states until France joined the war on their side. Afterward, Washington and the French naval fleet trapped a major British force at Yorktown, Virginia, causing England to abandon the fight in the colonies in order to better carry out its worldwide struggle against France and other European imperial powers.

So, when the English navy evacuated what would become the United States, hundreds of maroons and their families went with them. They were transported to English-controlled islands in the Caribbean and to Canada. Thus, today one can find their descendants in places like Nova Scotia and the Bahamas.

Of course, although their cause was not successful outside of the Dismal Swamp, the surviving maroons had absolutely no intention of becoming slaves! The maroons, therefore, retreated back into their all-but-impregnable fortress within the swamp. Others migrated further south to join up with the maroons already in Florida or in French-claimed lands as far west as present-day Louisiana. Others still went into Appalachia, mixing with the Amerindians there or trying to live cut off from the dominant white-controlled society as much as possible. Consequently, between the end of the Revolutionary War and the start of the Civil War, the Dismal Swamp maroons held onto their freedom inside of the swamp stronghold.

It was later discovered, moreover, that the maroons who lived inside of the deepest sections of the swamp had located enough dry grounds to build any number of settlements that included well-constructed living quarters and systems of log-covered and otherwise concealed pathways. Some of these homes, nevertheless, were built on high platforms for protection from wild animals and sudden changes in the swamp's water level. Furthermore, enough useful ground was found in order to plant crops and grow food which, in addition to their fishing, hunting, and trapping, allowed them to independently sustain themselves.

On the other hand, the white maroons living on the edges of the swamp relied on its still-heavy undergrowth to conceal their homes which were usually separate structures connected by winding, all-but-invisible pathways. An outsider could travel through these areas and never run into their dwellings.

As mentioned, those in the interior and those on the edges of the swamp cooperated in facilitating trade with the surrounding white-dominated society. This method of subsistence was maintained in addition to a certain amount of brigandage, mainly cattle rustling, for which the maroons bred a ferocious line of dogs.

Needless to say, the collective maroons would under no circumstances allow their people to go without the things needed to remain alive and safe, even if that meant mounting larger raids on the surrounding areas and coping with the resulting intensified searches of the swamp.

But mostly, from the end of the Revolutionary War up until the Civil War, the thousands of maroons known to occupy the swamp lived an independent existence, interrupted only periodically by mostly futile incursions and searches by posses, militias, or bounty hunters.

Freedom fighter Nat Turner and his rebels were headed for the Virginia side of the swamp, but their rebellion was suppressed before they could get there (although some may have made it). More than anything, the Dismal Swamp of those times was viewed and accepted as if it was a foreign, independent, hostile territory. It was a place, above all, never to venture into for fear of its fabled terrain and elusive, crafty, and untamed inhabitants. It was a "spooky place," or so the surrounding enslaved Blacks were taught to believe, and over time this myth kept most of them from seeking refuge there among the maroons. Thus, the losses that the plantation elites suffered because of the maroon presence in the swamp were not sufficient to alter the plantocracy's course, and the maroons therefore came to accept and absorb what they couldn't otherwise change.

When the cataclysmic events surrounding the beginning of the Civil War reached the maroons of the Dismal Swamp, a new generation of maroon guerrillas thrust themselves forward and almost immediately began to play a little-known strategic role against the slave-holding system. Emerging from the North Carolina side of the swamp in particular, the maroon fighters would eventually become so numerous and militarily powerful that they totally dominated and controlled whole counties and areas of the state. Of note is Henry Berry Lowery, one of their most effective leaders. After recruiting heavily among Blacks and Amerindians, mounted on fast horses, his forces would dominate large sections of the state for ten years, even after the war was over.

How, one may ask, could that happen in the very heart of the South?

It is true that since the end of the Revolutionary War the maroons were never numerous or militarily strong enough to venture out of the swamp except by stealth or during quick pinpoint raids. The Civil War, however, forced the majority of the white males who supported the slave system to join the fight against the Union Army elsewhere. To be sure, it was believed enough able-bodied men would be left behind to keep enslaved Blacks docile and terrorized. While that might have worked for a while, the maroons expanded their numbers by recruiting among Amerindians, fed-up "poor whites," and other Blacks who were beginning to flee in larger parties. Plus, one must remember that all of the maroons were masters at using guerrilla tactics: concealment, living off the land, improvising traps and deadly snares, the ambush, lightning raids and retreats. After proving their fighting qualities they could gradually depend on more and more of the enslaved Blacks, poor whites, and Amerindians to provide them with food and information about the weaknesses of the whites protecting slavery, munitions, and recruits.

So, within two years of the outbreak of the war the maroons had pulled together enough available forces. Some slavers, in fact, sent official documents to the Confederate government announcing their complete withdrawal from their cause and the Civil War altogether! Afterward, in those "liberated areas," the maroons and their allies set up a rudimentary framework for a new social order that the rest of the South would not know of until the reconstruction era.

Even so, in other areas of North Carolina and Virginia the maroons faced stiffer resistance. On the Virginia side of the swamp, undoubtedly, they had to be more combative simply because of the swamp's closeness to the heart of Confederate production at Portsmouth and because it was not far from the Confederate seat of government in Richmond. The latter, in particular, was always being threatened simultaneously by strong Union forces.

Therefore, these maroons were able to tie down and neutralize sizable numbers of Confederate troops through the use of their well-honed guerrilla hit-and-run tactics. The maroons, even when unable to defeat the Confederates militarily, still found other ways to strategically undermine their war effort, the morale of the troops, and their entire infrastructure. Due to their effective use of the Dismal Swamp, any Confederate officer worth his salt knew not to send men into maroon territory!

Certainly, the maroons' most effective blows came when they helped to liberate multitudes of enslaved Blacks! This is a subject that's rarely written about. But, if one wants to understand where the tens of thousands of mostly Black Union soldiers came from in those dark days when the North needed a lot of fresh troops in order to break the Confederates' will, then one must turn to the so-called "contrabands"—the thousands upon thousands of enslaved Blacks who were running away from bondage. Indeed, these contrabands provided the overwhelming majority of the two hundred thousand Blacks who fought for the Union. And the maroons of North Carolina and Virginia played a major role in that undertaking.

Just imagine all of Harriet Tubman's exploits in liberating hundreds of captives combined with John Brown's vision of the wholesale escape of captives, armed with the guns taken in his failed raid at Harper's Ferry, then multiply that hundreds of times. Only then is it possible to grasp the magnitude of what was achieved by the maroons.

Secondarily, the maroons' experience in cattle rustling was put to good use, causing the Confederacy, in areas where maroons were operating, to begin to suffer from starvation.

True to their loyalties, the white maroons who joined the Union force fought in the segregated "colored" units, although they didn't have to.

After the end of the war, the maroons would fully emerge from the swamp and play important roles in local affairs. Certainly, once we become knowledgeable of these hidden parts of history, we can better understand just why a country dominated by a white-supremacist culture and institutions would go out of its way to keep this history undercover.

The Seminoles

Let's examine another perfidious example of the mass deception and mis-education that surrounds this subject, namely, the so-called "Seminole Wars."

Scholars inform us that the word "Seminole" comes from the Creek Indian "simano-li," meaning "fugitive" or "wild." Furthermore, although it would later be applied to an entire ethnic group, originally—get this—it was used by Creeks to describe fugitive or runaway enslaved Africans—in particular those Africans escaping through Creek country to reach the "sanctuary" of Spanish-held Florida in the 1700s. By then, a section of the Creeks were breaking off from the main body of their tribe and also making their way to the same territory. The African Seminoles (who the Spanish dubbed "Negro Seminoles") were already present, so the ethnic name is as much theirs as the Amerindian Seminoles.

Thus, it's totally wrong to see Seminoles as Amerindians who befriended and mixed with Africans. Instead, this ethnicity is the result of a coming together of the two. This eventually happened in Florida because they both needed each other's help in defense from slave catchers and other Creeks not content with the separation.

To better grasp the deceit that continues to surround this subject, we have to closely examine what the Seminoles are best known for: the First and Second Seminole Wars. The first ended in 1819, and the second lasted from 1835–1842. In truth, there were other Seminole Wars.

Everyone is led to accept the misleading title "Seminole Wars," when in reality they started as slave-catching expeditions, and this fact always played a major role in the conflicts. The expanding plantation slave holders could no longer tolerate a sanctuary for their runaways in Florida. Over and over their emissaries and military commanders made it crystal clear to the Amerindian Seminoles that if they would detach themselves from the African Seminoles they would no longer be a target in the wars. Yet in popular depictions, the majority of literature, docudramas, and movies, one can hardly read about or see a Black person.

At the same time, the United States government eventually joined forces with the slavers and expanded the venture into a land grab. In fact, they had long been uncomfortable with Spain's occupation of the Florida peninsula. Florida changed hands several times, with England using the panhandle as a military base in the War of 1812. By 1815 the United States government decided to do something drastic about it.

So the Indian killer Andrew Jackson was sent to Florida to start the First Seminole War. The country's archives contain many of Jackson's own letters clearly spelling out his twofold mission of capturing runaway slaves and forcing Spain to give up Florida altogether. He failed to capture any significant number of runaways, but was successful in starting the war. Thereafter Spain was forced to "sell" Florida to the United States in 1819. The collective Seminoles, however, never gave in to Jackson and his soldiers, fighting pitched battles and eventually a full-fledged guerrilla war, until Jackson finally just withdrew most of his troops and simply proclaimed victory.

Sound familiar? For their part, the Seminoles migrated to areas not under control of the forces Jackson left behind. This consisted of just about everywhere except a few growing towns and the small number of settlements that Spain had founded. Consequently, until the outbreak of the Second Seminole War, African and Amerindian Seminoles built their own towns and settlements throughout the rest of Florida. In addition, they again established a strong base in agriculture and livestock production to sustain themselves and for trade.

Usually Africans and Amerindians lived in separate towns and settlements. Thus, the admixture between them never reached the degree that it did in the Dismal Swamp. Nevertheless, they still intermarried. One of these mixed marriages was to play a strategic role in later events. In addition, since the United States had nominal control of the peninsula, plantation owners began to acquire unused land and bring in enslaved Africans. Meanwhile, a substantial number from Florida and from out of state tried to get long-outstanding fugitive slave warrants served on African Seminoles, claiming to have owned the African Seminoles' ancestors and, by law, them too. Spain had, however, granted their ancestors freedom in return for serving in the border militia.

Therefore the African and Amerindian Seminoles began the practice of "adopting" each other as nominal slave and slave owner. This practice all but put a halt to the prosecuting of most of these old warrants. In return for this service, the Africans gave some crops to the Amerindians, but otherwise the African Seminoles were totally free. Both groups continued to peacefully coexist as they always had.

Still, things could not remain this way for two primary reasons. First, the plantation owners wanted to expand throughout the area. Second, the peninsula was still a sanctuary for "new" runaways from the local plantations and the neighboring states of Georgia and Alabama. In fact, to get a clearer picture, one must see Florida as a base from which fugitive Africans, for over one hundred years, would carry on a low-level guerrilla war with the neighboring areas in order to rescue their loved ones still in bondage, and to encourage others to join and strengthen their ranks. Complicating things for the slavers was the fact that nothing seemed to shake the African/Amerindian Seminole alliance.

Picture this: American emissaries and other government officials trying to negotiate slave-catching arrangements with Amerindian Seminole chiefs who had African Seminole interpreters and advisors. In addition, imagine the absurdity of trying to get certain chiefs to agree to turn over Africans whom they had known all their lives, some of whom were relatives, many of whom had been comrades in arms, and all of whom the chiefs had only known as free individuals. Yet since their ancestors had escaped slavery, they were now also supposed to be slaves and turned over to strangers. Finally, and this must be emphasized due to our own racial fears, there was a lot of selfless love between the African and Amerindian Seminoles—not lip-service love, but the kind of love that manifests itself in situations that endanger lives!

A clear example of the latter was the "blood pact" entered into by both parties at the prodding of Africans. This dictated that any Amerindian Seminoles who tried to deliver Africans into slavery were to be killed by their own people. History's most recognized Amerindian Seminole, Osceola, showed where he stood by killing a powerful Amerindian Seminole chief when it was discovered that the latter had broken the pact. Afterward and until his death, Osceola would be held in high esteem by the Africans. When he was captured during the war, it was discovered that his personal guards were mostly African Seminoles.

Earlier, Osceola was married to an African woman who was separated from him and put into chains during the couple's visit to a U.S.

government settlement. He was also jailed briefly, while his wife was sold into slavery and transported north.

This state of affairs came to a head in 1835, when a U.S. Army commander's plan to capture some Africans backfired after his guide, an enslaved African, led his soldiers into a prearranged trap. In the ensuing bloody encounter, an entire company of over one hundred American army soldiers was killed. The African Seminoles suffered only light casualties. Almost at the same time, Osceola and other warriors ambushed and killed the government official who had ordered the enslavement of his wife. Thereafter, all over the peninsula Seminoles opened generalized warfare against the U.S. government, and against all those believed to be in league with it.

The collective Seminoles, though extremely capable fighters when employing guerrilla tactics, still found themselves hard-pressed when the United States sent in massive numbers of army, marine, and navy troops, along with thousands of state militia, mercenaries, settlers, slave catchers, and adventurers. In particular, the Seminole women and children suffered terribly from the constant fighting and movement. Yet for seven years, they fought on.

In a testament to the resiliency of the African-Amerindian alliance and ties, neither group ever fell victim to ploys intended to divide them. In fact, they fought successive American commanders and new infusions of troops to a standstill, forcing the last commander to reject all direction and advice from Washington and the slavers, and concentrate his efforts instead on trying to get the collective Seminoles to agree to migrate to Oklahoma territory. There they could occupy lands in close proximity to other Amerindian ethnic groups who had also been forced to leave the East Coast—the Cherokee, Choctaw, Chickasaw, and their kin, the Creeks.

Wisely, the last commander also ignored the insistence of the plantation owners that he use his soldiers and sailors to insure that fugitive slave warrants be served on the African Seminoles. Instead, he either got the U.S. government to pay the slavers (out of tax monies) or, more often, just had his junior officers "cook the books," allowing any Amerindian Seminoles who were willing to migrate to "adopt" African Seminoles as their alleged "property" and take them along. Overriding all criticisms, he

roughly rebuked naysayers by noting that the last thing needed on a plantation was a veteran African Seminole warrior! Even so, the commander had
to transport respected African and Amerindian Seminoles west to inspect
the new settlements. And on their return he had to painstakingly locate
the Seminoles guerrilla hideouts and convince them to migrate.

Still, as is well known, the United States could never fully dislodge all
of the Seminoles. So once again it just declared victory, ended all hostilities
with the remaining Seminoles (whose direct descendants are still in Florida),
and got on with establishing plantation-based slavery all around them.

Was the struggle against slavery over for the African Seminoles?
Hardly! In fact, as soon the collective Seminoles began arriving in the
allotted Oklahoma areas, other slaveholders and former mercenary war
veterans who had fought with the Americans in Florida began their own
efforts to try to serve fugitive warrants against African Seminoles.

After a couple of near showdowns, most of the collective Seminoles left
Oklahoma for Mexico. On the way, thanks to their finely honed survival
and fighting skills, they were able to fend off attacks by hostile Amerindians
and whites alike. Since Mexico had already abolished slavery they applied
for asylum and land to work. For their part, the Mexican government was
glad to have them in their border regions, having learned of their legendary
fighting abilities during their recent war with the United States. Thus,
the Mexican government offered them large tracts of unused land if they
would agree to protect that section of their border from both marauding
Amerindians and whites from Texas. Both the African and Amerindian
Seminoles agreed, and up until the end of the American Civil War twenty
years later and the abolition of slavery, they effectively protected this area,
while otherwise establishing secure and productive settlements.

After the Civil War, however, many of the collective Seminoles returned and settled in the United States. Regrettably, the African Seminoles
lent their superior tracking skills to the U.S. Army's Buffalo Soldiers, and
both of these groups of Black descendants of enslaved people aided the
United States in the near-destruction on the Southwest Amerindians—a
very shameful episode in an otherwise illustrious history.

That aside, the Seminole Wars, in particular the Second Seminole War, remains a shining example of diverse peoples coming together to resist and overcome everything in their path, defeating all attempts to impose the barbaric system of chattel slavery.

Fabled renditions of America's "cowboys and Indians" and "Fort Apache" mythology are daily fare. You have to be a scholar to discover that out of all of America's so-called Indian Wars, the Second Seminole War was the most costly in terms of both human and material losses! And it's probably the only one they cannot boast of winning!

But, of course, it really wasn't just an Indian War, was it? So why talk about it?! Today, the Seminoles' descendants can be found in Oklahoma, Texas, and Mexico—all still fiercely proud of their distinct history and heritage, with many still speaking their own pidgin dialects and practicing their own customs.

The Underground Railroad

The storied and much-celebrated Underground Railroad (UR) is another subject that still demands study in order to firmly grasp its magnitude and historical significance, as well as to determine what lessons it holds that we may be failing to come to grips with. Here we will examine:

1. Its dimensions and its defiance of the government and popular sentiments; and
2. Why it was one of the two main causes of the Civil War and the "emancipation" of enslaved Blacks.

Submerged in a welter of stories that attempt to focus our minds and imaginations on the creativity, heroism, and sacrifices of so many, very rarely do we stop to examine the true magnitude and scope of the underground railroad and its historical accomplishments. But since slavery was such a lucrative moneymaker of an institution, a mountain of papers surrounded it. Many of these are still available for us to study.

It can confidently be said that by the beginning of the Civil War, there were more then one hundred thousand fugitive slaves in Canada, and thousands more in Mexico. Just about all of them received some direct or indirect assistance from the UR. Yet Mexico is usually not even mentioned as a destination on the UR. But it was, and our already-mentioned collective Seminoles played a key role.

Think about it: *over one hundred thousand runaways*, while four million were still in bondage in the South. That is roughly equal to the proportion all of today's Blacks in jail and prisons compared to the overall Black population of this country!

Canada became the main destination (other then the northern states) after the United States passed an aggressive Fugitive Slave Law in 1850—since England (Canada's ruler) had outlawed slavery and would tolerate no violations of its territory by slave catchers.

Mexico, on the other hand, was open to those fleeing from Texas. But once there, the escaped Africans would have to form "fighting alliances" with either our Seminoles or other Amerindians in order to protect their freedom from regular, aggressive slave-catching expeditions from Texas, a replay of the Seminoles' days in Florida.

Finally, an unknown number of runaways remained in cities and towns, organized to defend themselves, not counting those maroons still in the South's swamps, backcountry, foothills, and mountains.

Never before or since has this country had to cope with such a huge segment of its people offering such widespread, militant, and economically damaging opposition to its authority and control.

Still, the popular conception is that the UR and its abolitionist supporters had a free ride, which included overall support outside of the South. Notwithstanding its breadth and depth, that is far from the reality! Admittedly, in certain places like Oberlin, Ohio, and Boston, Massachusetts, abolition of slavery was supported by sizeable segments of the populace. But in most northern areas it remained a minority viewpoint. We know this because they could not get enough people behind them to stop the repressive arms of the state from interfering with their activities.

Furthermore, in a number of northern areas, rich and powerful people (and those in their employ) relied on slavery for their livelihood and profits. Banking, manufacturing of farm instruments, chains, shackles, insurance, and key political alliances all relied on the profits of slavery. No, the widespread and militant activities were carried on by the runaways themselves, and their UR supporters.

Consequently, abolitionists in many places were periodically assaulted, jailed and killed. Moreover, their homes and families were burned or attacked. They were arrested, imprisoned and never truly safe. Finally, the true abolitionist was one who either directly or indirectly supported the UR and thus also had to be ready to defend runaways, associates, and neighbors from armed and dangerous slave catchers, and from the authorities backing them. Contrary to what's usually highlighted, these were more often than not their own neighbors, looking to gain a reward for identifying and kidnapping "runaways" and "free" Blacks alike.

The so-called "Treason at Christiana" in 1851 is instructive concerning the plight of both runaways and abolitionists. Christiana, Lancaster County, Pennsylvania, is not far from Philadelphia—the main UR hub on the East Coast. Both were on the "Mason Dixon Line," the official divide between the northern and southern states and between Pennsylvania and Maryland; free and slave states. Thus, it was a secondary but still much used UR escape route.

Enter William Parker and his wife, two Black runaways from Maryland who worked a small farm near Christiana for about ten years. With them lived the wife's runaway mother, as well as their children. The farm itself was on lands leased to them by local white abolitionist. In addition, there were other Black farmers nearby, both free and runaways.

Parker and the others were not just farmers. In fact, they constituted an active, aggressive, and very effective armed section of the UR. As such, they had for years protected themselves, other runaways, free Blacks, and the UR traffic from slave-catching bounty hunters, who more often then not were from neighboring communities. They sometimes fought pitched gun battles with them, rode down and rescued kidnapped Blacks, and tried to rescue others from the local jail. With the passage of the Fugitive Slave Law of 1850, however, their situation worsened. That act "commanded" all citizens—both North and South—to actively assist in the capture of fugitive slaves. All of the slavers and bounty hunters were greatly emboldened by it. So, the stage was set for subsequent events in Christiana.

As it happened, a Maryland slaver received information that he could capture some of his runaway "property" in Lancaster County, Pennsylvania. Straightaway, he assembled his son, another relative, and others and proceeded to a federal courthouse in Philadelphia, where he obtained an official warrant to capture his property. In addition, he also appointed or hired a federal deputy and a city policeman to help in the undertaking.

Afterward, this posse took a train out to Lancaster County. Unknown to them, however, a UR courier was also on the train—in their very coach—watching their every move. A Philadelphia UR spy had sent word to the local "vigilance committee" of what had been learned about the warrant at the courthouse, prompting them to dispatch the courier to warn Parker and company. On the following day the posse bribed someone to tell them that the two runaways they sought were holed up on the Parkers' farm. The Parkers and others waited there for whatever was to come.

As things turned out, the slavers boldly entered the ground floor of the Parkers' home, while exhibiting the type of bluster one would expect, while the Parkers and other fugitives were on the second floor. Descending, Parker and some white abolitionists tried to get the slavers to leave, but to no avail. Thus, Parker's wife began to sound an alarm by sending blasts from a bugle out the window. That caused a slaver to climb a tree and shoot into the window, only causing her to duck down and continue to blow. In short order, other Blacks began to show up armed to the teeth.

Things then degenerated into a shooting, cutting, and fighting melee. Before long all but one of the slavers were either wounded or being chased through the countryside by the Blacks. The ringleader, moreover, after being wounded was "finished off by the women." No Blacks were seriously hurt.

In the aftermath, of course, the government brought a lot of repression down on the remaining Blacks and on the white abolitionists, going as far as to jail and try both groups. They were all exonerated however, and all of the runaways and their children escaped through the UR—except the elderly mother.

In Oberlin and other northern areas similar militant actions were taken: invading courtrooms and jails to forcibly rescue and spirit away fugitives, overpowering any guards or like-minded individuals, usually resulting in some abolitionist being arrested and tried.

Then, there were the "vigilance committees," UR "conductors" and "stockholders." These brave and committed individuals, along with their public agitators, newspapers, and a handful of elected officials, were the "technicians" of the movement, while its "heart and soul" were always the runaways themselves. The latter, as is well documented, used all manner of creativity, ruses, and violence, to escape on foot, by carriage, horseback, boat, and box. (Henry "Box" Brown was only one of a number of men and women known to have shipped themselves, as freight, to freedom.) And on most of these flights, the UR was involved in some way, north, south, east, and west.

Make no mistake, the UR was anchored by a cadre of truly selfless people, addressing each other with respect, warmth, and commitment: "Dear Friend William Still" (Philadelphia's brave, intelligent, and masterful vigilance committee head), "Dear Friend," "Esteemed Friend," "Dear Friend and Brother," "Truly thy Friend," "Thine for the poor Slave" and on and on. Whether motivated by religious convictions or otherwise, the dispassionate student cannot help but reach this conclusion. Indeed, a study of the huge amount of extant UR correspondence, coupled with what's known of the risks and sacrifices, makes any detractors seem like foolish or narrow-minded ideologues who (you can be sure) cannot themselves produce similar credentials.

Remember, this ain't no chess or debating club we're talking about! Harriet Tubman always went armed and vowed never to be taken alive. Levi Coffin had armed relatives to protect his person and home. John Brown helped Blacks in the North set up an armed section of the UR, like the Parkers in Lancaster County. And, for two decades after leaving

Florida, the Seminoles in Mexico fought off any number of large and small parties of slave catchers.

And consider: This wonderful correspondence could easily land the "Friends" and UR writers in jail—or worse!—if it were to fall in the wrong hands. Even more astonishing, they were not being paid to take these risks. They were not "drafted" by any government, and only a few were professional politicians.

Thus, the author having himself spent decades as part of a similar 1960s-generated movement, can readily recognize the same type of altruism that he's been fortunate enough to witness among his own comrades (latter-day "Friends").

Clearly, then, this moral and humane endeavor played a major role in forcing the entire country to ultimately involve itself in a bloody clash to resolve the issue of slavery. Yes, the emerging industrial system in the North, depending as it did on "wage slavery" was on a collision course with the South's system of "unpaid labor." Nevertheless, on the eve of the Civil War there were more millionaires (slavers) in the Mississippi Delta then could be found in all areas outside of it—a southern aristocracy that had absolutely no intention or incentive to abolish slavery. If anything, they were busy trying to spread it to the lands from which the Amerindians were being pushed off. Consequently, if the UR and the abolitionists had not forced them to panic and secede from the Union—provoking the Civil War—there's no telling how many more decades their system could have survived!

Thus, the UR stands as the most militant egalitarian movement this country has ever seen. Others have come close: the women's suffrage movement, the labor movement, the civil rights movement, and the anti-Vietnam war movement. But it cannot be argued that any of those movements had to tackle and defeat the most heinous form of oppression known: chattel slavery!

In a separate category, however, must be placed the Black, Native American, Puerto Rican, and Chicano liberation movements. Militant is not a word that fits these struggles' needs. They need revolutionary changes, something never sought by the UR or most abolitionists.

From my studies it seems as though history is reluctant to bring forth the type of mass selflessness displayed by the participants in the UR except once every few generations. Maybe the following generation(s) just feel as though they should rest, and collect and enjoy the fruits of their forerunners' sacrifices.

That said, the author challenges readers to more closely study the resistance to slavery in North America, then look in the mirror and ask yourself: just where do you fit in the historical drama? How do you measure up to the generations described here, which had so much effect on events that today's oppressors try very hard to keep their *real* accomplishments hidden?

Recommended Books

Aptheker, Herbert. *To Be Free: Studies in American Negro History.* New York: International Publishers, 1968.

Forbes, Ella. *But We Have No Country: The 1851 Christiana, Pennsylvania Resistance.* Cherry Hill, NJ: Africana Homestead Legacy Publishing, 2010.

Giddings, J.R. *The Exiles of Florida.* Baltimore: Black Classic Press, 1997.

Learning, Hugo Prosper. *Hidden Americans: Maroons of Virginia and the Carolinas.* New York: Routledge, 1995.

Loren Katz, William. *Black Indians: A Hidden Heritage.* New York: Athenaeum Books for Young Readers, 1997.

Price, Richard. *Maroon Societies: Rebel Slave Communities in the Americas.* Baltimore: Johns Hopkins Press, 1996.

Still, William. *Underground Railroad.* New York: Dover, 2007.

Liberation or Gangsterism
Freedom or Slavery
(2006)

Each generation must out of relative obscurity discover its mission, fulfill it or betray it.
—Frantz Fanon[1]

INTRODUCTION

Within two generations the youth of this country have come full circle.

Starting off in 1955, young people were driven by two major motivations:

1. To acquire enough education or training, or through the use of their unskilled labor or street smarts, to land "good" jobs or establish hustles, to make as much money and obtain as many material belongings as possible;

2. To earn, in this way, a measure of respect and dignity from their peers and from society in general. This was the only path open for youth to learn to respect themselves as individuals with self-worth, not just as eating, sleeping, laboring and as sexual beings.

Here we'll take a look at how this limited consciousness was transformed by the emergence of a social vision and a struggle for liberation, and how the subsequent generation became trapped once again in a striving for material things that continues to dominate the lives of young people today.

PART ONE

The First Wave: 1955–1980

The civil rights movement in the South successfully motivated Black, Puerto Rican, Euro-Amerikan, Native Amerikan, Chicano/Mexicano/Indigenous, and Asian youth to use their time, energies, creativity, and

---

1   *The Wretched of the Earth* (New York: Grove Press, 1963), 206

imaginations to discover their true self-worth and earn the respect of the entire world, while struggling toward even broader goals that were not measured by one's material possessions. Over time, each segment cheered on, supported, worked in solidarity with, and/or discovered their common interests and closely linked missions connected to broader goals.

Thus Black youth elevated the civil rights movement to become Black power and Black liberation movements. Puerto Rican youth energized their elders' ongoing struggle to win independence for their home island. Euro-Amerikan youth attacked the lies, hypocrisy, and oppression their parents were training them to uphold in the schools, in society, and overseas. Native Amerikan youth were returning to their suppressed ancestral ways and fighting to regain control over some of the land. Asian youth were struggling to overcome a system and culture that had always used and abused them.

Indeed, all of them came to clearly see that education, jobs, money, hustles, and material trappings could not—by themselves—win them the victories they needed or the new type of dignity and respect they deserved.

Moreover, from 1955 to around 1975 these youth joined, formulated, led, and supported struggles—worldwide—against racial oppression and bigotry, colonialism, and the oppression of women and youth, thus winning themselves the respect, admiration, and gratitude of the world's oppressed as well as of their peers. Furthermore, they became people that society had to take seriously, as positive contributors who had much to give and who were willing to sacrifice to achieve their goals. These youth were more egalitarian than their parents; more capable of imaging a better world and fighting to realize it—while still remaining youthful and having a good time in the process. This earned them a much-deserved place in history.

From the Mountain to the Sewer

Yet, here we are, thirty years later, and the youth nowadays are ridiculed, having been stripped of that hard-earned freedom, self-respect, and dignity. They are again being told—over and over—that the only way to regain these things is to acquire education, skills, good jobs or the right hustle(s), and to once again accumulate as much money and material things as possible. They are told that this is the only way to win respect and dignity from their peers and society.

How the hell did we get back to 1955?

First off, let me make clear that even with all of the glorious strides that youth made within the first wave, they were not the only ones fighting for radical and in many cases revolutionary change. These young people were usually only the tip of the spear, the shock troops of a global struggle. They were motivated by youthful energy and impatience, with no time or temperament for elaborate theories. They were rushing forward into the fray, ill prepared for the tricks that would eventually overwhelm them.

So to understand what happened we must examine some of the main "tricks" used to slow down, misdirect, control, and defeat them. Without a point, a spear loses all of its usefulness.

Strategic Tricks Used Against the Youth

Understanding these tricks and their various guises and refinements is the key to everything. You will never really understand what happened to get us to the present moment or be able to really move forward until you become a master at recognizing them and at devising ways to defeat them. They remain:

1. Co-option;
2. Glamorization of gangsterism;
3. Separation from the most advanced elements;
4. Indoctrination in reliance on passive approaches;
5. Raw fear;
6. Drugs.

Co-option was used extensively to trick just about all of the first wave youth into believing that they had won the war. Strategically, among every segment of the youth that we can name—university students to lower-class communities—billions of dollars were made available. Supposedly these funds were to enable the youth to determine what should be done to carry out the far-reaching changes they desired. In reality they were being expertly monitored and subtly coaxed further and further away from their most radical and advanced elements, mainly through control of this funding. This was part of the strategy adopted by ruling-class foundations, by government, and by corporate Amerika for defeating the youth with sugar-coated bullets.

In time, consequently, substantial segments of these previously rebellious youth found themselves fully absorbed and neutralized by either directly joining foundations, corporations, university faculties, "approved" community groups, or by becoming full-fledged junior partners after winning control of thousands of previously out-of-reach political offices and government posts. The same trick is still being used today.

Glamorization of gangsterism, however, was then and continues to be the most harmful trick played against lower-class segments of youth. Males in particular were and continue to be the most susceptible to this gambit—especially when combined with a prolonged exposure to raw fear!

Let me illustrate by considering two historic groups which presently enjoy nothing less than iconic status among just about everyone who is aware of them. Yet, their documented history clearly shows how the trick was—and continues to be—played throughout this country. Therefore, the following is a brief—but clear—history of how the original Black Panther Party (BPP) was bludgeoned and intimidated to the point where its key leader(s) consciously steered the group into accepting the glamorization of gangsterism. Because this represented less of a threat to ruling-class interests, the BPP won a temporary respite from the raw fear which ruling circles in the United States had been leveling against them. In the process, however, these leaders who went along with this gangster emphasis totally destroyed the organization. Secondly, we will consider the Nation of Islam–connected Black Mafia, which had a different background. But the same two tricks were played against them. Left in their wake was a sordid tale of young Black men who were—again—turned from seeking to be liberators into ruthless oppressors of their own communities, never once engaging their real enemies and oppressors—the ruling class.

Hands down the original BPP won more attention, acclaim, respect, support, and sympathy than any other youth of their time. At the same time, they provoked more fear and worry in ruling class circles than any domestic group since Presidents Roosevelt, Truman, and Eisenhower presided over the neutralization of the labor movement and the U.S. wing of the Communist Party. The BPP was even more feared than the much larger civil rights movement. According to the head of the FBI, they were "the biggest threat to America." That threat came from their ability to inspire other youth—both in the U.S. and globally—to act in similar ways.

Thus there were separate BPP-style formations among the Puerto Ricans (the Young Lords Party), the Chicano/Mexican/Indigenous (the Brown Berets), Asians (I Wor Kuen), Euro-Amerikans (Young Patriot Party and White Panther Party), and even the elderly (Gray Panthers). Also there were literally hundreds of similar but less known groups! Internationally, in Algeria the BPP had the only official embassy established among all of other Afrikan, Asian, and South Amerikan refugee groups seeking such a status in that that (then) revolutionary country. Astonishingly, Black Panther Parties in India, the Bahamas, and Israel were spawned as well!

On the other hand the Nation of Islam (NOI) had been active since 1930. Yet it also experienced a huge upsurge in membership in the same period as the BPP, due mainly to the charismatic personality of Malcolm X and his aggressive recruitment techniques. This continued after Malcolm's assassination, fueled by the overall rebellious spirit of the youth looking for some group that would lead them in the fight against the system.

There is a mountain of documents that clearly shows how the highest power in this country classified both groups as class-A threats, ones that they wanted to either neutralize or destroy—even musing that if this goal could be achieved they could then use similar methods to defeat youth in the rest of the country. So how did they do it?

Against the BPP they used a combination of co-option, glamorization of gangsterism, separation from the most advanced elements, indoctrination in passive approaches, and raw fear—*every trick in the book.*

The ruling class's governmental, intelligence, legal, and academic forces were extremely alarmed at the growth and boldness of the BPP and related groups and their ability to win a level of global support. They devised a strategy to split the BPP and co-opt its more compliant elements, while at the same time moving to totally annihilate its more radical and revolutionary wing. In addition, they knew that they had the upper hand due to the youth and inexperience of the BPP membership. The government also had a deep well of resources and experience in using counterinsurgency techniques. These were developed and used as early as against Marcus Garvey's United Negro Improvement Association (UNIA) in the early 1900s, during the Palmer Raids against Euro-Amerikans of an anarchist or left-socialist bent in the 1930s—crushing the Industrial Workers of the World (IWW) and neutralizing other socialists—and in underground work that contributed to the defeat of Germany and Italy during World War II, the subsequent destruction of any real Communist power in Western Europe, the total domination and subjugation of the Caribbean (except Cuba) Central and South Amerika (except the fledgling guerrilla movements). And they had learned a great deal in their wars to replace the European colonial powers in Afrika and Asia.

Still, the BPP had a highly motivated cadre, imbued with a fearlessness little-known among domestic groups. The ruling class and its henchmen were stretched thin, especially since the Vietnamese, Laotians, and Cambodians were kicking ass in Southeast Asia and the freedom fighters in Guinea-Bissau and Angola also had their European allies—whom the United States supplied with the latest military hardware—on the run. So although inexperienced, the BPP still had a fighting chance.

The co-option depended upon the state being able to "neutralize" BPP cofounder (by that time an icon) Huey P. Newton, and then using him (combined with other methods) to split the BPP and lead Newton's wing along reformist lines, while forcing the still-revolutionary wing into an all-out armed confrontation before it was ready. In this way, the repressive forces hoped to either kill, jail, exile, or break the BPP's will to resist and send its cadre into an ineffective underground existence. What's more, even with the BPP's extraordinary status globally, no countries seemed to want to risk the wrath of the United States by openly allowing the BPP to train guerrilla units on their soil.

Surprisingly, therefore, Huey Newton was allowed to leave jail with a murder charge for killing a policeman still pending. Thus, the government and courts had him on a short leash. With that leash, they hoped to control his actions, although probably not through any direct agreements. Sadly, the still politically naïve BPP cadre and other youth who looked up to Newton could only imagine that they had "forced" his release. Today, some veterans from those times still insist on clinging to such tripe!

Yet it seems Newton had other ideas, and since he was not prepared to go underground and join his fledging Black Liberation Army (BLA), he almost immediately began to follow a reformist script that was completely at odds with his own earlier theories and writings. This script was also at odds with basic principles that were being practiced by oppressed people around the world to good effect. Further, he used his almost complete control of the BPP central committee to expel many veteran and combat-tested BPP cadre in imitation of the Stalinist and Euro-gangster posture he would later become infamous for—involving an all-out shooting war to suppress any BPP members who would not accept his independently derived reformist policies.

At the same time, and on a parallel track, U.S. and local police intelligence agencies were using their now infamous COINTELPRO operation to provoke the split between Newton's wing and other less-compliant BPP members, which was finally consummated in 1971 after Newton's shooting war and purge forced scores of the most loyal, fearless, and dedicated aboveground BPP members to go underground. There, they were joined by those other BPP members who were already functioning as the offensive armed wing. They were known by names such as "Panther Wolves," "Afro-American Liberation Army," and "Black Liberation Army," but only the last one stuck. The BLA had already become a confederation of clandestine guerrilla units of mostly Black revolutionary nationalists from any number of formations who were willing to accept the BPP's leadership and who also accepted Huey Newton as their minister of defense. But obviously Newton didn't see it that way.

Most telling, it was later learned that Newton's expensive penthouse apartment, where he and other central committee members handled any number of sensitive BPP issues, was under ongoing surveillance by intelligence agents who had another apartment down the hall. Thus, Newton and his faction were boxed in, unable to follow anything but government-sanctioned scripts—unless he/they went underground, which only occurred when Newton fled to Cuba after his gangster antics threatened the revocation of his release on the pending legal matters that the government still held over his head.

In addition to the glamorization of gangsterism, there was something else that various ruling-class elements had begun to champion and push on the Black lower classes, especially after they saw how much attention the Black Arts Movement was able to generate. Indeed, they recognized that this new tool could be used to misdirect youth who were attracted to military activities, while at the same time becoming hugely profitable. They had, in fact, already misdirected Euro-Amerikan and other youth with James Bond, I-Spy, Secret Agent Man, and other replacements for the "Old West/Cowboys-and-Indians" racist crap, so why not a "Black" counterpart? Thus was born the enormously successful counterinsurgent genre collectively known as the "Blaxploitation" movies: *Shaft, Superfly, Foxy Brown, Black Caesar,* and their like as well as the wannabe crossovers like *Starsky and Hutch* with its notorious Black snitch Huggy Bear. This was psychological warfare!

Follow the psychology: you can be "Black," cool, rebellious, dangerous, rich; have respect, women, cars, fine clothes, jewelry, an expensive home, and even stay high—as long as you don't fight the system or its cops! But if you don't go along with that script, get ready to go back to the early days, to shoot-outs with the cops and ending up in the graveyard, in prison, on the run, or in exile! You can still be cool even as a Huggy Bear–style snitch or his buddy, modern-day/futuristic rat—Cipher of *The Matrix*—who tried to betray Zion in return for a fake life as a rich, steak-eating movie star. Most importantly, no more fighting with the Agents! Get it?

To bolster the government's assault and to saddle the oppressed with a Trojan Horse that would strategically handicap them for decades to come, the ruling powers began to flood their neighborhoods with heroin, cocaine, marijuana, and meth. Yes, all of these drugs had earlier been introduced to the same areas by organized criminals under local police and political protection. But now, intelligence agencies were using them in the manner that alcohol had long ago been introduced to the Native Amerikans, and with the same intentions: to counter any propensity to rebel against outside control while also profiting from the misery of the ghetto.

So Newton began to indulge in drugs as a way to try to relieve the stress of all that he was facing. He became a drug addict, plain and simple. That, however, didn't upset the newly constructed gangster-cool that Hollywood, the ruling class, and the government were pushing—although many BPP cadre and other outsiders were very concerned about it. But Newton's control was by then too firmly fixed for anyone to challenge it, except the BLA, which by then was in a full-blown guerrilla war with the government.

At the same time, the reformist wing of the BPP did manage some noteworthy strides under its only female head, Elaine Brown. Newton's exile, provoked by his addiction/gangster lifestyle, caused him—on his own and without any consultation—to "appoint" Brown to head the Party in his absence. An exceptionally gifted woman, she relied on an inner circle of female BPP cadre, backed up by male party enforcers, to introduce some clear and consistent projects that helped the BPP to become a real local power. However, she pursued a reformist paradigm that could not hope to achieve any of the radical/revolutionary changes the BPP had called for earlier. In fact, within Newton's earlier writings, he had put the cadre on notice that a time would come when the aboveground would have to be supported by an underground in order to keep moving forward. Yet it was Newton who completely rejected that approach on being released from jail—although he still organized and controlled a heavily armed extortion wing called "The Squad" which consisted of BPP cadre who terrorized Oakland's underworld with a belt-operated machine gun mounted on a truck bed. They were accompanied by cadre who were ready for war!

In classical Euro-gangster fashion, Newton had turned to preying on segments of the community that he had earlier vowed to liberate. But, of course, the police and government were wise to him. Since there was no connection to a true underground, there was no rational way to ratchet up the pressure on the police, the government, and the still fully operational system of ruling-class control and oppression. Newton's BPP had been reduced to relying completely on methods that were officially sanctioned.

Consequently, we can see all of the government's efforts bearing fruit. Newton's faction of the BPP had limited itself to either a legal or underworld-style approach; ("co-optation" and "indoctrination in reliance on passive approaches") that were passive toward the status quo. He fell for the trick of severing all relations with the armed underground—the BLA—which would lead the BPP if it got to the next level of struggle (open armed resistance to the oppressors). This was "separation from the most advanced elements." Because of Newton's control, his faction was immersed in the glamorization of gangsterism. Finally, Newton and his faction, along with activists from other Amerikan radical and revolutionary groups, succumbed to the terror and raw fear that was being leveled against them. All but those who waged armed struggle were killed, jailed, exiled, forced into hiding or into continuing their activism underground.

Epilogue on Huey P. Newton and His BPP Faction

Elaine Brown guided her faction to support Newton and his family in exile, while orchestrating the building up of enough political muscle in Oakland to assure Newton's return on favorable terms. Thus he did return, and eventually the legal charges against him were dropped. Newton continued to use his iconic stature and renewed direct control of his faction to play the cool political-gangster role. Like any drug addict who refuses to reform, he kept sliding downhill, turning on old comrades and even on Elaine Brown, who had to flee in fear.

Sadly, for all practical purposes, that was the end of the original Black Panther Party. Checkmate!

Later, as is well known, Newton's continued drug addiction cost him his life, a sorry ending for a once-great man.

PART TWO

When you grow up in situations like me and Cliff . . . there is a lot of respect for brothers like [drug lords] Alpo and Nicky Barnes, those major hustler-player cats. 'Cause they made it. They made it against society's laws. They were the kings of their own domain.
—Touré[2]

The "Original" Black Mafia (BM)

Albeit a touchy matter to many, it's an irrefutable fact that the original Black Mafia was first established in Philadelphia, PA, in the late 1960s and has seen its cancerous ideas imitated and lionized by Black youth ever since. Moreover, although it's unclear how much the Nation of Islam (NOI) leadership knew or learned about the BM, there's no question of the local NOI's eventual absorption of the BM under Minister Jeremiah X Pugh. In fact, although the BM was originally just local "stick up kids" culled from neighborhood gangs, being swallowed up by the NOI eventually turned them into a truly powerful and terrifying criminal enterprise— completely divorced from everything that the NOI had represented since its founding in 1930.

2　*Never Drank the Kool-Aid* (New York: Picador, 2006), 130.

Sadly, most of the high-level tricks used by the government and intelligence agencies against the BPP were used again here—namely, co-option, the glamorization of gangsterism, separation from the more advanced elements, and raw fear. Thus, it must be understood that although the NOI and BPP had different ideologies and styles, most Black youth still saw the same promise in both organizations: the possibility of helping them to attain the self-respect, dignity, and freedom they most desired.

Interestingly, the puritanical NOI's dealings with the founders of the BM were similar to that of the Catholic Church's historical relationship to the Italian Mafia. The BM members who attended NOI religious services did so strictly on a religious basis, while still coming to the attention of the local NOI leadership as unusually good financial contributors. Within the lower-class Black community, everybody knew that they were hustlers, stick-up kids, or both. So just as the Italian Mafia contributed huge sums to the Catholic Church, the BM eventually did the same thing for Philadelphia's Temple No. 12.

The national NOI, however, had been under close scrutiny and surveillance by intelligence agencies for decades. In fact, by the time of his death, the FBI had in excess of one million pages of files on the Honorable Elijah Muhammad alone!

Consequently, the BM's financial contributors would have come to the attention of the intelligence agencies through this process of monitoring. Nevertheless, overshadowing all of this was the bloody assault the FBI and local police were leveling against other radical and revolutionary Black groups, like the local and national BPP chapters and branches, the Revolutionary Action Movement (RAM), and scores of smaller formations. Indeed, FBI agents first tried to recruit Minister Pugh as a snitch against the local BPP by telling him that the BPP was out to get him and supplant the local NOI, which the BPP viewed as competition for the loyalty of Black youth. Pugh, to his credit, didn't take the bait. He also avoided getting his Temple No. 12 involved in a war with the BPP. At the same time he must have suspected that his taking money from the BM had also come to the attention of the FBI, and that he was therefore vulnerable.

Miraculously, during the same period, Minister Pugh's name was removed from the FBI's "Security Index," which contained all the country's top-level threats—after Pugh had been on this list for years, and immediately following the report on his refusal to become a snitch. Why would they relax the pressure? Co-option! How did they think it would unfold? Was it to give Pugh and his temple—and their BM followers—enough rope to hang themselves? Or was it to get them addicted to a game that would ultimately be controlled by their professed enemies—the U.S government and its underlings—thus turning the tables on Pugh and forcing him to be less radical, more compliant, no longer as significant a threat as the BPP, RAM, and company?

For BM members, the glamorization fit right in. After all, why would a group of Black stick-up kids and gang members call themselves The Black Mafia? This was in the era of "Black Is Beautiful," when millions of Blacks began wearing afros/bushes and Afrikan clothing, and adopting Afrikan names—completely at odds with aping Italians! Why not name themselves the Zulus, Watusis, or the Mau Mau—like every young street gang was doing? Hollywood's projection of gangsterism was getting through!

Consequently, within a couple of years, the BM would uniformly be recognized as expensively dressed, big-hat-wearing, Cadillac-driving imitations of the Italian mafia. And sadly, this turned countless numbers of street gang members, former RAM cadre, and militants from dozens of other Philly groups—who were fighting oppression—into pawns who could then be used to further destroy their own communities.

There was then a third step in the process of separating these Black youth from the more advanced elements. It operated under cover of Pugh and other insiders continuing to preach Black nationalist doctrines among the youth who were in the street gangs and the prisons, never missing an opportunity to hold out the illusion that they could gain pride and respect—while fighting oppression—by joining what they believed to be a rebel group, one that was only awaiting the right moment to throw its lot in with the masses of Blacks who were waging either nonviolent or else bloody battles from coast to coast and on the Afrikan continent.

By tricking these youth into diverting their energies toward gangster-ism, Pugh and company were effectively separating them from the more advanced elements. True, many, if not most, bought into the rationale: that their extortion and drug-dealing proceeds were a tax that could be used to build the Nation. A few years later, that was dubbed "drinking the Kool-Aid," after Jim Jones and his CIA handlers tricked and forced hundreds of other Blacks to their deaths, committing suicide by consum-ing poisoned Kool-Aid. And undoubtedly Huey Newton had also tricked his people with a similar game, although decades later it was shown to be completely false! Yes, that money did build or buy some expensive homes, cars, clothing, women, and drugs—as well as a few school and businesses. But to fight oppression? Please . . . !

Then, the raw fear being leveled on the entire society had the most devastating effect on the BM as well. Otherwise how can one account for the way in which hundreds (if not thousands) of BM street soldiers—fearless enough to challenge Philly's long-established and ruthless Italian Mafia and its other mobs, along with most of its warring street gangs and independents, and who fielded headhunters who literally terrorized the city by decapitations—would demonstrate such a lackluster showing whenever it came to confronting someone in uniform?

I'll tell you how: their leadership had completely disarmed their fight-ing spirit by always pointing to the gun battles that the BPP/BLA and other Blacks were known for, and telling them not to resist the police until they (the leaders) gave the order—which never came. Ironically, after the police and FBI had succeeded in suppressing, jailing, exiling, and co-opting most of the BPP, BLA, RAM, and similar formations, they then discovered the BM and attacked it with a vengeance—while none of the BM put up anything resembling real resistance except to go into hiding. Minister Jeremiah also made a 180-degree turn, becoming a snitch after being caught in a drug sting.

Thus, their legacy is one of a ruthless group of Black thugs who spawned similarly ruthless crews—notably Philly's Junior Black Mafia (JBM), and the latest clone, Atlanta's Black Mafia Family. But the most harmful effect of their deeds and mystique has been to return a huge segment of Black youth to believing that the only way to gain any respect and dignity is through being the best and most heartless hustlers around. Thus, we come full circle from 1955.

To conclude, I used the BPP/BLA and NOI/BM because they present the best-documented examples. Both are surrounded by so much mythology that a true analysis is almost never attempted. Except, of course, by government intelligence sources, who use their findings to refine, update, and revise old tricks in order to continue to check and control this country's rebellious youth and persistently oppress the communities they occupy in line with the ruling-class agenda.

Concurrently, the middle- and upper-class youth—from all segments of the first wave—allowed themselves willy-nilly and with few exceptions to be fully co-opted as the new managers of the system they had once vowed to radically change. They became the champions of—and made a doctrine out of the necessity to always use and rely on—passive and legal methods, epitomized by their new saint, Dr. Martin Luther King Jr.

The Second Wave: 1980–2005

Thus, by 1980, the youth from the first wave had, for all practical purposes, been defeated, following which they collectively descended into a long, debilitating, agonizing, escapist period characterized by partying. Not discounting the fringe elements who had their hands full trying to rebuild their sanity and families, or trying to go back to school, or survive in prison or exile, everybody else seemed to be dancing on the ceiling—like the shell-shocked vets of World Wars I and II, or the posttraumatic stress sufferers of the Vietnam War.

The most misunderstood victims, however, were that generation's children, the second wave—from 1980 to about 2005. Those are the years when these youth either reached puberty or became young adults. Paradoxically, they were left in the dark about most of what had occurred before. Instead, they were left to the tender mercies of the reformed but still-rotten-to-the-core and ruling-class-dominated schools, social institutions, and cultural-propaganda machinery.

So among all lower- and working-class segments of the youth, Coolio's "Gangsta's Paradise" fit the bill. They were raised by the state—either in the uncaring schools, juvenile detention centers and homes—or by the TV sets, movies, video arcades, or in the streets. Within the greatly expanded middle classes—most notably among the people of color—the youth were back to the gospel of relying on getting a good education and a good job as their highest calling, intermixed with an originally more-conscientious element, which tackled politics and academia as a continuation of the first wave struggles. The upper class youth, however, were doomed to follow in the footsteps of their bourgeois parents, since the radical and revolutionary changes the first wave had sought failed to materialize.

Like a reoccurring nightmare, the second wave youth also fell victim to co-option, the glamorization of gangsterism, separation from the most advanced elements, relying on passive methods, the raw fear of an upgraded police state, and drugs. Left to their own devices, the lower-class youth began a search for respect and dignity by devising their own institutions and culture which came to be dominated by the gangs and hip hop. On their own, these things could be used for good or bad. But lacking any knowledge of the first wave's experiences, a new generation was tricked like their parents.

The Gang and Hip Hop Culture

Gangs are a working- and lower-class phenomenon that dates from the early beginnings of this country. They have also been common overseas. In fact, many of those who joined the first wave were themselves gang members—most notably Alprentice Bunchy Carter, the martyred founder of the Los Angeles Panthers and head of the notorious Slausons, the forerunners of today's Crips. As little as it's understood, gangs are in fact the lower classes' counterpart to the middle and upper classes' youth clubs—Boy Scouts/Girls Scouts, fraternities, and sororities. The key difference is the level of positive adult input in the middle- and upper-class groups. Hip hop is just the latest manifestation of artistic genius bursting forth from these lower-class youth—seeking respect and dignity.

> Orthodox hiphoppers speak about a holy trinity of hip-hop fathers: Herc, Afrika Bambaata, and Grandmaster Flash. But, like moisture in the air before it rains, the conditions were ripe for hiphop before the holy trinity began spinning. Hiphop's prefathers or grandfathers are James Brown, Huey Newton, Muhammad Ali, Richard Pryor, Malcolm X, Bob Marley, Bruce Lee, certain celebrity drug dealers and pimps whose names won't be mentioned here, and Al Pacino's Scarface.[3]

Alas, hip hop culture is daily being co-opted in ways so obvious it needs no explanation. But woe to us if we don't come to grips with how the second wave's gangs have been co-opted. This is an ongoing tragedy, moreover one that if not turned around will ultimately make the shortcomings of the first wave pale by comparison!

> Ronald Reagan and crack were hiphop's 80s anti-fathers: both helped foster the intense poverty and teenage drug-dealing millionaires as well as the urge to rebel against the system that appeared to be moving in for the kill, to finally crush Black America.[4]

Certainly the gangs have comprised a subculture that has historically been a thorn in the side of the ruling class, one that either had to be controlled and used or else eradicated. Usually that was accomplished by co-option

3   Ibid., 3.
4   Ibid.

and attrition, with older elements moving on or being jailed long enough to destroy the group. Our first wave, as noted, was able to outflank the ruling class somewhat, lending their prestige to the rank-and-file's acceptance of radical and revolutionary ideas, which have since been pimped by BM-style groups.

It is fascinatingly simple to understand how the second wave was tricked and continues to be bamboozled into destroying itself. The pillars upholding this giant con-game have become familiar to everyone through the movies, TV, street culture, and our own experiences with friends, family associates, cops, courts, jails, prisons, death, and our own unfulfilled yearnings for respect and dignity.

Gangstas, Wankstas, and Wannabes

All of these gangstas, wankstas, and wannabes crave respect and dignity more than anything! Forget all of the unformed ideas about homies wanting the families, fathers, and love they never had. That plays a part. But if you think that the homies only need more hugs, then you've drunk the Kool-Aid! Actually, even if you did have a good father, a loving family, and an extended family, everything in society is still geared toward lessening your self-worth because of your youth, race, tastes in dress, music, speech, lack of material trappings, etc. Therefore you will still hunger for some respect—because that will give you a sense of dignity within yourself. Even suburban middle- and upper-class youth confront this, although to a lesser degree. All of the beefin', flossin', frontin', self-trippin', violence, and bodies piling up around them comes from the same pursuit of respect and dignity.

This is how 50 Cent put it:

> Niggas out there sellin' drugs is after what I got from rappin'. When you walk into a club and the bouncer stop doin' whatever the fuck they doin' to let you in and say, "Everybody else wait. He special."—that's the same shit

they do when you start killin' niggas in your hood. This is what we been after all the whole time. Just the wrong route.[5]

Admittedly, at times this simple—but raw—truth is so intertwined with so many other things that it's hard to grasp. But nowadays the drug game, other get-money games, and most gangs do provide a sort of alternative family as well as a strong cohesion that is mistakenly called love. Let's cut through the distractions, and illustrate my point as follows:

When the second wave was left hanging by the defeated and demoralized first wave, it unknowingly reverted to methods of seeking dignity and respect that the first wave had overcome—through its struggle for radical and revolutionary change during a period when gang wars and gang-bangin' was anathema! The revolutionary psychiatrist, Frantz Fanon, in *The Wretched of the Earth*, notes that the colonized and oppressed are quick to grab their knives and use them against a neighbor or stranger, thereby in a subconscious way ducking their fear of directing their pent-up rage at those who are actually responsible for their suffering—their colonial oppressors.

So the primary activity of the notable early gangs like the Bloods, Crips, and Gangster Disciples was bangin', or gang-warring over "turf"—neighborhoods, schools, etc.—as well as over real or imagined slights. But the real underlying motivation was the desire on all sides to build their reputations and earn stripes—meaning to gain prestige in the eyes of fellow bangers. This translated into respect among their peers. It also caused these youth to bond with each other like soldiers in combat—the way a family bonds—only more so. Not surprisingly, many outsiders decreed that this bonding was "love," which then caused some youth to parrot that thought. But to exchange love you first have to love yourself. And the gang-banger, by definition, has no love for him- or herself—in fact, these young people are desperately seeking respect, without which anyone's idea of love is fooling itself.

---

5   Ibid., 43.

Example: if you "respect" your body you can also "love" your body and you would not dare destroy it with drugs or alcohol. But if you don't respect your body and you go on to destroy it in that fashion, then it follows that you have no love for it either.

The bangin' raged on for years, piling up as many bodies as the Vietnam War—each case elevating the attacker's or victim's stature in the eyes of their peers. During those early times the overseers of the oppressive system bemoaned the carnage while locking up untold numbers of bangers for a few years. But overall they did nothing to stop the problem.

Now here's where it get really interesting! Drugs, as noted, had been flooding into these same communities since the 1960s. Back then, however, it was mainly heroin, with marijuana and meth playing relatively minor roles. Remember *Serpico* and *The French Connection*, movies which exposed this? But the early gangs, to their credit, never got deeply involved in that. They saw dope fiends as weak and although they would blow some "sherm" or "chronic," it was just a pastime for them. They were serious about bangin'!

Consequently, the bangers were all co-opted, wedded as they were to their form of fratricidal gangsterism and totally separated from the remnants of the first wave, who they knew next to nothing about. At the same time the "good kids" were being indoctrinated in passive, legal (get a good education) approaches, while both groups were scared to death of the police! Despite the bangers' hate and contempt, any two cops could lay a dozen of them out on all fours at will.

Hence, Tupac's later iconic stature with them, since he could walk his talk:

> The fact [is] that while everyone else talks about it, Tupac is *the only known rapper who has actually shot a police officer*; the walking away from being shot five times with no permanent damage, and walking away from the hospital the next day and the rolling into court for a brief but

dramatic wheelchair-bound courtroom appearance—it's been dangerously compelling and ecstatically brilliant.[6]

But something was on the horizon that would cause a seismic shift in this already sorry state of affairs, altering things in ways that most still cannot or will not believe. Apparently, since this madness was contained in the lower-class communities, the ruling class's henchmen had no desire to do anything but keep their Gestapo-like police heavily armed and fully supported. Technology had made what they dubbed "the underclass" obsolete anyway. See, for example, Sean Penn and Robert Duvall's movie *Colors*.

Peep the Game

The South Amerikan cocaine trade replaced the French Connection, and CIA-controlled U.S. distribution of Southeast Asian golden-triangle-grown-and-processed heroin as the drug of choice in the early 1980s. Remember *Miami Vice*? As usual, this country's government intelligence agencies and the large banks immediately began a struggle to control this new cocaine trade. Remember, their goal was to control it, not to get rid of it, as their lying propaganda projects with the hyped-up "war on drugs"! Thus, they were contending with South Amerikan governments, militaries, and large landowners who controlled the raising, processing, and shipping of the cocaine—although for a few years these South Amerikan elites had to also do battle with a few independent drug lords, most notably the notorious Pablo Escobar and the Ochoa family–dominated Medellín Cartel.

Within this country, the youth gangs had next to nothing to do with the early cocaine trade which was then primarily servicing a middle- and upper-class white clientele. There were a few old-school big-time hustlers, along with some Spanish-speaking wholesalers who also had their own crews to handle things. After the fact, hip hop favorites such as *Scarface*

---

6   Ibid., 118.

and *New Jack City* are good descriptions of that period. But both films purposefully left out the dominant role that the U.S. government intelligence agencies played in controlling things.

I know you're down with all of that and love it! So let's move on.

In the mid-1980s, the United States began backing a secret war designed to overthrow the revolutionary Sandinista government in Nicaragua. The Sandinistas had fought a long and bloody civil war to rid Nicaragua of its U.S.-sponsored dictatorship in 1979. But after his secret war was exposed for the world to see, the U.S. Congress forbade President Ronald Reagan from continuing it. Like a lot of U.S. presidents, he just ignored Congress and had the CIA raise millions to recruit mercenaries, buy or steal military equipment, and continue the war.

That's how and why crack and the mayhem it has caused came upon us. However, you won't see Hollywood or TV giving up that raw truth—with a few exceptions, like Black director Bill Duke's *Deep Cover*, starring Laurence Fishburne, and *Above the Law* with Steven Seagal. Otherwise, you have to search hard to see the facts portrayed so clearly. Later I'll explain why.

Most people have heard that crack was dumped into South Central Los Angeles in the mid-1980s—along with an arsenal of military-style assault rifles that would have made a first wave BPP member ashamed of how poorly equipped s/he was. Needless to say, the huge profits from the crack sales, coupled with everyone being strapped, magnified the body count! Since crack was also so easy to manufacture locally and so dirt-cheap, just about anybody in the hood could get into the business. Gone were the old days of just a few big-time hustlers—except on the wholesale level.

But make no mistake, the wholesale cocaine that was sold for the production and distribution of crack was fully controlled by selected CIA-controlled operatives. So to all you around-the-way dawgs who have been bragging about how big you were/are, an organizational flow chart would look something like this. At the top would be President Ronald Reagan, vice president and former CIA director George Bush Sr., the national security advisor, the secretary of state, General Secord, Colonel Oliver North, major banking executives, Central and South Amerikan military and government leaders, arms dealers, mercenary pilots, and drug lords like Escobar and the Medellín Cartel (originally), Justice Department attorneys, U.S. Navy and Coast Guard officers, U.S. Customs and Border Patrol officers, state and local police officers, county sheriffs and deputies, and their successors in office. Then, at the bottom of the barrel: you, dawg!

Now, I know you already understood in your hearts that there were some big dawgs over you, but I'll bet you never guessed that the game came straight out of the White House or that you were straight-up pawns on the game board. If that sounds too wild, then tell me why it is harder to find any government, CIA, military, or bankers like George Bush Sr. and his crew in prison than it is to win the lottery? Yeah, they double-crossed Noriega, Escobar, and the Medellin Cartel and made Oliver North do some community service, but that's all. The real crime lords—the government, CIA, military and banking dons—all got away. True, after Congresswoman Maxine Waters made a stink about it the CIA was forced to launch two investigations, and post its findings and admissions of drug dealing on its official website.

Now, dawg, y'all were played! Face it. That's what happened to you OG's from the '80s. But like Morpheus said in *The Matrix*, let me show you how deep the rabbit hole goes.

Gradually, the U.S. government was forced to crack down on the cocaine coming through Florida. By then the South Amerikan cartels and their allies in governments and military circles had found new routes through Mexico. At first, the Mexican underworld was just a middleman. But it quickly recognized a golden opportunity and essentially seized control of most of the cocaine trade between South Amerika and the United States. The Mexicans forced the South Amerikans into becoming junior partners, responsible for the less-profitable growing and processing, after which the Mexicans would purchase mountains of cocaine for trans-shipment overland, smuggling it into the United States and its wholesale markets that produced oil-and-automotive-industry-type profits.

One might wonder how and why the South Amerikans—powerful players—would go for a deal like that? As ever, the answers can be found among the Machiavellian and serpentine maneuverings of the U.S. and Mexican governments. You see, in the 1980s the Mexican government was overseeing an economy that was so bad that for all practical purposes it might have gone belly-up bankrupt. Indeed, the United States and its underlings within the International Monetary Fund (IMF) and the World Bank (WB) were forced to periodically give Mexico millions upon millions in loans in order to save its economy, in return for further unfair trading concessions. Note that the United States was then, and remains today, extremely vulnerable to what happens in Mexico. Common sense and past experience told them that the worse things got in Mexico, the more destitute the already dirt-poor Mexican majority would become, forcing millions to search for a way into the United States to find the means to feed themselves and their families. Rather than keep prevailing on the IMF to continue lending Mexico money, the rulers of the United States saw another way to temporarily plug up this hole in their control of international finance.

Thus, another unholy alliance was formed. This one was between the U.S. State Department, the CIA, the big banks and other usual suspects on one side, and their Mexican counterparts—including the first fledgling cartels—on the other, with the South Amerikans now in a junior partnership role. However, I don't want to give the impression that it was all arranged diplomatically, neat and tidy. Far from it! It evolved through visionaries among the usual suspects placing their ideas before selected insiders and working to craft an unwritten consensus, the same way that (along with Cuban exiles in Florida) they had earlier created the cocaine trade to fund its growth around Miami. Only this time, it would be Mexico's underworld that would eventually land in the driver's seat due to its ability to take the kind of risks called for, a geographic proximity to the U.S. border, and (most importantly) a strong desire to avoid confronting the U.S. and Mexican governments—as Pablo Escobar had. Thus, the Mexican drug lords were more than willing to guarantee that most of their profits would be pumped back into the moribund Mexican economy through large building projects, upgrading the tourist industry, large-scale farming, and other clearly national ventures. In addition, and on the messy side, their gunmen were becoming experts at making reluctant parties fall into line by offering them a stark choice between gold and lead.

Nevertheless, avoid thinking that the Mexican or South Amerikan underworlds ever became anything more than hired hands of the big dawgs in the U.S. government and their partners in the banking industry, who always remained in control. In fact, under President George Bush Sr., the invasion of Panama—a major hub of offshore money laundering—was ordered when their hired hand, Manuel Noriega, became unmanageable in 1989.

These hired hands would ensure that the chosen corrupt politicians would garner sufficient votes in the Mexican elections by bringing in plane-loads of money that the South Amerikan gangsters and government/military partners would make available as part of their overhead expenses. More importantly to the United States, however, a major part of the profits would be pumped into the Mexican economy in order to forestall its looming bankruptcy.

Consequently, by the mid-1990s, the Mexican underworld had established the super-powerful Gulf, Juárez, Guadalajara, Sinaloa, and Tijuana cartels. Moreover, they had consolidated their power by not only controlling who was elected to key political posts in Mexico, but also by perfecting the art of bribing key local, state, and regional police heads as well as strategic generals in Mexico's armed forces. Check out the movie *Traffic* and the Antonio Banderas/Salma Hayek *Bandalero* and *Once Upon a Time in Mexico*. Again—after the fact—you'll see Hollywood spilling the beans. But don't let the fancy stunt work lull you into thinking that there's no substantive truth to the plots of these films!

Remember, Mexico's cartels would not be able to function without the collaboration and protection of the highest levels within the U.S. establishment. Just as the CIA has openly admitted it was an illegal drug merchant during an earlier period you can believe nothing has changed—except the partners!

The hilarious part is that none of the wannabe real gangstas in the United States know that in reality they are low-level CIA flunkies. Or else they can't wait to get out of prison and become undercover government agents—slinging crack. Alas, most think it's crazy to believe that the government of the United States would allow its cities and small towns to be flooded with cocaine. They cling to the illusion that they are something more than pawns on a chessboard.

But you have to go beyond the idea that this whole thing is just a plot to destroy Black and Brown peoples—a favorite though short-sighted theory. Otherwise, there is no way to see just how deep the rabbit hole really is. I repeat: The main objective was to pump billions of dollars into the Mexican economy in order to avoid a complete meltdown and the subsequent fleeing to the United States of sixty million or more Mexicans out of its then ninety-plus million inhabitants. It would have been a migration that dwarfed the numbers who actually did cross over, and are just beginning to make their presence felt.

The big dawgs in the United States probably didn't know just how they were going to control the fallout, although they surely knew there would inevitably be some as a result of their cocaine/crack tax. They routinely tax alcohol, gambling (from the lotteries to the casinos), and even prostitution in certain areas, don't they? So yeah, a clandestine operation to use cocaine to rescue Mexico and stave off an economically induced invasion of the United States by a population made poverty-stricken by five hundred years of colonialism, slavery, peonage, neocolonialism, and the theft of over one-third of their country by the United States in the nineteenth century was an indirect tax.

Sadly, though, the first wave degenerated into the glorification of gangsterism; the second wave's hunger for respect and recognition fueled the gang carnage; and the hip hop generation provided youth with vicarious fantasies to indulge their senses with the hypnotic allure of the temporary power that the drug game could bring them. All this led youth in the United States back to emulating the first wave's *Superfly* and *Scarface* days. Others also see that this is true:

My theory is that nine times out of ten, if there's a depression, more a social depression than anything, it brings out the best art in Black people. The best example is how Reagan and Bush gave us the best years of hip-hop. . . . Hiphop is created thanks to the conditions that crack set: easy money but a lot of work, the violence involved, the stories it produced—crack helped birth hiphop. Now I'm part conspiracy theorist because you can't develop something that dangerous and it not be planned. I don't think crack happened by accident. . . . Crack offered a lot of money to the inner-city youth who didn't go to college. Which enabled them to become businessmen. It also turned us into marksmen. It also turned us comatose.[7]

With the deft moves of a conjurer, the big dawgs in the United States seized upon all of this and began to nudge various elements around on the international chessboard—as part of their giant con game. Moreover, these big dawgs in the United States had very little choice regarding who they would sacrifice in order to gain some relief from their manufactured domestic crisis. I'll tell you why!

Cocaine in its powder and crack forms is so addictive with everyone who uses it regularly—the rich and famous, the Hollywood set, corporate executives, lawyers, doctors, weekenders, entertainers, athletes, college kids, suburbanites, hood rats, hustlers, pipers, etc.—that its demand is guaranteed! In this sense, it's just like alcohol and tobacco, which have never been successfully suppressed in the United States for long.

It follows then that despite all of their propaganda about "Just Say No" and the bogus "war on drugs," the big dawgs never had any intention of even trying to eradicate the use of cocaine. At the same time, however, the Black and Brown communities were becoming major headaches that,

---

7   Ahmir Thompson in ibid., 298–99.

if left unchecked, could evolve into a real strategic threat. Yes, crack had turned their lower-class neighborhoods into lucrative mainstays of the big dawgs alternative taxing scheme. However, the urgency to deal with what happened as a result was graphically driven home by the non-Black/Brown communities' consumption of more (mostly powder) cocaine. And the trade in the Black/Brown hoods and barrios was accompanied by an unforeseen, exponentially rising rate of ever-more-sophisticated drug-related violence, especially once the gangs got seriously involved.

As I've pointed out, the gangs were mainly just pursuing the goal of earning respect prior to getting involved with hustling drugs. The carnage connected with that was not a real concern to the big dawgs. But unlike the earlier dumping of heroin into those communities, accompanied by the comparatively isolated violence of the Black Mafia–style groups, (whose violence, though terrifying, was also more selective) the widespread availability of crack and assault rifles led the big dawgs to understand that this was different. If they did not deal aggressively with the ultraviolent, inner-city politics then, like the Mexican cartels, this reality threatened to become less predictable—once the gangs realized that the money and power they now had would not, of themselves, provide the kind of respect and dignity they sought. To understand why, just consider the rich and famous hip hop artists who continue to wild-out because they still lack the respect and dignity that comes with struggling for something other than money or power—in short, for some type of cause.

Anyway, the hip hop generational favorite TV drama *The Wire* lays out the entire phenomenon pretty much the way it actually played itself out in Baltimore and other urban areas. In fact, the fictionalized TV series derives its sense of reality from an earlier long-running exposé featured in a Baltimore newspaper. This is another after-the-fact but still-useful piece to study. Indeed, the show depicts the earlier years of the Black gangs getting involved in the crack trade and clearly illustrates my point about the gangs evolving into proto-cartels, then getting strategically neutralized.

That's why the "prison industrial complex" was formed! It was formed as a tool to neutralize the second wave before it woke up to the fact that—despite their money and power—young people were being used and played like suckers. This was an itch that the more astute of the big dawgs feared money would not soothe. Thus, all of our draconian gun-related and mandatory sentencing laws were first formulated on the federal level, where most of the big dawgs have their greatest power. They were then forced upon the states. It was all to ensure that the second wave would never be able to consolidate any real power. Precisely because they were proving themselves to be such ruthless gangstas in imitation of their Hollywood idols, coupled with the potential power derived from their share of the undercover tax being extracted from their communities, the big dawgs chose to step in every time they got too big. This happened on average every one to three years, then everything they acquired was taken. The martyred hip hop icon The Notorious BIG put it all together in his classic song—rightly entitled "Respect":

> Put the drugs on the shelf
> Nah I couldn't see it
> *Scarface, King of New York*
> I wanna be it . . . Until I got incarcerated
> kinda scary . . . Not able to move behind the steel gate
> Time to contemplate
> Damn, where did I fail?
> All the money I stacked was all the money for bail.[8]

Let's get another thing straight! I mean the question that continues to have short-sighted people chasing ghosts about why powder cocaine and crack are treated so differently. Within the big dawgs' calculations, there was no reason to punish the powder cocaine dealers and users as harshly as they were punishing the crack crowd. Racism was not the

---

8   *Ready to Die*, Bad Boy Records, 1994.

driving motive. Rather, it was the potential armed threat within these proto-cartels! The big dawgs witnessed a clear example of what could happen by looking at the Jamaican posses that cropped up in the Black communities at this time. These involved young men from the Jamaican and Caribbean diaspora. Like the second wave youth from the United States, they were also a product of the degeneration of the attempts by the lower classes to throw off the economic and social effects that were the legacy of slavery and colonial oppression. Led by the socialist Michael Manley, and inspired by the revolutionary music of Bob Nesta Marley, their activity can be glimpsed in the later Steven Seagal *Marked for Death* and DMX/Nas *Belly* movies. The Jamaican posses were the Black Mafia on steroids!

Moreover, their quasi-religious nationalism, coupled with their ability to operate in Jamaica and in the Caribbean with heavily armed soldiers, put the big dawgs' teeth on edge. Their ten thousand or so were nothing compared to the hundreds of thousands waiting in the wings in the Black and Brown communities!

The cry from the big dawg mouthpieces in Congress was about the gunplay, not so much the drugs. What was not spoken of, however, were the big dawgs' anxieties about stopping these gunslingers before they got over their mental blocks about using their weapons against the police or the system. They wanted to stop them while they were still hung-up on imitating their Hollywood and Euro-Mafia icons—who made a mantra out of instructing their gunmen not to use their weapons against the police. Indeed, with few exceptions, the second wave allowed itself to be disarmed and carted off to prison like pussycats!

Add to all of this the unforeseen windfall of thousands of new jobs in prisons for the rural communities that were being destroyed economically by capitalism's drive for fuller globalization. These conservative rural communities are vital to the big dawgs who needed their fanatical religious support.

We must struggle against the shortsighted view about racism alone being the driving motive that fueled the construction of the prison industrial complex. Instead, if you do a follow-up and add your own research, you'll be able to detect and document the who, when and where of how the big dawgs set everything in motion, as well as how they continue to use us as pawns in their giant, international con game.

CONCLUSION

Ask yourself the following questions:

1. How can we salvage anything from the way the first and second waves allowed their search for respect and dignity to degenerate into gangsterism?
2. In what ways can we help the next wave avoid our mistakes?
3. What can we do to contribute to documenting who the real big dawgs behind the drug trade are?
4. Why have they never been held accountable?
5. How come our families and communities are the only ones to suffer?
6. How can we overcome our brainwashing?
7. How can we truly gain respect and dignity?
8. In what ways can we atone for our wrongs and redeem ourselves, our families, and our communities?
9. What are some of the ways to fight for restitution and reparations for all those who have been harmed by the government-imposed (undercover) drug tax?
10. How can we overturn the Thirteenth Amendment of the U.S. Constitution and finally abolish slavery in the United States?

Once you've answered these questions and begun to move to materialize your conclusions, you will then have made the choice between Liberation or Gangsterism: Freedom or Slavery.

Recommended Books

Bowden, Charles. *Down by the River*. New York: Simon and Schuster, 2003.

Fanon, Frantz. *The Wretched of the Earth*. New York: Grove Press, 1961, 2005.

Griffin, Sean Patrick. *Black Brothers Inc.: The Violent Rise of Philadelphia's Black Mafia*. London: Milo Books, 2005.

"Inspector General's First and Final reports on Iran-Contra and the Illegal Drug Trade," https://www.cia.gov/library/reports/general-reports-1/cocaine/contra-story/pilots.html.

Mutaquim, Jalil. *We Are Our Own Liberators*. Montreal: Abraham Guillen Press, 2000.

Parry, Robert. *Lost History*. Arlington, VA: The Media Consortium, 1999.

Shakur, Sanyika. *Monster: The Autobiography of an L.A. Gang Member*. New York: Grove Press, 1993.

Webb, Gary. *Dark Alliance*. New York: Seven Stories Press, 1998.

**Respect Our Mothers
Stop Hating Women
(2010)**

This essay is mainly for men, although it will also make some women examine some of the ideas and practices in which they indulge. With exceptions, men love or at least have loved their mothers—or so they think.

This fiction of loving our mothers has also translated into "respect" for mom more than for most other women. Plus, men will (mostly) protest that they don't hate women. Guys like me are experts in deceiving themselves in this manner. I deceived myself a lot—despite, in my youth, practicing the vilest forms of woman hating, attempting to be the ultimate street thug during the heyday of Philadelphia's street gang craze in the 1950s and early 1960s. Afterward, I was an equally insane, ruthless, low-down, dirty, drug-dealing hustler.

Nonetheless, after becoming politically conscious, I further deluded myself into believing that being a "revolutionary" made me a champion dedicated to the uplifting of all humanity. It turned out, however, that I had just transferred many of my woman-hating practices to another arena. That's the special fate of male revolutionaries who put so much stock in the testosterone-dominated armed struggle.

One can see a similar paradigm being followed by men who come from "the other side of the track." Stan Goff—who's white, while I'm Black—followed this same macho script:

> In a distinguished career in elite Ranger, Airborne and Special Forces counterterrorist units, Stan Goff went to Vietnam, Guatemala, El Salvador, Grenada, Panama, Venezuela, Honduras, South Korea, Colombia, Peru, Somalia, and in 1994, Haiti. There he refused to turn away from the implications of his own experience. . . . *Hideous Dream* is a revealing look inside U.S. foreign policy, inside the elite echelon of the Special Forces and inside the racist history of American imperial domination of Haiti. It is also a deeply personal account of a man trapped between his emerging political

consciousness and the cynical mandates of his life as a professional soldier.[1]

But Goff has also grown a great deal in his understanding and commitments to truly egalitarian social change. He has written books and essays, and he organizes in the streets to help bring this about. So here I'll quote from his writing to help make my points: Two former "macho men"—once from opposing camps—are now joined in an effort to prevent others from making the same kinds of anti-women mistakes they made.

Some of the knee-jerk men are already thinking: "This guy's talking to the nut cases. I don't hate women. In fact, I really love women more then I feel comfortable discussing!" What's really being said there is "I love sex! Period." Of course, that's how most males are made. But don't get that confused with what's really being pointed out here. It's similar to when the plantation owners in the American South used to swear to outsiders about the supposed affection they had for their "niggras"—especially after the North's abolitionists began to make inroads with their anti-slavery efforts prior to the outbreak of the Civil War. What the slavers (too) were saying was; "I love what all my niggras can and are doing for me."

In a passage from Stan Goff's *Sex and War*, he writes about how the related "male power is not simply father-right but sex-right. It's about men having access to the bodies of women in a relationship of domination and subjection."[2]

That's not love; it's exploitation like master and slave. To really get a handle on all of this we must clear away centuries of built-up diversions that hinder us from simply accepting the reality of so many woman-hating practices, by going to the root of the problem: the ancient and still-operational, institutionalized, and culturally ingrained practices of a system known as "patriarchy."

---

1   Stan Goff, *Hideous Dream* (New York: Soft Skull Press, 2000), back cover.
2   Goff, *Sex and War* (New York: Soft Skull, 2006), 196.

Patriarchy and the Roots of Women's Oppression

Patriarchy as a system of male dominance over women emerged some 5,000–6,000 years ago among certain tribes living in the central Asian steppes north of the Black Sea. . . . The Kurgan People were able to make warfare and conquest of other tribes and their territory the main source of their wealth. The secret . . . was not their superior intelligence or culture, or some kind of genetic superiority, but mainly more efficient means of transport, namely tamed horses and camels, and their more efficient means of destruction, namely bows and arrows and spears and other long distance weapons. . . . This monopoly over efficient means of destruction, however, changed not only the relationship between those tribes and other tribes, but also the relationship between humans and nature and also, in particular, the relationship between men and women. . . . It also changed the whole conceptualization about the originator of human life. Whereas before it was clear that women were the beginning . . . of human life, this logic could now be turned upside down. A new logic could be created, namely that of "He who kills is." . . . "He who kills is" has remained the core of all patriarchal logic until today.[3]

There have been exceptions, in particular in Sub Saharan Africa, due to women being responsible for the production of 80 percent of the food—at least up until European colonialism. But even there, and everywhere else inhabited by humans, patriarchy has developed and held sway until this

---

3   Veronika Bennholdt-Thomsen and Maria Mies, *The Subsistence Perspective: Beyond the Globalised Economy* (London: Zed Books Ltd, 1999), 32–33.

very day. Patriarchy's most virulent manifestation, however, developed with the early European capitalist system and has since metastasized into patriarchal capitalism, which dominates the world today. It is a male-dominated system that's totally irrational and can never hope to satisfy the needs or desires of its participants.

"In a system that is driven mainly by the motive of constant growth of money and because capital cannot say 'It is enough,' there is no concept of sufficiency."[4] Nonetheless the history of our species runs counter to any idea that we are beings who have not in the past, or cannot today, satisfy our needs and wants—when not indoctrinated into believing otherwise. "Capitalism had to transform needs into wants and addictions by producing ever more fashionable 'satisfiers.' . . . Only when thirst will no longer be quenched by water but only by Coca-Cola or wine or beer is it possible to extend production of these beverages limitlessly."[5]

Even with patriarchal capitalism dominating our world, most of the needs of its billions of inhabitants are still met in other ways.

> Economists define growth as the increase of all goods and services produced and marketed in the course of one year in one country, . . . GDP or GNP (gross domestic product, or gross national product). . . . [But] the bulk of the work done on this planet is *not* included in this indicator, namely the work of housewives and mothers, the work of subsistence farmers and artisans, most of the work in the informal sector, particularly in the South, and, of course, the self-generating activity of mother nature. All this production and work does not *count*. On the other hand all destructive work—like wars, environmental and other accidents, oil spills, arms production, trade and so

4   Ibid., 54.

5   Ibid., 55.

on—is included in GDP, because it "creates" more wage labor, more demand and economic growth.[6]

For generations some thinkers have been explaining how irrationally an economic system like capitalism functions, mostly to be ignored, vilified or silenced in other ways. Here's a quick rundown on just why capitalism—ultimately—does not work:

> In non-capitalist subsistence . . . *use-values* are produced for the satisfaction of limited human needs. When they are exchanged in the market, use-value is exchanged for use-value, for example, potatoes against apples. Marx called this the "simple circulation of goods." His formula is C-M-C (Commodity –> Money –> Commodity). But the capitalist production process has a different beginning and aim. It starts with money and its aim is more money . . . M-C-M′ (Money –> Commodity –> Money′) . . . In the next production round the increased money (money′) is again invested with the aim of again producing *more* money (money′′). And thus ad infinitum. Use-value production and exchange-value production realise two different economic goals: the one life, the other money. The aim of use-value production—we also call it subsistence production—is fulfilled with the satisfaction of limited, concrete needs. It makes no sense to work longer once one has produced the things—or services—one needs for a good life. Exchange-value production, on the other hand, is by its very logic unlimited. Its aim is extended accumulation of ever more money, or abstract wealth.[7]

---

6   Ibid., 56–57.
7   Ibid., 57–58.

Money—Or, Until the Wheels Fall Off

In this logic lies the basic clue for the understanding of the capitalist growth mania, not in insatiable human greed, as some think.
—Veronika Bennholdt-Thomsen and Maria Mies[8]

A final but very important aspect must be touched on here. "A subsistence perspective can be realised economically only in smaller, regionally limited decentralised areas. Only in such regional or local economics can production and consumption be integrated in such a way that the interests of the producers and the consumers are not antagonistic."[9]

Although patriarchal capitalism is a world-wide system, it cannot be grappled with or defeated using its methods: massive, regimented, faceless armies of dissidents who will also fall victim to an inability to adequately understand, and thus empathize with, the needs of other dissidents who are geographically and culturally removed from them. The antithesis of global patriarchal capitalism, therefore, must be a global, decentralized localization, that nevertheless still shares a common need to be rid of patriarchal capitalism's exploitation and domination. We must develop ways and means to coordinate our efforts in order to accomplish such a goal. Failure to both decentralize and (ultimately) coordinate will allow patriarchal capitalism room to develop new and better ways to continue to pursue its goal of accumulation.

Many of my readers already desire and work toward the realization of egalitarian goals—they believe—but by now may be troubled by some of what I've written so far. Let's call them "left alternative thinkers." It seems to me that many of these thinkers have been confused by a blind following of doctrines and practices of what I'll call "patriarchal socialism."

---

8   Ibid., 58.

9   Ibid.

We discovered that women's work to reproduce . . . labor power did not appear in the calculations of either capitalists or of the state, or in Marx's theory. On the contrary, in all economic theories and models this life-producing and life-preserving subsistence work of women appears as a "free good," a free resource like air, water, sunshine. It appears to flow naturally from women's bodies. . . . We began to understand that the dominant theories about the functioning of our economy, including Marxism, were only concerned with the tip of the iceberg visible above the water, namely only capital and wage labor. The base of that iceberg under the water was invisible, namely women's unpaid housework, caring work, nurturing work . . . the production of life or subsistence production. . . . And finally we saw that nature herself was considered to be a "free good," to be appropriated and exploited with no or little costs for the sake of accumulation. Therefore we called all those parts of submerged "hidden economy" which are under the water in our iceberg metaphor—nature, women and colonised people and territories—the "Colonies of the White Man."[10]

Even the followers of Marx, Mao, Che, Nkrumah, Cabral, Newton, and George Jackson fall woefully short in grasping the true nature of patriarchy, even though they strive mightily to overcome capitalism. The author fit into that category, too, until as recently as four years ago anyway.

"In revolutionary practice, women were relegated to being revolutionary helpmates with certain exceptions and the most immediate forms of women's oppression—often in the home—went unrecognized or were 'deferred' for resolution within the socialist project until after the revolution."[11]

---

10   Ibid., 31–32. "White Man" here stands for the Western industrial system.

11   Goff, Sex and War, 182.

Even though we've all seen those iconic posters of the woman guerrilla, rifle in hand and baby on her back, how many posters do you know of *male* guerrillas with babies on their backs?! Even during times of war the "life preserving" work of women appears as a free good, a free resource, that appears to flow naturally from women's bodies.

That's patriarchy at work: propaganda designed to encourage women to support and participate in movements labeled "anti-oppression." It's a sleight of hand that's hidden by patriarchal socialization. Thus we inadvertently propagate our own blindness about how the patriarchal woman-mother stereotype is perpetuated.

And it's apparent that those tens of thousands of women guerrillas who participated in the wars of national liberation from Angola to Vietnam to Nicaragua, as well as anti-oppression struggles globally, have all but been forgotten today, except by those who lived through those times or by the diligent student or researcher: "Everyone knows who Dr. Martin Luther King Jr. was. Only some know who Ella Baker was. Yet her contribution to the Black Freedom Struggle was contemporaneous with King's and just as significant."[12]

In the United States, one can locate scores of streets, buildings, programs and even a national holiday named after black men who contributed to the civil rights and Black liberation movements of the last hundred years. But one would be hard pressed to find a dozen named for Black women. Without being a student of the subject, everybody has images of black women and children being set upon by cops or dogs, or being dragged away and arrested. We can visualize the sisters in their huge afros showing defiance in the front ranks of all manner of struggles during that same period. If it wasn't for the capitalists recognizing that a dollar could be made recording those images, we would really be at a loss!

Earlier, I quoted Veronika Bennholdt-Thomsen and Maria Mies concerning the fight against patriarchal capitalism and about decentralization. Here's something from our comrade who spent decades in the

---

12   Ibid., 182

U.S. military and should know a thing or two about the strengths of centralization and decentralization, and how this fits with his/our desire to dismantle patriarchal capitalism.

> Women have been able to contest for power with men more effectively at the local level where these communal networks (more often than not organized by women) were strongest, and that "the more centralized, bureaucratic, and trans-local working-class organizations are, the easier it is for men to monopolize decision making and marginalize women."[13]

Again quoting Johanna Brenner, he continues:

> Limitations on women's participation were cultural (definitions of leadership, and notions of masculine authority and the role of women in the public sphere) but also material. In the first instance, caregiving responsibilities restricted women's leadership beyond the local level. Until quite recently most women union leaders and organizers were single, childless or had grown children.[14]

Once again we see patriarchal privilege manifesting itself in order to keep the women union members from effectively exercising power, albeit without really saying so or even recognizing it. The women union members were expected to do the bulk of the work in raising the children, and to the union men that seemed natural. Of course, in 2010, an ever-growing number of men do the bulk of work in raising children, usually because the capitalist class has discovered it can discard large sections

---

13   Johanna Brenner, "On Gender and Class in U.S. Labor History," *Monthly Review* 50, no. 6 (November 1998): 1–15.

14   Goff, *Sex and War*, 172.

of higher-paid men and replace them with lower-paid women, leaving couples with little option but to switch roles. Yet most men and women still adhere to patriarchal norms: the men resenting the women for taking their jobs, and the women accepting women's (patriarchal) wages for work they know men are or would be paid more to do. The overwhelming majority would not dream of blaming or challenging the real culprits, the twin pillars of capitalism and patriarchy.

Once again Goff comments on centralization and its history in supporting patriarchy:

> As resistance struggles begin they are more local, and increasingly as the struggle transforms into a nationwide (and even internationalized) coordinated one, from war of maneuver to war of position, from guerrilla to conventional, the organizational tendency is to centralize. Given that many forms are necessarily centralized and translocal, the question becomes how to be intentional about preventing sectoral patriarchal defaults from kicking in.[15]

I would wager that most men who consider themselves to be combating capitalism's many ramifications—whether they consider themselves to be seeking "socialist" solutions or not is besides the point, since another wager says that they fit the bill otherwise—have not seriously wrestled with the issues presented so far about patriarchy. That's been left for some future time, until after the primary problems of national, racial, and class oppression within the capitalist framework are solved. This author lived this position as well, until former macho-man Stan Goff's writings, coupled by earlier shoves by a couple of women comrades, forced me to go back to school where I discovered the neglected writings of radical feminism. In fact, it took another former macho-man to provoke me to read titles such as *Ecofeminism* by Maria Mies and Vandana Shiva. At that

---

15   Ibid.

time, feminism evoked for me visions of middle class, pampered, northern white women who were struggling to be like the ruling class capitalists. Of course, many so-called feminists fit that bill. But I was floored to be introduced to some real radical revolutionary feminists from whom I've learned more in a few years than I did in the previous few decades!

Many of my white comrades believe that most other whites become more open to seriously examining their racist views and practices only after being patiently and intelligently engaged by other whites, and work hard challenging others in that way. Similarly, the radical feminists say the main task of true liberation-minded men is to challenge other men to first recognize how deep a hold patriarchy has on all of us, then move forward to help them really fight patriarchal capitalism. In my case, they were right.

"We need to organize a community of organic and academic intellectuals and activists who are committed to the refoundation of a revolutionary left that makes gender, national oppression, and ecological science as central to its theory and practice as class and—here is my own wish—that we recruit, educate, and incorporate those with military backgrounds (especially women) into this revolutionary process."[16]

Getting Off the Patriarchal Capitalist Merry-Go-Round

Not convinced? Of course you're not. Most men have gone their whole lives being socialized to either exploit women or simply ignore—as much as possible—the obvious disadvantages that a majority of women are forced to live with. Furthermore, the most exploited or brutalized man still believes in his heart that he's better than any woman. This is one of the reasons for so much otherwise-senseless violence against women. To men, it's the pecking order, similar to the way many whites feel about non-whites in matters dealing with race. Yet most men also know—deep inside—that the world we live in is very, very fucked up! Bear with me. If

16   Ibid., 187.

I get too graphic, the Agents (as in the movie, *The Matrix*) will keep you from reading this. Things are so bad that this film is as close as Hollywood likes to come in depicting the control exercised over our lives. It raked in untold millions and has become a classic. And, as in the movie, we don't really know who's unplugged from the Agents. Those who are unplugged must keep trying to stay out of the Agents' way as they search for ways to defeat the Matrix. Let's face it: every attempt to fight patriarchal capitalism (our Matrix) has failed. Yet most of the male-dominated efforts today are still trying to get the job done with the same tools (ideologies and ideas) that our matrix has repeatedly defeated for centuries.

A new vision is needed. And, ironically, like in *The Matrix Revolutions*, maybe it's time that we look to some wise women to help guide us, like the Oracle and the woman head of Zion's council of elders.

Allow me a little digression here, in case the reader is thinking my Hollywood references have no place in this discussion. Patriarchy is so clever and deep that an anti-establishment blockbuster like *The Matrix* can be stolen from the original script of an African American woman by two white movie-making brothers. And its legions of fans will remain in awe of these men producing a sci-fi movie that so clearly mirrors patriarchal capitalism's development—a very rare thing indeed! Yet it was another anti-woman undertaking from its beginning:

> Sophia Stewart filed a federal lawsuit in the U.S. District Court of California against Hollywood defendants Andy and Larry Wachowski, Joel Silver, and Warner Brothers alleging copyright infringement of the movie *The Matrix* and the *Terminator* movies' original script. . . . Stewart, a Black woman from the Bronx, New York, now living in Salt Lake City, Utah, filed her case in 1999 after she saw the Matrix. . . . She was certain that it was based upon her own manuscript, "The Third Eye." It was copyrighted in 1981, '83, and '84. . . . Ms. Stewart sent her manuscript to an address given by the Wachowski

Brothers. . . . "Third Eye" is an epic plotted in the past, present, and future—about a woman whose baby is part of a prophecy—or "the one." There is also a Terminator-like figure that comes from the future to protect the baby so that the prophecy is fulfilled. Considering herself a very conscious observer of society, Stewart wrote the script as a counterbalance to the impression left by the "Blaxploitation" films of the 1970's. "I am the oracle," she said. "I write myself in my work. I know two white boys are definitely not the oracle." There were so many changes made and ghost writers for *The Matrix* and *Terminator*. Holding out for more meaningful legal retribution, she rejected the initial court settlement. "The rich steal because they're greedy; the poor steal because they're needy," asserted Stewart. "Some people said they were just validated because they could not believe it was the Wachowskis' because they would never explain anything about the movie," she said. "They never went on any talk shows. The first *Matrix* went through seven different plot changes and copyrights. America will be throwing stones at the Wachowski brothers because they pulled the Milli Vanilli on everybody." The defendants have filed several unsuccessful motions to have the lawsuit dismissed. If successful, Stewart will receive damages from both trilogies. She could receive one of the largest payouts in copyright infringement history.[17]

My digression reflects so many aspects of patriarchal capitalism that I'll just leave the reader to ponder them, while I hope you will now be more open to the remainder of this essay, which also requires that we dig more deeply into our already-molded ideas and practices.

---

17   *Philadelphia News Observer*, December 8, 2004, and February 23, 2005.

The new vision that's needed is *not* really new. It must contain aspects of ways of life that have been practices (and to a degree are still practiced) by what we call "underdeveloped" societies. It is a way of living that is more balanced and sustainable than what "developed" societies have become addicted to, a way of living and of viewing life that is going to be very hard for the reader to accept because I will not have enough space to adequately take you through the steps that led me my conclusions. A few assumptions that underpin most peoples' economic, social, and world-views can be touched on, however: the fallacies of pursuing a catching-up-with-the-rich (or "developed") strategy; the reliance on technological fixes for all problems, and the belief that a good life can only be had by societies and individuals who have access to the trappings that surround the middle and upper classes of the global North.

> A way out of this destructive and irrational system of commodity production cannot be found in catching-up development and technological fixes, even if technological alternatives could be quickly found to end and repair some of the environmental damage caused by industrialism. . . . If, for example, we note that the 6 per cent of the world's population who live in the United States annually consume 30 per cent of all the fossil energy produced then, obviously, it is impossible for the rest of the world's population, of which about 80 per cent live in the poor countries of the South, to consume energy on the same scale. . . . But even if the world's resource base was unlimited it can be estimated that it would be around 500 years before the poor countries reached the living standard prevailing in the industrialized north; and then only if these countries abandoned the model of permanent economic growth, which constitutes the core of their economic philosophy. It is impossible for the South to "catch-up" with this model, not only because of

the limits and inequitable consumption of the resource base, but above all, because this growth model is based on a colonial world order in which the gap between the two poles is increasing, especially as far as economic development is concerned.[18]

Do not think that the present author or the activists whose books he's been liberally quoting are anti-technology; we're not. Basic and well-known facts are here being unhinged/liberated and presented without concern that they might trample certain sacred cows that have prevented many of us from questioning what we've been doing for a long time.

> These facts are widely known, but the myth of catching-up development is still largely the basis of development polices of the governments of the north and south as well as the ex-socialist countries . . . if one tries to disregard considerations of equity and of ecological concerns it may be asked if this model of the good life, pursued by the societies of the North, this paradigm of "catching-up development" has at least made people in the north happy. Has it fulfilled its promises there? Has it at least made women and children there more equal, more free, more happy? Has their quality of life improved while the GDP grew?[19]

Those of us who live in the United States in the twenty-first century cannot but come to the conclusion that even the bulk of the middle classes, to say nothing of its lower classes, are not experiencing happiness, even in the midst of so many material possessions. Our ubiquitous media thrives on delivering statistics to attest to our consumerism, added to the TV images of people trampling each other in a headlong rush to purchase the latest

---

18   Maria Mies and Vandana Shiva, *Ecofeminism* (London: Zed Books, 1993), 60.

19   Ibid., 60–62.

gadget or article of clothing that they believe will make them happy. If not, then millions turn to their search engines, overeating, prescription drugs, TV sports, video games, cyber-sex, channel surfing, and any number of other addictions that patriarchal capitalism daily produces in order to keep them hooked.

"It has been found that in the United States today the quality of life is lower than it was ten years ago. There seems to be an inverse relationship between the GDP and the quality of life. . . . The affluent society is one society which in the midst of plenty of commodities lacks the fundamental necessities of life: clean air, pure water, healthy food, space, time, and quiet."[20]

The primary contradiction (materially) is that not only is the catching-up strategy not viable for most of us outside of the privileged classes, but that patriarchal capitalism's trajectory cannot even be sustained for the most privileged sectors of society, forcing these societies to throw tens of thousands to the wolves every day, while trying to hold the starving millions from the global South at bay, and engaging in an ongoing war to steal their resources.

Look at how the former "privileged" workers in the Midwest of the United States have been forced out of their labor-aristocracy jobs, to become homeless, jobless, and all but destitute—not knowing how they're going to feed themselves and loved ones once their (formerly taboo) hand-outs run out. And on the bottom—overall—are women and children.

Our radical feminists have been advocating for decades that our new vision must be what they term a "subsistence perspective." For a number of years, I too had been thinking along those lines. But I was not strong-minded enough to totally go against everything I'd previously championed. And most of my comrades were also stuck in the same dead end. So I remained in limbo, beating a dead horse. But now that I've read these writings and further researched the subject, I also believe that a subsistence perspective is the vision that holds promise. There are certain reservations that I harbor,

---

20   Ibid., 61.

but on a scale of one to ten, they would register a two. On that same scale, my current clarity about what needs to be done, and my determination to pursue it is a nine. (Nothing is a ten, except maybe hindsight.)

In fact, others are being forced to adopt a similar strategy even though they may not use the word "subsistence" in their explanations. That word tends to generate misunderstanding about what is being advocated. Here's an example of what is actually meant:

> The World Wide Fund For Nature *Living Planet Report* 2006 pointed to Cuba as the only nation in the world to have achieved sustainable development. . . . Some large state farms were transformed into cooperatives, where large machinery was replaced by human and animal labor. . . . In cities, unused plots of land were turned into urban farms . . . and gardens, increasing food production, providing employment for 30,000 people in Havana alone. . . . In Havana, these now supply 100 percent of the city's fruits and vegetables and are supplemented by urban patios, which number 60,000 in Havana. . . . They have developed pasture techniques to increase milk productivity and help recycle nutrients. . . . Specialist[s] work closely with farmers, learning from each other and overcoming the artificial gap between manual and mental labor. In electricity, Cuba uses a variety of renewables: biomass, mainly from waste products of sugar cane . . . hydroelectric, which is small in scale and largely used for local needs, biogas, produced from the decomposition of organic waste, . . . solar energy, . . . wind farms. Santa Clara University develops eco-materials for use in small-scale localised production of housing, . . . low-energy fire clay bricks, . . . laminated bamboo sheeting, . . . light but strong micro-concrete roofing tiles. . . . Wildlife and biodiversity are also protected in Cuba. . . . Now forest cover has risen

to 24.3 percent. Cuba's internationalist solidarity and its building of the Bolivian Alliance for the Americas (ALBA) with Venezuela, joined by Bolivia, Nicaragua, Dominica, Honduras (under Zelaya), Ecuador, St. Vincent and the Grenadines, and Antigua and Barbuda, with its policy of humanitarian, economic and social cooperation through non-market, non-profit-based exchanges show the only sustainable and workable basis to deal with the effects of climate change. Socialism is good for the environment.[21]

Nowhere in that article was the word "subsistence" used. But although Cuba and other ALBA countries continue to do a lot of good—often under the "socialist" heading—what they're doing is a lot of what subsistence-perspective advocates believe is needed for a new vision. *If* they also work as hard to root out all forms of patriarchy—that's the dividing line between a subsistence perspective and patriarchal socialism.

Maria Mies and Veronika Bennholdt-Thomsen summarize some of the "main features of a new subsistence paradigm":

1. *How would work change?* There would be a change in the secular division of labour: Men would do as much unpaid work as women [childcare, elderly care, care for the sick and infirm, household duties]. Instead of wage work, independent self-determined socially and materially useful work would be at the centre of the economy. Subsistence production would have a priority over commodity production . . . .

2. *What are the characteristics of subsistence technology?* It must be regained as a tool to enhance life, nurture, care, share, not to dominate nature but to cooperate with nature. . . . Technology should be such, that its effects could be "healed" and repaired.

---

21   David Hetfield, "Socialism Is Good for the Environment," *Fight Racism Fight Imperialism* 214 (April–May 2010).

3. *What are the "moral" features of subsistence economy?* The economy respects the limits of nature. The economy is just one subsystem of the society, not the reverse ... The economy must serve the core life system [which militates against the patriarchal capitalist—unspoken—morality that says: "War is an extension of politics, and politics is the tool best suited to increase one's economic worth short of war"; thus anti-core life system—RMS]. It is a decentralized, regional economy ....

4. *How would trade and markets be different?* Local and regional markets would serve local needs.... Local markets would also preserve the diversity of products and resist cultural homogenization. Long distance trade would not be used for meeting subsistence needs. Trade would not destroy biodiversity.

5. *Changes in the concepts of need and sufficiency.* A new concept of satisfaction of needs must be based on direct satisfaction of all human needs and not the permanent accumulation of capital and material surpluses by fewer and fewer people. A subsistence economy requires new and reciprocal relations between rural and urban areas, between producers and consumers, between cultures, countries and regions. The principle of self-reliance with regard to food security is fundamental to a subsistence economy. ... Money would be a means of circulation but cease to be a means of accumulation.[22]

It is imperative that this new vision not be lumped in with the talk about "green energy" and the other fashionable ideas about saving the planet from global warming. In none of these schemes do the advocates make the bottom line what it needs to be: the absolute destruction of the ideals and institutions that define and help patriarchy to continue its exploitation and brutality toward women that has been going on for thousands of years. We must even reject some of those ideas that claim to put destruction of capitalism up front, patriarchal socialism included.

---

22   Bennholdt-Thomsen and Mies, *Subsistence Perspective*, 62–63.

Conclusion

The liberation of women is not an outcome of revolution. It is the precondition for it.
—Stan Goff[23]

By now some of you men will be saying, "Yeah, Maroon, you make some good points. I'll have to check out what you're saying. But what has all of this got to do with "Respect our mothers"? You're totally out of order to suggest that we don't respect our moms! Forget about all those other BI_ _ _ _ _ (I mean women). I've always respected my mom! In fact, I think you and Stan Goff done got y'alls in, now in y'alls old age, y'all are feeling all guilty and shit. Fall back on us young brothers. It takes time to digest and adjust to all these changes. Plus, how do we know that women ain't gonna act crazy too?"

Let me end by saying everything written here speaks to ways that women have always—as a whole, all of our mothers for sure—been forced to the bottom of the bowels of patriarchal capitalism's Matrix-like slave ship. So if you and I are not working to destroy that setup, then we cannot really say we respect our mothers.

Stan Goff ain't Morpheus, I ain't Neo. Bennholdt-Thomsen, Maria Mies, Vandana Shiva, and company ain't no shape-shifting oracle. But I believe in much of what they have written (here and elsewhere), primarily because much of it aligns with my own thinking and reasoning. So I ask you to take the red pill. Get a hold of their writings and let them show you how deep the rabbit hole goes.

Note: The alternative spellings "womyn," "wimmin," "humyn," etc. have not been used here in order not to confuse the reader, because the conventional spelling of those words has been used by all of my quoted radical feminist sources. That does not mean I reject such alternative spellings. That's a subject for another work.

---

23   *Sex and War*, 177.

Recommended Books and Articles

Bennholdt-Thomsen, Veronika. "Subsistence Production and Extended Reproduction." In *Of Marriage and the Market: Women's Subordination in International Perspective*. Edited by Kate Young, Carol Wolkowitz, and Roslyn McCullagh, 41–54. London: CSE Books, 1984.

Bennholdt-Thomsen, Veronika. "Toward a Theory of the Sexual Division of Labor." In *Households and the World Economy*. Edited by Joan Smith, Immanuel Wallerstein, and Hans-Dieter Evers, 252–71. Beverly Hills, CA: Sage, 1984.

Bennholdt-Thomsen, Veronika. "Women's Dignity is the Wealth of Yucatan." *Journal of Interdisciplinary Economics* 3, no. 2 (1991): 327–34.

Goff, Stan. *Hideous Dream*. New York: Soft Skull Press, 2000.

Goff, Stan. *Full Spectrum Disorder*. New York: Soft Skull Press, 2004.

Goff, Stan. *Sex and War*. New York: Soft Skull Press, 2006. http://www.insurgentamerican.net/download/StanGoff/Sex-n-War.pdf.

Mies, Maria. *Patriarchy and Accumulation on a World Scale: Women in the International Division of Labor*. London: Zed Books, 1999.

Mies, Maria, and Vandana Shiva. *Ecofeminism*. London: Zed Books, 1994.

Mies, Maria, Veronika Bennholdt-Thomsen, and Claudia von Werlhof. *Women: The Last Colony*. London: Zed Books, Ltd., 1988.

Mies, Maria. "Women, Food and Global Change: An Ecofeminist Analysis of the World Food Summit–Rome," Institute for the Theory and Practice of Subsistence (ITPS) November 13–17, 1996, Bielefeld.

Mies, Maria, and Veronika Bennholdt-Thomsen. *The Subsistence Perspective: Beyond the Globalized Economy.* London: Zed Books Ltd., 1999.

Shiva, Vandana. *The Violence of the Green Revolution.* London: Zed Books, 1991.

Shiva, Vandana. "Food Security: The Problem," in *Seminar* 433, New Delhi, India, 1995.

Shiva, Vandana. *Captive Minds, Captive Lives: Ethics, Ecology, and Patents on Life.* New Delhi, India: 1995.

Shiva, Vandana, Afsar H. Jafri, and Gitanjali Bedi. "Ecological Cost of Economic Global Isolation: The Indian Experience," Prepared for the UN General Assembly Special Session on Rio + 5.

Democracy, Matriarchy, Occupy Wall Street, and Food Security (2011)

Interviews conducted by Bret Grote

How would you define democracy?

In its broadest sense, to me, democracy is the ability of the individual to exercise self-determination in the core areas of economics, education, entertainment, labor, law, politics, religion, sex, war, and peace, taking under consideration the need to both support and guide children until they can responsibly exercise this self-determination on their own.

If one falls victim to believing what Marimba Ani calls "rhetorical ethics" (the practice that has held sway surrounding the word "democracy"), then you would dismiss my definition as superfluous. Nowadays, however, more of the masses globally are accepting the fact that except for a small minority, democracy is something they do not exercise in any of these core areas.

So the question we must ask ourselves is: "How do we construct societies where the individual is able to broadly exercise self-determination?"

Do you find the concept of democracy to be useful to popular movements?

For the already-mentioned reasons, the exercise of democracy/self-determination is paramount at every stage of a popular movement, and for such an effort to remain true to the word "popular." After all, individuals usually feel a need to look out for their own interest. To promote and support democracy/self-determination goes hand-in-hand with that need. If a popular movement deviates from this, then it too will fall into the practice of utilizing rhetorical ethics—if it continues to call itself "popular."

What was the relationship between democracy and the Black Panther Party?

Here, I'll have to step on a lot of toes. The Black Panther Party (BPP)—with which the Philadelphia Black Unity Council (my parent group) merged in 1969—was never a democratically run organization. It, too, used rhetorical ethics to justify its methods, both internally and to the public at large. It championed the "Leninist vanguard party" concept that had been used during the Russian struggle against the czar. Subsequent to that, close copies of those practices have spread throughout the world before the BPP adopted it. I've been researching and studying those instances for about forty years, and I have yet to find a single "vanguard party" that really exercised what I have defined as democracy/self-determination.

Such groups have and continue to champion the establishing of popular movements—as I've defined them—but their motives are to try to control such movements and use them as a battering ram to weaken or defeat the state in order to give the vanguard party a chance to "seize state power," then set itself up as a new ruling elite. The histories of vanguard parties leaves no doubt about that.

The BPP, however, was a youthful formation that served a historical purpose: giving youth of color—and later youth in general—an introduction to a form of radical politics that was little-known to them previously. Little did they know that the methods they chose to use were contradictory to the ends they sought. Thus early on they began to experience friction from members who actually believed in the rhetorical ethics the leadership relied on, while the leadership failed to act toward the rank-and-file democratically—within the traditional vanguard party "democratic centralist" organizational rules.

That forced the BPP leaders to resort to naked terror and violence—both internally and within the communities. (See what the womyn BPP head Elaine Brown wrote in her book *A Taste of Power*.) Eventually that, along with the struggle to keep the state from destroying them (see the FBI's COINTELPRO program of unlawful actions against the BPP) plus their youthful inexperience caused the original BPP to disintegrate. It left members in prison, exiled, disillusioned, and with shattered lives.

Only a fraction of those former BPP members remain active in ways that justify their earlier sacrifices and efforts.

Unfortunately, newer BPP formations have not been provided with enough insight into this subject to help them fully weigh both the strengths and weaknesses of the original BPP. Indeed, some of the newer formations are hostile to any real critiques of the original BPP, a practice held in common with most Leninist vanguard parties, historically.

To our rescue has come the multiple popular movements that the Arab Spring has inspired: the Wisconsin state workers, Georgia and California prisoners' actions, and Occupy Wall Street. Here, we're witnessing a promising trend that contains the seeds that can develop into a much-needed popular movement, one that can be democratic and self-determining, capable of challenging the minority for control in the already-mentioned core areas.

Would you say you are a latecomer to the feminist movement?

Yes! In fact, although I've been a committed activist since before the assassination of Martin Luther King Jr. in 1968, it has only been in the last six years that I've awakened to the best of what feminism is, and the history of that movement. Moreover, I'm ashamed to admit that in this area I too have long practiced a purely rhetorical ethic, paying lip service. Since before 1968, I claimed to be struggling for the uplifting and freedom of all, while never fully grasping that my entire worldview was steeped in and rested on patriarchal/male-supremacist ideas and practices—feminism's opposite and mortal enemy.

My New York–based comrade Fred Ho is the first person to put it all together for me. In the transcript of a speech I read, he made an excellent case for how the ancient practice of matriarchy was once a widespread and egalitarian phenomenon, and why today we must again study how we can utilize some of those principles in order to address the ills that humynkind faces.

Nonetheless, I was so stuck-on-stupid that I continued in my male-supremacist ways, incorporating Fred Ho's ideas in a rhetorical ethic to hide my psychological conditioning. I'll explain.

It took the writings of Stan Goff—a former career military man (Special Forces, Rangers, Delta Team; Vietnam, Grenada, Somalia, and other operations veteran) who had rejected the oppressive policies that he had spent his life defending, adopting instead a form of radical politics and activism—to get my full attention. This level of machismo is venerated within the patriarchal/male supremacist worldview. He was "my kind of guy."

In Goff's third book, *Sex and War*, he really got my interest by offering long and insightful quotes to bolster the points he was making, quotes by radical and feminist writers and activists. They were passages so full of meaning that they stimulated me to begin to research the full works of the wimmin mentioned—powerful feminists like Maria Mies, Vandana Shiva, and Veronika Bennholdt-Thomsen. They are activists, scholars, and grassroots organizers with groundbreaking books like *Ecofeminism* (Mies and Shiva), *Patriarchy and Accumulation on a World Scale: Women and the International Division of Labor* (Mies), and *The Subsistence Perspective: Beyond the Globalised Economy* (Bennholdt-Thomsen and Mies). I've learned more from their critiques than from most of my previous twenty-five years of study and activism. More importantly, those works and further study, reflection, and discussions, caused me to radically alter my worldview and my political views.

Thus, when comrade Fred Ho and I recently got together, I was finally ready to join his efforts, which you, too, can examine by looking at appendix 2 of this book.

What were the primary obstacles—psychological, social, or otherwise—to your being receptive to the feminist movement?

Psychologically and socially—like most males—I was conditioned and socialized from birth to accept and even to seek violent solutions to most problems: the pirates, cowboys and Indians, war movies, James Bond, gangsters, boxing, football, martial arts, hunting, and on and on. Little boys get toy guns, toy soldiers, football gear and then "graduate" to get (or want) real guns and go to war—with somebody!

Fred Ho and Maria Mies point out that for thousands of years men first bamboozled wimmin out of acquiring and maintaining the knowledge and tools (weapons) of the martial arts, before going on to subsequently use that knowledge and those weapons to totally subjugate wimmin and nature—the foundations upon which patriarchy rest.

Unknowingly, I became a member of that patriarchal cabal almost from birth, and remained a loyal member even after I thought I was struggling in the Black Panthers and Black Liberation Army for egalitarian ends. Our effort was destined to leave patriarchy/male supremacy in place, even if we had otherwise been successful.

It is depressing to know that it took me over sixty years to stumble upon a feminist who had the kind of "credentials" I could trust, in order to pay proper attention: the "macho" Stan Goff. Therefore I believe that men—the more respected the better—are the best advocates to persuade other men about feminist ideas and practices. (Fred Ho and his comrades more correctly use the word "matriarchy/matriarchal," but for this piece I'll continue using "feminist.")

Finally, it's my opinion that the leading feminist/matriarchal thinkers and activists are heads and shoulders above all others in offering up a worldview that we can utilize to help rescue ourselves and the environment from this worsening crisis we've allowed ourselves to be manipulated into. Everyone needs to look into their ideas and programs.

What are the strengths and weaknesses of the Occupy Wall Street Movement?

Occupy Wall Street (OWS) has brilliantly changed the narrative and relationships of opposing forces—not by the "occupations," which by themselves could be equaled or even eclipsed by a number of other street demonstrations from the right and left. (Let's not forget that Tea Party activists "occupied" venues for a while too.) That's not to belittle the beautiful people of the OWS-inspired occupations and related ongoing actions.

Rather, OWS's strategic strength and paradigm-shifting breakthrough is encompassed in the awesome "We are the 99 percent" slogan. That alone instantly won to our side 99 percent of the inhabitants of the globe! It was a masterstroke that forced the ruling minority into a defensive position that it will be extremely hard for them to get out of. Indeed, the ruling elite's only response has been to use police force, which leaves the OWS movement in control of the narrative. Others inspired by OWS are themselves thinking of ways that they, too, can make their grievances known.

It's like the rebellions (so-called "riots") during the "long hot summers" of the 1960s. Each rebellion fueled later rebellions, because the underlying conditions were so widespread—until there were simply not enough police/national guard troops to fully repress them. The genie was only coaxed back into the bottle after billions of dollars were spent on social programs, President Johnson's "Great Society" being the best known.

Today, however, the ruling minority will be both unwilling and (finally) unable to fully co-opt the 99 percent financially, unless they commit "class suicide," because, they would have to agree to reorder the system so radically, and give back so much of the wealth they've stolen, that in the end they would have "killed the goose that laid the golden egg."

The ruling minority won't even accept the pleas of their more far-sighted spokespeople, like Warren Buffet and Bill Gates, who see the handwriting on the wall. These individuals are begging others in their class to at least act as if they care by paying their taxes—an appeal which is roundly ignored and ridiculed. It is the U.S. elite's equivalent to Queen Marie Antoinette's famous declaration: when the starving masses of Paris said they had no bread, she responded, "Then let them eat cake." Nowadays, it's "Go to the mall and buy a flat-screen TV."

Control of the narrative will continue to be the main strength of the OWS movement for the foreseeable future. But in order to effectively be more proactive, OWS must address a glaring weakness: the present physical disconnect between it's activists and the exploited and super-exploited people of color—numbering in the tens of millions in the United States alone. This is a segment of the country that has always suffered more (per capita) than the rest of its 99 percent. I'll not address how the global 99 percent breaks down in that regard, except to say that the global South has historically been at the bottom of the barrel in most respects. But I know the United States better, so I'll address things here and leave it to others to break down the situation elsewhere.

In the United States, people of color—except for a minority of rich and "middle class" individuals—are worse off than the rest of the 99 percent (per capita) in every category: homelessness, joblessness, home foreclosures, lack of health insurance, new diagnoses of HIV, deportations, immigrant homes broken up and separated, children in foster care, drug and crime-ridden communities, imprisonment, probation or parolees, loss of voting rights, loss of access to local, state and federal social welfare programs, horrible schools, being forced to live in toxic communities, and the list goes on.

What's important is OWS's moral strength, which really rests on its avowed pledge to rescue this country's vast "middle class" from sliding further backward—into the poverty that the majority of the people of color already find themselves in. Yet, the middle class itself is not yet ready to take the steps that are necessary to pursue a protracted struggle to reach those ends. And the people of color have yet to see that it's in their interests to hit the streets in massive numbers in order to alter the class composition and goals of this movement. Most people of color view OWS as a "white thing," or so I've been told, not recognizing that their mass participation is needed to help OWS mature into a true mass movement.

To complicate this lack of participation by people of color is the failure of their traditional "leaders" to mobilize them behind OWS. This failure, I believe, is a product of these leaders' egos: they feel a deep sense of jealousy and envy toward this young upstart movement, which has accomplished more in weeks than they have in the last three decades. And the hostility of OWS to the old charismatic leadership style—these "leaders" believe—threatens to make them useless. It's an extremely shortsighted calculation! In fact, their accumulated knowledge and experience could be invaluable if they would control their egos and begin to see themselves more as organic intellectuals than as the old-style leaders for whom there was some justification prior to the spread of modern communications. The Arab Spring makes that style superfluous, reactionary, and a drag on forward progress.

That said, it's my belief that OWS and those traditional influential personalities within the people of color communities still desperately need each other!

In *The Wretched of the Earth*, Frantz Fanon tells us that during the Algerian independence struggle, the more advanced elements initially believed they could bypass the traditional leaders among the oppressed and go directly to the masses with their compelling logic and arguments against the French colonial system. They failed, however, and were isolated, killed, exiled, and imprisoned.

After studying things while in prison, they decided on their release to seek the help of the traditional leaders as a necessary compromise. This position later bore fruit, although both elements—the forward thinking fighters and the traditional leaders—continued to struggle to control the dynamics of the independence movement.

OWS, I believe, must pursue a similar strategy in order to acquire help in mobilizing the masses among the people of color in the United States. An influx (beyond the relatively small numbers we see) of people of color into the OWS movement will provide a bridge between the forward elements in OWS and that vast middle class that's needed if OWS is to be successful, but who need time in order to realize they must hit the streets too. And the people of color will benefit by being in a position to educate OWS regarding the necessity of putting their needs and concerns "on the front burner," because they are the proverbial "canary in the coal mine"—meaning, whatever kills the canary will later kill the coal miners if not attended to.

OWS must seek out not only the known influential individuals in the people of color communities, but also the smaller groups who are working for change. OWS can also launch its own initiatives in those communities—wherever that's deemed possible and useful.

What are economic alternatives to the current domination of big banks, war profiteers, and the profit-drive system?

On November 25, 2011, on *Democracy Now!* ("Occupy Everywhere: Michael Moore, Naomi Klein on the Next Steps for the Movement Against Corporate Power") a similar question was raised: "How does the OWS movement move from the 'outrage phase' to 'the hope phase,' and imagine a new economic model?" Both Michael Moore and Naomi Klein addressed that, but I just want to comment on a few things Naomi Klein said—namely, that after the Seattle protests and the later hysteria, war, and repression following 9/11, many radical activists "put their heads down and started building the economic alternatives to that model we were protesting in Seattle, Washington, in Genoa, and around the world. Now we have ten years of those experiences." She goes on to tick off many of these experiences that I would encourage you to read about by searching for this interview on the *Democracy Now!* website.

One aspect of the prefigurative work that strikes me as part of the bedrock is working toward food security. There's no need to detail how fragile most people's food acquisition is—in particular as it relates to healthy food and the terrible eating habits and subsequent poor health in this country. Suffice it to say that the majority of the 99 percent are on shaky ground here, primarily because we are prisoners of the large corporations that dominate everything we eat. They actually mass-produce, process, and sell foods that have been proven, over and over, to be like slowly drinking poison—a poison that is profitable (for them).

Thus, food security is designed to lessen our dependency on those corporations, making us healthier and saving money, and bringing us back to a respect for nature in the process. After all, we can't struggle as much as is needed if we are as sick as most of us find ourselves to be. Such an effort is already being carried out by the parent group of the prefigurative initiative that Fred Ho is a part of: Scientific Soul Sessions (SSS). Go to www.scientificsoulsessions.com. One of their guides to food security rests on the practice of Mel Bartholomew's "square foot gardening" (www. squarefootgardening.com).

SSS writes, "According to Bartholomew, for urban settings, four square feet is all that is needed to grow vegetable gardens to feed two adults year-round. Rooftops, sidewalks, parks, front and backyards, common areas of buildings could all become food-growing sources with minimal alteration and costs. Indeed, children and the elderly could be organized to tend to such gardens, and thus enhance the curriculum of math, science, and other fields in the tasks of farming."

It is imperative, however, that we don't start believing that such prefigurative efforts, or others not mentioned here, are "the answer" to everything that will be needed to bring about the deep and broad-based changes needed for twenty-first century. Such mistakes were made after the high tide of the 1960s–1970s era. And those who made that mistake allowed the exploiting minority a chance to study how to better hold on to their ill-gotten power and wealth. Now we all face a much more ruthless and sophisticated foe.

Thus, prefiguration must work hand-in-hand with broad-based movements to bring about the changes needed. OWS is on the cutting edge of that side of the equation.

The Question of Violence
(2012)

Editors' note: The essay below originally used the pen name "Tank" in order to hide Maroon's identity. As indicated in the Author's Note in this volume, Maroon risks considerable danger and increased torture when targeted words such as "violence" appear in anything he writes or reads. But, as Maroon instructs those of us who are editing this book: "Lenin, during the height of czarist repression, used a pseudonym, but the crisis we face today demands as much clarity as we can muster." So Maroon has told us to go ahead and publish this essay, his most recent, in his name.

I t may seem less serious, but I'm going to liberally use references from "pop culture" (movies) in your training. We will not have access to the kind of aids the most sophisticated states and corporations use to train their people. So I'll be directing you to movies that will serve a similar purpose. And keep in mind that the operators of the most deadly military drones are essentially trained on TV/movie/game-like simulators.

Creative revolutionaries face the probability that they will have to defend themselves as they labor to educate and mobilize others to understand and organize in response to the universal ecological, economic, social, and cultural crises that we are discussing. Further, we must attempt to use all available means to aid those global masses who reach the point of recognizing that a thoroughgoing revolutionary change must be embarked upon, both to save themselves and as much of our ecosystems as possible. To this end we must move aggressively to replace the present reality with one that is ecosocialist and matriarchal.

Thus, the "question of violence" must be tackled from the beginning. It would be *suicidal* for creative revolutionaries, and the diverse elements we hope to join with, to be caught off guard believing that our collective situation will be adequately handled without being fully prepared to defend ourselves against the global forces of financial, corporate, transnational, state, and surrogate capital. These forces show signs of assuming a twenty-first-century neofascism—with its sham elections and its historical, ever-growing violence toward and domination of wimmin, the indigenous, national minorities, nonheterosexuals, and our entire ecosystem. A posture and practice that has led to the normalization of what has been called "exterminism," or "ecocide."

Creative revolutionaries must work to establish a *prefigurative praxis* in order to help educate and train ourselves and others in ways of tackling the question of violence, and violence itself.

Demystifying Violence

As a phenomenon violence exists throughout the universe. Turn to your Weather Channel or Animal Planet cable stations and you will witness violence that would be hard to classify as anything else. The footage of hurricanes, tornadoes, volcanic eruptions and other "natural" occurrences fit that category. Similarly, the stalking, chasing, killing and devouring of prey by a vast array of animals and insects is hard to define as anything other than naked violence. Our species likes to cling to the fallacy that we are distinctly different than these "lower" life forms, and are thus outside of this violence equation—a position no scientist can accept. As scientific revolutionaries, we too agree with those other scientists.

Homo sapiens as a species has thousands of years of recorded history, and in that record, the serious student cannot find any period (anywhere) that is free of violence between members of our species, or between *Homo sapiens* and the animal and insect worlds—to say nothing about the violence we inflict upon our habitats! And since recorded history is the laboratory for the study, analysis, and understanding of social science, which includes how *Homo sapiens* interact with each other and with the flora and fauna that surround us, then it is safe to say that violence is (like it or not) a natural occurrence. It is, however, a condition we can seek to escape from, in the same way that other animals and insects seek to escape the violence of predators and of nature.

What's called "nonviolence" is often juxtaposed as the opposite of violence by those who want to believe that our species can somehow remove ourselves from the violent universe of which we are a part (a tiny part!), while continuing to participate in the violent phenomena that are responsible for our existence (such as the violent movement of tectonic plates that continues to shape the very ground under our feet).

Counterposing nonviolence to violence, however, totally confuses the *progression* of these phenomena. One cannot properly understand violence without recognizing its *kinetic* aspect: the motion of material bodies and the force and energy associated with that motion. This is a state that the already-mentioned examples of violence exhibit. We cannot violate the laws of physics, which dictate that a body in motion cannot be checked without a body possessing an equal or greater counter motion. So we have to look elsewhere if we want to locate an *opposite kinetic energy* to serve that purpose, since nonviolence by its very description cannot be scientifically understood to contain a *counter kinetic energy.*

In fact, *the opposite of violence is counterviolence:* a kinetic energy-force that is capable of providing a counter motion, thereby satisfying the laws of physics, and can also serve as a check on the forward or reverse movements of violence. All things being equal, this is what can lead to a *synthesis between the two,* which would then be nonviolence.

Such violent kinetic forces can be shown to be present *internally* (in *Homo sapiens*) where, for example, stress hormones might cause the individual to suffer anxiety, which is only relieved by medications or by therapeutic exercises designed to counteract that force.

Historical, Scientific Analysis of Violence and Nonviolence

How did so many get it wrong, and continue to do so? Two historical examples and one from the Bible, which are most often relied upon to substantiate the "nonviolence as a direct counter to violence," can help us answer that question. The two historical examples are the struggles led by Mohandas K. Gandhi (1869–1948) and Martin L. King Jr. (1929–1968). The biblical example is what is written about the historical or mythological Jesus Christ.

These three men are said to have been avowed believers in and practitioners of nonviolence as a way of achieving radical or revolutionary social change against violent powers. And it's accepted wisdom that all three were eventually successful in overcoming their violent antagonists with this method. Gandhi is credited with leading the movement that forced the British to leave India; Martin L. King Jr. is lauded for leading the civil rights movement that destroyed segregation in the United States. And Jesus Christ inspired the creation of a new religion (since he was born into the Jewish faith)—a religion that subsequently went on to become the worldview of the violent power that decreed his death: The Roman Empire.

There is no disputing these basic facts. But once we begin to dissect and analyze the events surrounding these victories we quickly discover that the nonviolence preached by these three men was *not* the counterforce that checked the violence that was being leveled against them and against the movements they led.

In the case of Gandhi and India, one can easily see that he started his nonviolent campaign during a time when the British Empire was very strong. They were fond of bragging about how "the sun never set on the British Empire." And that remained true after World War I. That war, in fact, made the British Empire even stronger, since it acquired even more colonies after the conflict. In India, Gandhi and his movement was no more than an occasional concern to the British, due mainly to the British penchant for overreacting toward peaceful protesters. They killed scores, causing many others to join the movement in sympathy. Gandhi and his people could have gone on in that fashion for who knows how long, winning occasional reforms that had the effect of reinforcing the hold of the British on the country.

Moreover, the British could ill afford to allow a nonviolent, unarmed movement in one of its major colonies to *force* them to leave, because such an example would have provoked its other numerous colonial subjects in lands on four continents to think about emulating those methods. Thus, the British had to decide to either allow further defections from their empire, or to wage bloody and costly wars to suppress them—in order to hold onto the colonies that provided the British with untold wealth.

Thus for twenty five years (1914–1939) Gandhi and his movement in India could not get the British to budge on their demand for self-rule.

That situation was radically altered only after Adolf Hitler's Nazi regime in Germany invaded Poland in 1939, which marked the beginning of World War II. That war went on until 1945, with the British Empire playing a major role along with its allies, chiefly Russia and the United States. This was a war that forced the British to their knees, in a life and death struggle that threatened to subjugate even their home island of England, Wales, and Scotland. Eventually this struggle stripped them of their global colonial possessions. It is this turn of events that, one can easily understand, served as the *counterviolence* to the British Empire's *violence*—which was otherwise holding Gandhi's *nonviolent* movement in check.

In fact, during that war, when the British forces in India were weaker than they had ever been, Gandhi refused to join with other Indians who wanted to step-up their noncooperation campaigns. Nor would he sanction such efforts by others. Apparently he had been given promises from the British that they would look favorably upon his efforts after the war (if he continued to *cooperate* with them). Since the British also needed—and received—the help of tens of thousands of Indian colonial soldiers to help save their empire, an arrangement similar to the one Frederick Douglass, the African American abolitionist, had made with President Lincoln and the Union forces during the American Civil War, became possible. We will expand upon this thought later.

Not only was the British Empire under direct attack from Nazi Germany, its Italian and Japanese Axis allies and their surrogates, but Britain also being blackmailed by its main ally—the United States—and its president Franklin Delano Roosevelt. The latter was claiming to stand for the right of all people to be able to exercise self-determination. This sent a signal to the British colonies that they had a powerful backer in the United States—an ally that the British could not go against, since the bulk of the war materiel Britain needed to save itself came from the United States.

Roosevelt was *not* concerned with true self-determination, however. He was instead attempting to strip the British of their colonies, so that this country (the United States) could begin instituting an indirect, and more efficient, form of exploitation that came to be called "neocolonialism."

This is the backstory that is rarely introduced into the debate about Gandhi and his use of nonviolence in the struggle for Indian independence. Hollywood muddied the waters even more with their Ben Kingsley, Candice Bergen, and Martin Sheen movie, *Gandhi*.

Thus one can see that Gandhi's nonviolent noncooperation campaign *did not* free India from British rule at the end of World War II (in 1947). Instead it was the *counterviolence* of the Nazi, Italian, Japanese and their surrogate Axis powers that *neutralized the violence of the British Empire*, and allowed Gandhi's *nonviolent* movement in India to obtain independence through a *synthesis* between the *kinetic* forces that dominated these events.

When we *fully* examine the case of Martin L. King Jr. and the gains made by the civil rights movement in the United States, we can easily recognize similar counterviolent forces working to neutralize the violence being leveled against that movement. In this case, the counterviolence came from two major arenas: the police and military forces of the United States government, and the rising anticolonial struggles in the (so-called) Third World—the latter being closely associated with Russian and Chinese Cold War opposition to the United States.

The civil rights movement began with Rosa Parks's refusal to give up her bus seat in segregated (apartheid) Montgomery, Alabama, in 1955. One could say that its high points were reached within a decade, marked by the signing of a number of laws that essentially destroyed the monopoly which segregationists had on political and social institutions in the United States.

During the same period, anti-colonial struggles were being waged across the globe—in Vietnam, throughout the African continent, in Cuba and South America. And though these anti-colonial fighters claimed to be unaligned with the United States, Russia, or China, in reality most of them were receiving a massive amount of assistance from all three parties. Tens of millions of dollars in military supplies and training were being received from Russia and her Eastern European bloc allies, and from China. And the United States—desperate to not allow its Cold War foes to dominate the fight for the Third World—*also* provided millions in funding and covert support through the CIA and other agencies. This was a continuation of Roosevelt's effort to undermine the British Empire during World War II, which had expanded to undermine French and Portuguese colonial holdings—with Russia and China now in the race as well.

Many of these struggles were guerrilla insurgencies that threatened to directly involve the Cold War adversaries in direct military clashes—such as when Russia tried to transport nuclear-armed missiles to Cuba, or when both Russia and China both butted heads with the United States over the arming and training of Vietnam during its war against American invaders.

We can see from all of this that the efforts of Martin L. King's nonviolent movement were *not* taking place in a vacuum. In fact, the iconic scenes of civil rights demonstrators—children, wimmin, and men—being clubbed, bitten by dogs, mowed down by fire hoses, dragged away and locked up, were *also* being viewed around the world. Such scenes were a terrible problem for the United States, whose representatives were busy trying to convince foreign multitudes—who were themselves victims of such treatment from their own colonial rulers—that they should ally with the United States once they gained their freedom.

Consequently, the United States government's big picture foreign policy concerns were being undermined by the segregationists, and the rulers of the United States subsequently introduced their own government *counterviolence* (or its threat) by way of the FBI, United States Marshals, National Guard, and regular U.S. Army soldiers at key intervals—on the side of the *nonviolent* civil rights movement.

It's ludicrous to believe that heavily armed and historically terroristic forces like the Ku Klux Klan, the Mississippi Sovereign Commission, and other fellow travelers—entities who controlled all arms of government on both a local and a state level, and owed their positions, power and lifestyle to the generations-old segregated/apartheid arrangements—would stand by while an (essentially) unarmed civil rights movement stripped them of those advantages. It is ludicrous, at least, *unless* they knew or believed that a potential counterviolence was ready, willing, and able to enter the struggle against them. This was particularly true in a region of the country that had never fully recovered from an earlier physical/military struggle that the ancestors of the segregationists had blundered into and lost.

So here, too, it's the violent segregationists, trying (like the British in India) to hold onto their privileges, whose use of *violence* is checked by the *counterviolence* (or threat of it) by some other—the United States government forces, which are embroiled in a Cold War struggle for the future control of the Third World—which must therefore appear to the world as a "just" actor, allowing a movement wedded to *nonviolence* to prevail. It is *another synthesis of the forces we are analyzing.*

Let's now closely examine this question in relation to the historic or mythological Jesus Christ. Here we'll use the written records, despite the obvious inconsistencies and distortions they contain. It's clear that Jesus was "a man of peace," who taught his followers to use nonviolence and other commendable practices toward others. A reading of "The Sermon on the Mount" (Matthew 5–7) leaves one with little to criticize. And after his clash with the Jewish and pagan (Roman) powers of his time—a clash that led to his crucifixion and death—Jesus still staunchly continued to advocate nonviolence in all affairs:

> You have heard that it was said "An eye for an eye and a tooth for a tooth." But I tell you not to resist an evil person. But whoever slaps you on your right cheek, turn the other to him also.[1]

After Jesus' death his disciples and tens of thousands of his subsequent followers tried to emulate such nonviolent methods. And it's absolutely true that many of them were subjected to the most horrible abuses, tortures, and deaths—all because they would not abandon the core of his teachings. They were placed in arenas where they were set upon by wild and starving animals, who tore them apart before devouring their bodies while crowds cheered, drank, and feasted. Many were forced to

---

1   Matthew 5:38–39.

flee from place to place, even to live underground, hidden like insects in catacombs or in caves.

That went on for hundreds of years in Africa, Asia and Europe, until 312 AD, when the pagan Roman ruler, Constantine I, defeated another ruler in battle and said the victory was due to the "Christian God." This same God had by then gained moral currency among many otherwise pagan Roman soldiers and citizens. Constantine went on to become the first Roman Emperor to promote Christianity throughout the lands over which he ruled.

Recalling our earlier examples, the most likely explanation is that Constantine co-opted the moral currency that he knew had gained strength among his soldiers and subjects. He factored that in with his efforts to motivate them to sacrifice themselves to help him defeat a rival leader in battle. A "spiritual" conversion of Constantine is more problematic.

At any rate, starting with Constantine and continuing up until the present day, the nonviolence that Jesus taught is never followed by those who otherwise profess to follow his teaching—once they get their hands on the levers of power! The violence of Christianity is well recorded—during their many bloody crusades to "the Holy Land" and the later near-extermination of the indigenous peoples of North and South America, the enslavement of the aboriginal peoples of Australia and Asia and of non-Christian Europeans alike. All of this leaves us to note again that there is a clear pattern: The pagan Roman violence that put Jesus to death (or allowed it to occur), and which persecuted and killed his nonviolent followers for centuries, was only halted (against those of his followers who were true to his teachings) after the pagan ruler Constantine became a champion of Christianity and brought a counterviolence along with him. At that point nonviolence could be practiced—except in the cases of the Christians' wars, or their subjugation of "others," including wimmin and nature.

Nonviolence, Moral Force, and Counterviolence

All life seeks to live and Homo sapiens, as one form of life, has an ability to recognize the same motivations in other life forms. We are capable of empathizing with those urges. That empathy creates a *moral force* that we call "*right*," juxtaposed to forces seeking to hinder this life or its recognizable supports. The opposing force we call "*wrong*."

When confronted with *violence* this moral force (in the mind of the *Homo sapiens*) creates anxiety. If not relieved, that anxiety builds until it begins to exhibit external manifestations that seek to resist the wrong on its own terms: *counterviolence*. Wrong can attempt to circumvent this process by turning the life it's harming into something *other* than life; into a lifeless *object*. That objectification relieves the anxiety that came from the recognition that life was being harmed.

Thus the moral power latent in nonviolence *cannot* overcome violence until it generates into a counterviolence with enough power to satisfy the laws of physics—as earlier laid out.

Once again we have the kinetic forces of violence and counterviolence that are capable of being balanced and forming a nonviolent synthesis—within the realm we call *morality*.

Nothing here should suggest that we are advocates of, or champion violence, or that we fail to recognize how nonviolence can be utilized for radical and revolutionary social change. Our earlier brief histories of various movements show otherwise. As revolutionaries, however, we firmly hold that our entire existence is threatened by ecological and socioeconomic factors that make exterminism or ecocide an imminent danger. That threat does *not* allow for a centuries-long process of raising moral consciousness until counter forces emerge to confront the violent forces that are propelling this runaway train. We therefore will remain firm in doing what our historical and scientific analysis suggest we must, while always remaining open to other well-founded arguments.

Fear, Terror, and Pain

Revolutionaries hold, moreover, that the *real* problem here is not violence, which as already noted, will continue to be a part of our existence. No, we believe that it is the *fear, terror, and pain* that most *imagine*, which clouds one's reasoning. It is this which clever and ruthless abusers and exploiters use to manipulate us, mystifying the extent to which they will use violence against us. Fear increases the power of violence, while terror and pain magnify fear *beyond* reasoning!

Fear itself is a *natural* and *necessary* combination of reactions among *Homo sapiens* and other life forms. Fear can be understood as a kind of yellow or "caution light" that is meant to alert us to a threat of one kind or another. But like a caution light, it is *not* designed to bring everything to a halt. On balance fear—like the caution light—leaves one's mind in charge, to decide what to do next: to go forward, stop, or make some other adjustment, as *clear reasoning* suggests.

The *outer body's* reaction to kinetic violence and any accompanying pain includes its own mechanisms to protect itself. Once a certain *unbearable* threshold of pain is reached, the body's defenses will simply render one unconscious and incapable of feeling anything more—unless revived. And the body will continue to protect one's inability to experience such levels of pain until death.

An example is the U.S. Congresswomyn Gabby Giffords, who was shot in the face and head at close range. After a long recovery, she expressed absolutely no memory of any pain associated with being wounded. Untold numbers of others who have suffered similarly traumatic wounds have said the same thing.

The *mind* similarly has its own defenses when being confronted with or subjected to unbearable (internal) kinetic violence and pain. As already mentioned, the mind will seek shelter in anxiety to *escape* stress, and if the pain associated with the experience becomes unbearable, it will slip into paranoia, develop phobias, schizophrenia, and a more debilitating range of mental disorders. This can be arrested but will reappear periodically in the form of conditions like posttraumatic stress disorder/syndrome.

The *actual* pain caused by even the most extreme kinetic violence is both physically and mentally bearable. Once that is fully grasped, such an understanding can lead the individual to become *less susceptible* to those who use fear and pain to *terrorize*. And if one does not come to grips with these facts, she or he will remain open to being controlled by them—as the writings of the ancient advisers on war and politics, Niccolo Machiavelli (1469–1527) and Sun Tzu [historians disagree but place him in the period between 722 and 481 BC –editors] make clear.

In *The Prince*, Niccolo Machiavelli rhetorically asks future rulers whether they believe it best to be loved or feared by their future subjects. He then proceeds to answer his question by detailing a number of reasons one in such a position should seek to be loved, but then outlines how fickle such love may prove to be and ends by saying, "Fear never fails!" Ever since those words were penned, Machiavellian rulers and power-seekers alike have clung to his advice about the reliance on fear—*even more than naked violence!*

In *The Art of War*, Sun Tzu offers to give an ancient Chinese ruler a vivid lesson about how—in the hands of a master—fear, terror, and violence can be manipulated to achieve one's ends. The ruler directs Sun Tzu to proceed with his demonstration by using the ruler's concubines who are present. Straight away Sun Tzu orders a number of these ladies to form rows, with two of them being told that they would serve as officers under Sun Tzu, and the others would be the troops in their mock force. Sun Tzu subsequently uses the concubine officers to determine if the entire troop knows their left from their right and other simple commands. He was told that they did. He then instructs all of the concubines to turn in a certain direction on his order—to which all the concubines just giggled among themselves.

Sun Tzu bristled and said, "If commands are not clear and distinct; if orders are not fully understood, it's the commander's fault." He once again asked whether they all understood his earlier questions about their left, right, etc., and was again told that they did. On being given that assurance Sun Tzu again ordered that they perform certain movements and once again all of the concubines giggled without following his orders. Sun Tzu then said, "If commands are not clear and distinct; if orders are not fully understood, it's the commander's fault. But once orders have been made clear, and the troops still disobey, it's the fault of the officers." Sun Tzu then sternly ordered the rulers' palace guards to behead the two concubine officers for failing to see that his orders were carried out.

Before the guards could carry out the order they are stopped by the ruler, who had until then been paying little attention to the demonstration. Sun Tzu then informs the ruler that having been appointed the commander and given a task to carry out, he has no need to follow any command that contradicts his fulfilling the appointed task. He thus once again sternly orders the palace guards to behead the two concubine officers, and they do.

Sun Tzu then returns to the remaining concubines and appoints two new officers, and once again relays his orders to the troops through them. Now *sufficiently terrified*, all of the concubines execute order after order in perfect form.

The ruler, though saddened by the loss of the two concubines and miffed by how Sun Tzu overrode his wishes, still recognized that Sun Tzu had displayed an uncommon understanding and use of power, fear, violence, and terror. He swallowed his bruised ego in order to place Sun Tzu in his service.

Finally, during the Great Depression of the 1930s, U.S. President Franklin D. Roosevelt, in trying to offer the citizens under him who were experiencing extreme hardships and despair an encouraging way of looking at their plight, often stated "there is nothing to fear but fear itself." Creative revolutionaries advocate viewing and analyzing things from a scientific perspective. We *too* believe that Roosevelt's words hold a lot of truth and that so many continue to get it wrong about how exploiters and abusers manipulate violence, fear, and terror to keep them down. In fact, both Machiavelli and Sun Tzu's methods *do work* on those *unaware* of these methods; on those who are *untrained* in ways to neutralize them. We will here lay out a theory toward a *praxis* designed to overcome that shortcoming.

Prefigurative Training in Controlling Fear and Terror

For thousands of years armies have been facing off against each other, then advancing to engage in brutal and bloody mayhem that would leave battlefields a scene of utter horror. Hence the saying that "the field of battle is a land of standing corpses." In ancient times—outside the arrows and missiles catapulted at them, and the cavalry charges—the fighting was done face to face, where swords, daggers, axes, pikes, and shields allowed warriors a chance to react and attempt to survive this ordeal. The Mel Gibson movie *Braveheart* is an excellent portrayal of such battles.

With the widespread introduction of gunpowder, muskets, and cannons in the middle ages, however, that all changed. Cannon fire could sow havoc in the ranks of soldiers like never before, and massed musket fire could follow up on that havoc, before the traditional hand-to-hand combat began. Holding one's ground under cannon and musket fire was a much more terrifying ordeal than the arrow and catapult barrages, or even the cavalry charges. Consequently, for a long time commanders and armies wrestled with the best ways to neutralize these new terrors.

Gradually the best trained soldiers of fortune and mercenaries learned how to stand their ground against these weapons, something that allowed them to charge dearly for their services. But in the seventeenth century a French officer named Jean Martinet introduced a standardized system that proved itself capable of turning new recruits into soldiers who could also stand their ground under cannon and musket fire that tore up the terrain and left huge holes in their ranks, while assaulting the ears with the terrifying sounds and filling the battlefield with smoke and the screams of injured soldiers.

Martinet was a severe drill instructor—so severe that his name became a part of the English language. It means "one who stresses a rigid adherence to the details of forms and methods; or a strict disciplinarian." Martinet's training methods were learned and replicated by armies all over the world, most notably the Prussian army officer Friedrich Wilhelm von Steuben, also known as Baron von Steuben (1730–1749), who by the age of sixteen learned them as a serving Prussian army officer in a region of today's Germany. His career came to the attention of Benjamin Franklin, who was in Europe trying to drum-up support for the insurgent American revolutionaries. Franklin got von Steuben to sail to America and in 1778 met George Washington, who was in command of the American forces.

He was charged by Washington with turning the raw American recruits into soldiers who could stand up to the veteran British troops: which meant standing their ground against cannon and massed musket fire before repelling bayonet charges. These were raw recruits who had previously used hit-and-run tactics. This was a task Baron von Steuben—using the principles Jean Martinet had made popular—excelled at.

History tells us that von Steuben's training of the Americans under George Washington was primarily responsible for turning them into the kind of fighting force that was able to stand up to the otherwise superior British forces until France came into the war—a development that subsequently forced the British to admit defeat and withdraw, allowing the Americans to become independent.

Even today, hundreds of years later, the American army and most others *still* utilize the same basic techniques to prepare their forces to face the terrifying ordeal of live fire, and afterward forcing themselves to put one foot in front of the other to advance against the same deadly menace. The secret that Martinet and Baron von Steuben understood was the necessity of getting raw recruits to *practice* following instructions in drill formations, while at the same time suppressing their fears of the terrifying sounds and events that their drill instructors *simulated* by firing cannons and muskets around them. In a nutshell, that meant they had to learn to accept the fear they were feeling, while still trying to concentrate on what they were being told to do. That meant the recruits would have to practice meeting and overcoming each pang of fear they were feeling and not allow it to cloud their reasoning, terrorize them into panic, or paralyze their movements.

Using these same principles, our praxis rests on a simple but effective *daily* practice each individual *must* integrate into their lives in order to *simulate* the Martinet/von Steuben formula for teaching soldiers to face and control their fears. To accomplish that feat you must daily face something that you're afraid to do, then go ahead and do it! Even if it's a little thing like getting out of bed the first time the alarm or music awakens you, or to not procrastinate regarding something you should do. Perhaps it will be to speak up about something you know you should raise your voice against, or any other of the numerous things one fears facing every day: *Just do it!* And once you practice *drilling yourself* in this manner—over and over—it will in time become second nature. Even though you'll *never* lose the fears, those fears will no longer paralyze you and cloud your reasoning about what needs to be done. They will not terrorize you and leave you open to being controlled by such emotions.

Another leg of our praxis is individual and group training in *self-defense*, which is especially important for *all* wimmin and girls—something we'll expand on at length later. Self-defense as taught by martial artists (all the martial arts schools are equally good for our purposes here) is valuable, as well as self-defense training with firearms, while following *all* of the legal requirements. Both the unarmed and the armed self-defense training will go a long way in our efforts to demystify our understanding about the fear and terror that most people experience when faced with individuals or groups who themselves are trained in the fighting arts and are armed. Such training will keep others from terrorizing us into submitting to their whims *without thinking*.

Further you must begin to follow what all athletes understand. You must "train your brain for pain." You will be able to gradually accomplish that through your martial arts training, or by some other exercise routine that also causes you to exert yourself. That will help you eliminate any thought that you can *ever* arrive at a place in life where you can avoid pain. A desire to reach a place where you can avoid pain puts you at the mercy of Machiavellian individuals, who depend on people that fear pain. By training your brain to tolerate pain, you will be conditioning yourself to be able to bear-up under it—although one must never see this practice as accepting or advocating masochism!

An added benefit relates to the saying in the martial-arts world that "training is everything—and everything is training." Here our praxis is training one to further overcome the fear of pain, while at the same time improving both your physical and mental health.

An example of how an individual can withstand being subjected to one of the most brutal and sophisticated uses of fear, terror, and pain against them can be found in the person of an individual who was arrested and charged with being the mastermind behind the September 11, 2001, attacks on targets in the United States. Creative revolutionaries obviously do not condone the acts carried out that day. But our goal here is to use a scientific approach to analyze this example, which clearly illustrates and reinforces the arguments already put forward.

The individual in question is a man from the Middle East who has been identified as Khalid Sheik Muhammad (KSM). He was subjected to a brutal and sophisticated application of fear, terror, and pain, administered by forces in the service of the U.S. government. They sought to extract information from KSM which they claimed would help them capture others in his circle, as well as thwart other actions designed to harm America, its friends, and its allies. And the main tactic used by the U.S. government agents was the brutal torture technique called "waterboarding."

KSM—we are told—is a man in his thirties or forties, of small to average size and apparently highly educated. He is a professed Muslim, but not overly zealous in his practice of that religion. Instead, he is skillful in manipulating its precepts to serve the political ends he and his group sought—ends that varied to fit the political objectives of a number of related groups that collected under a broad umbrella. He came to public attention through acts of terrorism that he self-promoted and publicized on the Internet. These acts seemed to be designed to attract recruits among a fringe of Muslim extremists.

Later we are told that KSM "masterminded" the September 11 attacks, after receiving backing from Osama bin Laden's group, although KSM never played any direct physical role in any of the actions carried out that day. He was subsequently captured in Pakistan and eventually handed over to U.S. agents at the notorious prison camp at Guantanamo Bay, on U.S.-occupied Cuban territory.

The torture technique of waterboarding has a long, sordid, and brutal history. We can trace its use (at least) to such infamous regimes as the long-running and ultra-sadistic Catholic Inquisition of the latter part of the Middle Ages, down through the Imperial Japanese military and secret police during the Second World War. It's unclear when United States forces began to use it, and even now there's a heated debate (in some circles) whether or not it should be classified as "torture"—something the reader can decide after reading this.

The technique generally involves strapping an individual's body and head to a table blindfolded, then raising the foot of the table until the individual's head is substantially lower than their strapped-down lower legs and feet, while placing a cloth across the individual's nose and mouth. Then water is continually poured over the cloth. Since the head is lowered, the water goes both up the nostrils and into the mouth, and the victim begins to gasp for air, which prevents proper breathing, or swallowing water fast enough to catch their breath—simulating what one feels while drowning. And since the victim is strapped down and blindfolded, the inability to struggle against the drowning sensation is terrifying! The torture is interrupted only to periodically interrogate the victim.

Such simulated drowning is clearly painful, provoking a deep fear of being subjected to the ordeal again after once suffering through it. The pain begins with the fear that comes from being blindfolded and strapped down (totally defenseless!), intensifies in anticipation of the torture, continues through the horrible ordeal brought on by simulated drowning, culminating in the heightened fear that one will not be able to avoid another round of the ordeal, and also not knowing at what point one may actually drown!

Terrifying any way you size it up!

It's been reported that a number of KSM's fellow captives at Guantanamo Bay were also waterboarded a dozen or more times before providing the interrogators with enough information to get them to stop. The reports go on to say that KSM, however, was waterboarded well over one hundred (close to two hundred) times! This apparently took place over an extended period. It's also asserted that KSM too eventually provided his interrogators with valuable information. But what's of more interest to us is how he managed to withstand the ordeals for so long, especially since he's reported to have been subjected to the waterboarding many, many more times than his fellow prisoners.

After the fact, some analysts have raised the idea that KSM was somehow able to determine that his interrogators/torturers were limited in the number of times they could subject him to waterboarding during each session. Apparently this theory is based on the belief that waterboarding victims beyond a certain number of times during a session would in fact cause them to drown, thus defeating the ability of the interrogators to get information. It's clear from the sheer brutality of the procedure that no type of *humane* considerations limited its use! One must also assume that KSM's captors believed that waterboarding was the most effective tactic available. If not, then why would they stick with it so religiously? How (or if) KSM had in fact discovered that such limits were in place is never addressed.

Returning to the question, however, of "how did he withstand this ordeal for so long?" our analysts believe that KSM disciplined himself to control his mounting fear that came from the pain of feeling as if he were drowning, not allowing this to begin clouding his reasoning and terrifying him into forgetting that his interrogators did not want to really drown him since that would render the information that they believed he was in possession of useless. These analysts also believe that KSM somehow guessed the approximate number of waterboardings he would be subjected to in any session, and was able to keep his fear, pain, and terror in check by being able to think clearly enough to keep a count of each waterboarding until that number was reached and the session would have to end.

Some would speculate that his religious beliefs account for his ability to withstand the torture for so long, and this no doubt played a part. But the fact that *none* of his fellow Muslim cohorts, who underwent the same ordeal, were able to stand anywhere near the number of waterboardings that KSM did—before they succumbed and fully cooperated with their interrogators—leads one to believe otherwise.

Whatever the true situation, the public acknowledgement—by analysts closely associated with the U.S. government—that its agents subjected KSM to such brutal and prolonged violence causes most people's imaginations of how fearful, painful, and terrifying that must have been, to totally overshadow the fact that KSM demonstrated to the world that our fears are, more often than not, our worst enemies!

Before moving on it would also be helpful to memorize a few lines once taught to children in a song: "Whenever I feel afraid / I hold my head erect / and whistle a happy tune / and no one ever knows I'm afraid. / Make believe you're brave / and the trick may take you far. / You may be as brave / as you make believe you are."

The reader should note that I too have experienced and used all of the foregoing, in one way or another, in over fifty years of swimming in an ocean of testosterone-dominated environments; something I will elsewhere elaborate more fully.

Toward a Matriarchal Prefigurative Praxis in Controlling Male Violence

Violence among *Homo sapiens* is *overwhelmingly* a male phenomenon. Even though history exhibits wimmin rulers and common people also indulging in violence, their numbers, motivations, and opportunities for such actions pale in comparison. This male violence can be roughly divided into two categories: *exhibitionist* and *exploitative* violence. Sociopathic male violence is an exception to the rule, and its origin is mainly due to chemical imbalances in the brain.

Exhibitionist violence among males is closely associated with the individual's need to be recognized—a seeking to reinforce his self esteem; his Freudian *ego*. This search for recognition all too often flatters itself by hiding under the self-congratulatory "machismo/macho" designation. But we will continue with the more sober term: "exhibitionist."

The testosterone hormones prevalent in the male *Homo sapiens* are a source of exuberance. It is believed—as in other male species—that this is connected with their desires to exhibit to wimmin a readiness to pass on their superior genes. This exuberance, if not channeled or restrained, can lead to destructive aggression.

Historically, and up until our time, we can witness the prominent display of exhibitionist violence among men in the arena of competitive sports, primarily contact sports. From the ancient Greeks and Romans we have a wealth of examples that show entire societies wedded to the notions that men and boys (in particular) need such outlets for their aggressions, and for their desires to be recognized above the crowd. That remains true today, although some societies have also allowed wimmin and girls to compete for accolades as well.

Moreover, clever rulers have utilized these competitive desires among men and boys, not only to distract their societies from more pressing matters through attention to sports, but also by utilizing sports as a training ground to prepare men and boys for waging war. This is ultimately connected to the universal practice of rewarding soldiers with medals for their exploits during wars. Such medals are coveted by soldiers as recognition of their sacrifices and valor, and when worn allow the wearer to stroke his own ego—like throwing a fist in the air after winning in the sports arena.

Similarly, the worldwide, misogynist "gangsta" genre of the hip hop culture is a male, macho parody of exhibitionist violence. Here too, ironically, we witness wimmin and girls competing for these accolades.

More troubling is the fact that this male exhibitionist violence has also permeated the minds, practices, and circles of otherwise brilliant and well-meaning revolutionary thinkers. Such theorists as the renowned Frantz Fanon, icons like Malcolm X and Kwame Ture (formerly Stokely Carmichael), and others have unconsciously conflated the necessary utilization of defensive revolutionary violence, in seeking meaningful revolutionary socioeconomic and cultural change, with what they believed was a need for males to use "revolutionary violence" to also "liberate their minds and spirits" from the subservience imposed on them by the vestiges of slavery and the colonialism/neocolonialism of their times.

These individuals failed to recognize that their "revolutionary" worldview would still leave in place the entire male-supremacist/patriarchal framework, an edifice that we can term "the father of oppression." The destruction of this edifice will signal the *true* liberation they sought.

Otherwise, the "revolutionary violence" they formulated must also be recognized for what it is: exhibitionist, ego-based male violence.

That leads to our second category: male exploitative violence. Here we find thousands of years of patriarchy/male supremacy in homes, communities, and in societies at large. I have elaborated at length on patriarchy elsewhere, so I'll concentrate here on how violence plays a major role in relation to it, primarily in the arena of warfare but also in the rapes of wimmin and girls in *all* settings. This exploitative violence has also been driven by the already-mentioned male exuberance, unchecked by wimmin, once males won control over an evolved skill set and accompanying technologies associated with the martial (fighting) arts. This control can be traced back (at least) to four thousand years before our times, but it did not always exist.

As already touched upon, this exploitative violence is also linked with male exhibitionist violence in warfare—whether of the reactionary or "progressive" (so-called revolutionary) kind. The reactionaries openly seek to use violence to maintain and expand their domination and exploitation of wimmin, of "others," and of nature, while progressive-leaning "revolutionaries" struggle to introduce more equality into the socioeconomic and cultural reality. For as far back as we have records, males have sought to restrict warfare to a strategic struggle between themselves, relegating wimmin to a supporting role except under the most dire circumstances. At the same time, in the progressive camp, their rhetoric tended to give wimmin an opening to *force* their way into these struggles, on the side of the "revolutionaries." And these wimmin generally performed well in *both* camps, as unarmed or armed supporters.

Nonetheless, at the ending of these conflicts, if the reactionaries prevailed the wimmin would experience even *more* exploitation than before, while if the progressives won out the wimmin would be afforded a measure of what they had been struggling for, but little by little they *too* would be manipulated and then *violently* forced into more subservient positions.

And rapes of wimmin and girls are also inseparable from patriarchy! For thousands of years, wherever *Homo sapiens* could be found, men have first monopolized the uses of violence, and then gone on to rape wimmin and girls. To help facilitate these rapes, men struggled to suppress or eradicate the ancient precepts and customs underpinning the matriarchal paradigm that originally controlled human societies—customs and practices that supported wimmin controlling their own bodies. The male entitlements that the patriarchal cabal was fighting to institute—where the bodies of wimmin and girls would belong firstly to the men in power, who could then divide them among their "subjects" as they saw fit—had been unheard of in matriarchal society.

During warfare (especially) the raping of wimmin and girls is both exploitative and exhibitory violence. In the first instance the rapist is exploiting the wimmin and girls bodies for sexual gratification, and in the other instance rapes carried out in the company of other men are seen as a perverse "sport," where the men *compete* with each other to carry out their rapes in the most sensational ways.

Under patriarchy the monopoly of violence which men exercise helps them construct societies where the relationships between men, wimmin, and girls are so unbalanced that the wimmin and girls can often be seen as *forced* to participate in them. Thus, their submission to sexual unions essentially constitutes another form of rape.

Violence is also prevalent in the form of intragender rapes of males on males and wimmin/girls on wimmin/girls in closed situations like jails and prisons. This form of rape is also abetted by the patriarchal cultural construct that dictates that violence may be used to force others to satisfy one's sexual desires. Thus, in such closed institutions, these rapes are largely ignored by both the authorities and occupants.

The global capitalist economic contradictions, along with the ecological devastation that is the product of centuries of unbridled misuse of the Earth's ecosystems, are propelling the rapid disintegration of societies across the planet. In such communities, we are witnessing something that resemble the Mel Gibson *Mad Max*, *The Road Warrior*, and *Beyond Thunderdome* movie trilogy. The forces that still "control" whatever state power functions in these territories are themselves entrenched in a struggle with other forces that are attempting to independently satisfy the survival needs of those around them. In many of these communities there is a three-way struggle between the truncated state, struggling subsistence elements, and a welter of warlord-style drug gangs and cartels.

In certain areas, the warlord gangs have teamed up with the local arms of multinational corporations. They serve as protectors/assassins against the indigenous inhabitants who are suffering a loss of their customary access to and control over the land and/or water. At times the truncated state, corporations, and warlord gangs have joined together against the indigenous communities. This creates a neofascist breeding ground.

In most cases the communities struggling to survive on a subsistence level are prey to all these neofascist elements. Being mostly unarmed, they have to remain on perpetual guard for signs that their lives may be taken directly by one armed group or another, or because they were caught in the struggle between them. Yet in a few notable instances those who remain unarmed have managed to interject themselves (Mohandas Gandhi–style) into the struggles occurring around them—with mixed results, specifically in Liberia/Sierra Leone, Colombia, and in the U.S. city of Philadelphia, Pennsylvania. And in each of these cases, wimmin provided both the leadership and the bulk of the courageous and tenacious activists.

Liberia and Sierra Leone suffered through prolonged, brutal civil wars in the last twenty years. One of the main instigators of these conflicts found himself in the dock at a war crimes trial in Europe. And in early 2012 that actor, the previous president of Liberia—Charles Taylor—was convicted, and sentenced to spend the rest of his life in prison.

During the war, a truncated state under Taylor experienced a push by many armed insurgents to liberalize the socioeconomic and cultural fabric of Liberia, while next door in the country of Sierra Leone a similar civil war was being waged by its own armed factions. In both countries the degree of brutality included the widespread practice of cutting off the arms and legs of civilians if any faction considered them hostile or unsupportive.

The root causes of both conflicts date back centuries, to when the two states were created—in the campaigns by the United States and European powers to expand and consolidate their holds on the continent of Africa. Up until the civil wars that concern us, those same campaigns for domination were still taking place, though they had most recently morphed into a neocolonial proxy fight over the resources of both countries. Among the main resources being fought over were the diamonds that Sierra Leone has in abundance. Charles Taylor and his supporters in Liberia, along with allied forces in Sierra Leone, were trying to control the mining and selling of these precious stones to the United States, Europe, and other buyers.

Enter a small group of wimmin in Liberia who began to demonstrate daily and agitate for an end to these civil wars along with the widespread suffering they produced. These wimmin were *unarmed*, and thus followed the Gandhi/Martin L. King Jr. style of nonviolent civil disobedience struggle. But for a very long time (as in Gandhi's case) they were all but ignored by both the government and the armed groups fighting around them.

A break came for them when international forces began applying pressure on Taylor and his allies in Sierra Leone due to a brilliant campaign launched on the international level to boycott the diamonds that fueled so much of the fighting. These "blood diamonds" (as they were called) then became a liability. The worldwide pressure around their purchase began to make them all but useless—and they would remain so until a settlement could be reached to end the boycott. Plus, all sides were showing signs of being exhausted by the ongoing warfare.

Consequently, all sides to the dispute began negotiations to end the conflicts. And although they were not invited to take part in those talks, the wimmin who had for years demonstrated and agitated in Liberia for peace now began to do so outside of the venue where the negotiations were taking place. Meanwhile, the male-dominated armed groups inside immersed themselves in an orgy of macho posturing that threatened to reignite the bloodshed. At this moment the wimmin interjected themselves into the impasse in a very dramatic and forceful way: among the various ethnic groups present at these talks, the viewing of naked bodies of wimmin who were not related by blood was taboo. So the demonstrating wimmin began to disrobe and display their bodies, after failing through other means to get the bickering men to move toward a settlement of the conflicts.

Such a bold and unexpected gesture caused chaos and consternation among the males at the talks. Some of them recognized that their hand was being forced by these wimmin, and they attempted to use force against the wimmin, while other males intervened to prevent any physical harm coming to the wimmin. Afterward the wimmin publicly threatened to continue to disrobe every time the men met—until the men reached a settlement. This threat finally motivated the men to move forward and formally reach a settlement. Through a chain of events, this eventually led to Charles Taylor being forced to leave the presidency, and a womyn (Ellen Johnson Sirleaf) being elected as president in his place. Taylor was later tracked down, arrested and sent to the war crimes court in Europe.

The experience of these *unarmed* Liberian wimmin once again displays the dynamics of *violence* on the part of one side, being met by *counterviolence* on the other side, then *synthesized* by the wimmin disrobing—an act that caused oscillations between the exhausted armed groups and helped them recognize that the peaceful solution the wimmin sought was the only way out of the impasse. Thus, a nonviolent ending was achieved.

When we examine our case study from Colombia we witness a similar power struggle between its truncated government forces and drug gangs on one side, leftist guerrillas of the Revolutionary Armed Forces of Colombia (FARC) on the other side, and an *unarmed* wimmin-led segment of Afro-Colombians in the middle. The government was fighting to beat back the FARC, as well as to control portions of Colombia that have been autonomously administered and occupied by Afro-Colombians since their maroon (fugitive slave) ancestors defeated all efforts by their Spanish owners to capture or kill them back in the eighteenth and nineteenth centuries. This land is valued for gold deposits and fertile countryside that the government and drug gangs want to use to raise both coca leaves (for cocaine) and palm-oil plants for biofuels. But it is land that the Afro-Colombians have been occupying as both subsistence farmers and small-family gold miners for centuries.

The violent guerrilla war that has been going on in Colombia for two generations only reached this area with any force in the last two decades. Since then many Afro-Colombians have been killed or forced to flee the area altogether, as the government and drug gangs used the war as a cover for their own designs to take over these lands.

As in the case of the conflicts in Liberia and Sierra Leone, the situation of the hard-pressed Afro-Colombians also came to the attention of the international community. And once again supporters of the Afro-Colombians began to apply pressure that has *forced* the government and its drug-gang allies to curtail their most aggressive incursions into the Afro-Colombian areas. The FARC too has been forced to abandon most of its activities there. Moreover, it is a wimmin-led and dominated Gandhi/Martin L. King Jr.–style mass organizing movement that has since held at bay a camouflaged effort by both the government and the drug gangs to continue their conquest of these districts through less bloody means—relying more on intimidations, individual assassinations, and rigged courts to move the Afro-Colombians off the land.

As in Liberia and Sierra Leone, here too these wimmin-led groups are proving to be courageous, tenacious, and brilliant strategists and tacticians, capable of recognizing how to maneuver *between* the violent armed groups and around the threat of counterviolence against them—by using economic pressures and the threat of military intervention from the international community in order to seek a nonviolent solution that will help them keep their land. Here, however, the situation is fluid, and demanding of one's attention, as well as support for the Afro-Colombians' just struggle, while also drawing what lessons we can from their example.

Mothers in Charge (MIC) is an organization in Philadelphia. It was founded and is primarily composed of the mothers of young people who were killed in that city's violent street incidents. In the United States, the country that fashions itself as being the most "advanced" on our planet, these mothers once again faced the same basic dynamics that were on display in Liberia, Sierra Leone, and Colombia: communities caught up in a vortex of violence between warring nonstate actors and a government of reduced power. Thus here too these grieving mothers' pleas to bring an end to this (drug-fueled) violence fell on deaf ears, as their communities were engulfed in violence from all sides (between the government—which was complicit in the drug trade—and the warring drug gangs).

Starting with a handful of mothers of the slain youth, these courageous wimmin began regular patrols of their communities. Though unarmed, they boldly confronted young people, and—acting like *their* mothers—chided and pleaded with them to think about the disruptive and deadly activities they had brought to the community. The wimmin followed these youth around so that they had no peace. And (mostly) the young people, being caught off guard by these wimmin, and feeling uncomfortable responding in their usual violent way, would simply move their drug-dealing activities to other locations in order to avoid an escalation of the confrontations.

The police, of course, then tried to exhibit more concern than usual, mainly to impress the MIC wimmin and try to *co-opt them as an auxiliary*. But MIC remembered how the police had been unresponsive to their suffering and complicit in the drug trade, so it resisted the co-option, though it did begin to work along with the police—on its own terms.

Over time MIC won a great deal of respect and support from many community members and from various other organizations involved in similar "anti-violence" activities. Yet, without a broader vision for radical/revolutionary socioeconomic change, MIC has reached a plateau. It will be difficult for the group to advance beyond its present activities in order to tackle the terrible economic, political, social, cultural, and ecological problems that are choking their communities and the entire planet.

In order to move beyond the constructive but still rudimentary efforts and successes that our three examples have highlighted, to move firmly in the direction of a *prefigurative praxis* that has the capability of controlling male violence, drug gangs, neofascist governments, and warlordism, we must *expand* upon the understandings that have been put forward by earlier thinkers and activists.

The brilliant radical feminists Veronika Bennholdt-Thomsen and Maria Mies have written:

> For millennia the model has been violent revolutions (and wars) in the patriarchal men's houses and it is still so today. And what has it accomplished? How has it formed men's and women's psyches? This model of violence and counterviolence has by now created a male identity that sees its ideal in a Kalashnikov-waving Rambo figure. One of the biggest problems of our time is the Ramboization of our young men.[2]

Earlier we put forth our position in regards to the questions of violence and counterviolence that our feminist authors show so much concern about. Let us now expand further in a spirit of addressing their valid concerns. To do that we will move on to one of our "training modules," which we will call "A Prefigurative Matriarchal Interpretation of Crouching Tiger/Hidden Dragon" (CTHD).

From our point of view CTHD serves as a perfect training module, because this movie is centered on an epic struggle between patriarchal forces and an aspiring matriarchal womyn, who risks everything to seize the tools she needs to overcome male violence and control. To follow our reasoning you too must view CTHD.

The movie begins with our aspiring shero being kidnapped by a youthful bandit leader. Coming from a privileged and pampered background, the outdoors, adventure, and novelty of our shero's struggles with this bandit leader, coupled with her own combative personality, cause her to feel liberated in this environment. She subsequently falls in love and willingly joins her one-time kidnapper to roam freely and live day-to-day. Between our shero and her bandit-lover the patriarchal customs of her upbringing don't apply. They are both simply outlaws on an equal footing.

---

2   Bennholdt-Thomsen and Mies, *Subsistence Perspective*, 211.

Since our shero was the daughter of a high official, however, they both knew that they would be under constant threat from the soldiers charged with tracking them down. Thus her bandit-lover prevailed upon her to return to her home so the search would be called off. This would also give our shero a chance to decide if their feelings for each other could survive the separation. He promised to again seek her out once things cooled down. Then the two of them could decide if their love still held.

In another part of the country our shero's future antagonist was ending a distinguished career as a legendary policeman, an upholder and bulwark of the entire patriarchal establishment. Sometime after our shero returned home, this patriarch is summoned to retrieve the legendary Green Destiny sword that had been stolen from the local ruler's home, the ruler being our shero's father. Also on the trail of whoever took the Green Destiny was another career policewomyn, who was a close confidant of the patriarch. Thrown into the mix was another career policeman and his daughter, who were searching for a notorious womyn outlaw and assassin known as the Jade Fox.

These characters engage in a series of fantastical martial-arts-based fights and chases, choreographed to highlight the superb skills of the wimmin fighters in particular. While at the same time it becomes increasingly clear that underneath all of this sword play and leaping about is really a struggle being waged by the forces dedicated to upholding the traditional and long-established patriarchal order, and our (now) *two* sheroes who are dead set on risking all to bring it down. Our young shero believes that by possessing the Green Destiny she will solidify her effort to destroy patriarchy, while her mentor (the Jade Fox) seeks to continue as part of the same battle, joining our young aspirant as another outlaw assassin.

The career policewomyn as well as the daughter of the elderly policeman searching for the Jade Fox, we note, though also excellent martial artists, are both *staunch* supporters of the patriarchal establishment!

So here in our training module we witness being played out Bennholdt-Thomsen and Mies's "violence and counterviolence," *but with a decided twist:* Our shero and her mentor *are not* in Bennholdt-Thomsen and Mies's "patriarchal men's houses." In our interpretation of CTHD our shero and her mentor are using the captured Green Destiny and their stolen martial arts skills to destroy the patriarchal "men's house," then to usher in a new matriarchal order—which we assume the Green Destiny's "magical" powers will allow them to accomplish.

As he had promised, our shero bandit lover does eventually make his way to her home to ask her if she still loves him, and if she does to come away with him. This is a turn of events that our shero had dismissed from her thoughts, although she still does love him. Since he is in grave danger in the city, our shero sends her lover off and promises to again meet up with him *after* she has fulfilled her more pressing goal of overturning patriarchy. Failing that, she promises to meet him at a sacred "magical mountain" where all wishes can be fulfilled.

Thereafter our shero begins in earnest to spread her message about the new matriarchal order by casting off her aristocratic clothing and donning peasant garb, then visiting a male-dominated tea house where she immediately causes a stir among the ruffians there. As she suspected, both her presence in this male environment, and her possession of the legendary Green Destiny, cause all of the macho martial artists to first try to bully her, blustering and trying to intimidate her verbally, then to provoke a fight with her. Once again our shero puts on a masterful display of fighting skills that leaves the tea house a wreck and sends all the "tough guys" scrambling to find her patriarch in order to seek his help against this "crazy womyn!"

With her mentor, the Jade Fox, having earlier been killed, our shero is now totally alone in her quest. Having failed to earlier win over the sympathetic career police-womyn, she is now continually pursued by her patriarchal antagonist. His male-supremacist conditioning can see nothing in her skills and extraordinary personality except a promising student underling whom he hopes to develop further as another upholder of the patriarchal establishment, totally failing to grasp our shero's hate for that order!

Our shero's bandit-lover, meanwhile, had made it to the magic mountain and awaits her there, longing to be reunited with his true love so that the two of them can resume their lives in the outdoors, intoxicated with whatever daily adventures they encountered and with each other.

Alas her bandit lover, though accepting her as an equal and otherwise free of the traditional patriarchal restraints that he knows she detests, still has no clue that her vision is of a matriarchal order that could be *fully* shared with others. Accepting the fact that she has failed in her quest, our shero makes it to where her bandit lover awaits. But instead of accepting his proposal, our shero throws herself off the magic mountain in the memory of a legend that one who sacrifices herself will be granted a wish by the "magical spirits" there. We have to assume that her dying wish is the eventual fulfillment of her quest for a matriarchal order.

Let us use this interpretation of CTHD to present our ideas about a prefigurative praxis designed to address the concerns that Bennholdt-Thomsen and Mies present about "violence and counterviolence," the connection of these things to "the patriarchal men's house," and how this has formed men's and women's psyches. It is our firm conviction that the root of the problem is not the violence itself (as we've already said), but instead the historical domination and manipulation of when, where, and for what purposes violence has been practiced, while at the same time agreeing fully with Bennholdt-Thomsen and Mies about violence in the patriarchal men's house. Thus we've interpreted our shero's actions and motivations as an idealized struggle to overturn patriarchy (the "men's house") and replace it with a matriarchal order. This does not deny the role violence plays in life, but struggles to control its practice.

In our CTHD training module we must point out a few obstacles that our sheroes were not able to overcome—centuries-old contradictions that contributed to their inability to defeat the patriarchal forces arrayed against them. Moreover, these same entrenched interests and mindsets continue to hold sway and will remain the Achilles' heel of any movement to defeat patriarchy and all forms of oppression/exploitation that stand in the way of our establishing a matriarchal ecosocialist order, unless they are understood and defeated.

Briefly, the alliance between our young shero and the Jade Fox was plagued by an inability of our shero to recognize that her privileged background and the sense of entitlement that came with it had absolutely no place in the struggle to defeat the patriarchal order. Thus her smug sense of superiority to the Jade Fox was a fatal flaw. Proceeding in that manner allowed this class contradiction to fester and eventually led to a lack of trust, which in turn led to a lack of coordination in their efforts to defeat their common foes.

Both our shero and the Jade Fox had unique qualities: our shero was able to utilize her captured knowledge of the martial arts and the Green Destiny to develop into a prodigy that even the Jade Fox could not equal. Yet, the Jade Fox had been steeled in her hatred for, and determination to defeat, their foes by a lifetime of struggles and abuses that our shero could only imagine.

Thus the Jade Fox was not prone to the kind of vacillations that are always a challenge to the upper class rebels that our young shero symbolizes. In this case, the vacillations led our young shero to try to save the patriarch, who remained hell-bent on keeping her and all wimmin underfoot, and who especially was responsible for the death of her main ally, the Jade Fox. This course of events could only have been avoided by our young shero committing *class suicide*. First, she had to control her ego in order to better absorb the lessons the Jade Fox still had not made available, and which would take years to fully grasp—how to truly become one with the lower classes. It was not enough to simply wear peasant clothing and mix with them outside of her patrician compound.

Then there was the career policewomyn, who symbolizes the tragic middle strata. She has contact with conscious and highly motivated individuals who are striving to bring down an oppressive and exploitative order and is truly sympathetic to that fight. However, because of her conditioning and cognitive dissonance, she cannot bring herself to fully reject her present behavior and alliances. She thus cannot join those who caused her to begin to question her ideas and actions.

In the career policewomyn's case, it was the search for the "love" of our young shero's patriarchal foe that obscured her lack of self-esteem. Meanwhile, her unworthy love object exhibited a sense of patriarchal entitlement that only a masochist could otherwise mistake for love.

Not much can be said about the career policeman's daughter who zealously aided her father in his pursuit of the Jade Fox. Her youth and filial sense of duty and loyalty to her father's mission shows us the inertia that can be found in all youth who simply are following in the footsteps of the previous generation, and will continue to do so until counter-ideas and forces can offer an alternative that they can adopt as their own.

Finally, our shero failed to take the time and make an effort to direct her young male lover into a more productive role. His love for her opened him to a total rejection of his patriarchal conditioning (he was already an outlaw), which could have gradually made him into a valuable partner in her quest to establish the matriarchal order. This would have been a far more satisfying way of life than the bandit existence, of which he had already tired.

These all are aspects of this training module that we must consider and build upon.

So how do we exercise this prefigurative praxis beyond what we have previously discussed, keeping in mind that a rejection of violence altogether is contrary to everything we know about history and science? We begin by adopting the principle of *matriarchal control* of the kind that our shero was struggling to bring about. Along with that we too need our own version of a special weapon. Thus our *Green Destiny* must be defensive counterviolence. This counterviolence must be answerable to our matriarchal order, and guided by the matriarchal, ecosocialist principles put forth by Scientific Soul Sessions [see appendix 2 of this book].

Reinventing the Commons: Prefigurative Professional Training

Bennholdt-Thomsen and Mies, in their already-mentioned work, call on us to "reinvent the commons" and "not . . . to be fooled by the enclosure of language."[3] Taking their advice and applying it to our scientific and historical understanding we put forth the view that understand-

---

3   Ibid., 141, 152.

ing "the commons" as a concept requires first of all a recognition of the historical fact that from its inception *patriarchy began the first enclosures: the circumscribing of wimmin and girls.* This fact can be substantiated by any student of history. And as has been discussed, violence was the main tool used to accomplish that enclosure, which remains in force up to the present day.

Thus creative revolutionaries will "not be fooled by the enclosure of language"—any language or explanations (no matter how artful) that do *not* acknowledge this fact. Further, we here put forward the strategy of "reinventing the commons: prefigurative professional training" as a step toward addressing what happened historically. And we will use as guides the examples of two successful historical instances of earlier peoples reinventing the commons. We will refer to the agitation for and subsequent introduction of African Americans into the Union forces during the American Civil War, and the later deserters and mutineers from the Russian czar's armed forces who were introduced into the ranks of the Russian Revolution's Red Army after World War I. An understanding of these historical events will help us develop our prefigurative praxis and provide us with our Green Destiny weapon.

First, we must accept the fact that patriarchal, capitalist, financial, corporate, neofascist, and cartel/gang-controlled groups have at their disposal an overwhelming monopoly of the tools and ability to use violence. Under whatever flag they operate, and however much they fight among themselves, they *all* fall within Bennholdt-Thomsen and Mies's definitions, using this violence to (primarily) benefit "the men's house." But the weapons of violence and skills involved are *all* products of centuries upon centuries of enforced and stolen sweat, toil, creativity, and sacrifice on the part of untold millions of wimmin, girls, and "others." Nature too has been devastated in that accumulation of power, though here we will concentrate on how this process relates to *Homo sapiens.*

From a matriarchal/ecosocialist standpoint, those skills and weapons that have been accumulated and monopolized are a part of the stolen commons. They are skills and weapons that wimmin, girls, and "others" have been circumscribed from obtaining, to use for their own benefit, or else to prevent their use altogether. More importantly, *no* matriarchal/ ecosocialist order has any real chance of standing up to any serious effort by those who have these weapons and skills, unless that matriarchal/ ecosocialist order does as our shero did: *capture the Green Destiny weapon.* This is what the African Americans who joined the Union forces during the U.S. Civil War did, and what the deserters and mutineers did during the Russian Revolution.

Let's consider our example from the American Civil War. That provides a case study of how the African American abolitionist Frederick Douglass, and other lesser-known individuals, recognized that with the outbreak of war between the Union and Confederate forces, this struggle would provide an opportunity for African Americans in the northern states and the fugitive slaves in Canada to *reinvent the commons of their time.* That commons then only extended to men of European background in the Northern states, and consisted of rights and privileges that were *not* extended to wimmin, indigenous peoples, Chinese, or Africans in those areas. Violence is what enforced this state of affairs!

As is well known, President Abraham Lincoln and the entire Union establishment had absolutely no goal for the Civil War except to force the Confederate states back into the Union. Thus, from the outbreak of the war in 1861, up until the Emancipation Proclamation at the end of 1863, African Americans in the northern states, Canada, and the states in rebellion had *no* assurances of deriving any benefits from the war.

Even so, long before the Emancipation Proclamation was signed, Frederick Douglass and many, many other African Americans applied an enormous amount of pressure on Lincoln and the Northern leaders to allow African Americans to join the Union forces. They correctly saw that the root cause of the war could only be resolved by the most extreme bloodletting. The decades-old abolitionist movement's peaceful tactics had failed to overcome the entrenched economic interests in the South (and North) that were in fact opening up new western slave territories. This was a fact that no amount of peaceful reasoning could change!

So to force the issue, Douglass and thousands of African Americans in the North and Canada began recruiting to and volunteering to serve with the Union forces. One can see a portrayal of this in the excellent Denzel Washington, Matthew Broderick, and Morgan Freeman movie, *Glory*. This is a movie that, incidentally, also illustrates the exhibitionist violence that we spoke of earlier on the part of otherwise well-intentioned individuals. The title of the movie itself, along with the stirring scene where the African American soldiers are singing and "testifying" about how they want to be remembered if they are killed in the coming battle are examples of this.

Most unbiased historians believe that even though the North possessed a huge advantage in war production and railroads to deliver troops and materiel to the battle areas, it still remained unable to win a decisive victory against the dogged southern fighters without a new and massive infusion of soldiers. Even the European immigrants who filled the ranks of the Union army as soon as they stepped off the boats wasn't enough—a fact that caused a bloody backlash among Irish immigrants who rioted against being essentially forced to fight as soon as they arrived on U.S. soil. *Gangs of New York* is a movie that depicts these events.

Frederick Douglass and others were able to get Lincoln to allow a certain number of African Americans to fight, and as *Glory* seeks to show, they proved themselves to be as good as the other Union soldiers. Still the *true* determining moment came when Lincoln realized that the North could not decisively win without the influx of thousands of African Americans into the Union forces: two hundred thousand is the number (by most estimates) during the Civil War.

In our view, this mass of African American troops was the Green Destiny weapon that assured the success of Frederick Douglass and others in their struggle to reinvent the commons in the United States. We further believe that had the Confederate/slave-holding states held out for a stalemate in the Civil War—something that only the African Americans soldiers prevented from happening—slavery would have remained in practice in the southern states. Even though the commons was reinvented to the point that African American males of a certain age gained the vote, and all African Americans were freed from chattel slavery, African American wimmin, Europeans, Asian and indigenous peoples were *not* allowed to vote and continued to suffer other debilitating forms of exploitation, discrimination, and abuse. Those segments of the country had *not* found their own Green Destiny weapon, and thus remained circumscribed with regards to the commons.

Alas, the African Americans subsequently allowed their Green Destiny weapon to slip from their hands and were then forced back into a *new* form of slavery called "Jim Crow." But that does not negate their earlier accomplishment of reinventing the commons. This is an example that must be studied, learned from, and expanded upon.

Moving to our next example, you can benefit from viewing another *training module* movie in order to better follow our reasoning: how the deserters and mutineers captured their Green Destiny weapon from the Russian czar's forces, then went on to use it to reinvent their commons during the Russian Revolution. The movie in question is the classic *Dr. Zhivago*, starring Julie Christie, Omar Sharif, and Rod Steiger. The movie is a love story, set during a tumultuous early twentieth century Russia. It is chock-full of references to real historical events. It begins with the movie's narrator, a Russian general in search of his lost niece, his late brother's daughter—that brother being the movie's namesake: Dr. Zhivago. The narrator only appears briefly in the movie, but his voice details how their Green Destiny weapon was captured, and thereafter used to reinvent their commons.

The main womyn character is the beautiful Lara (Julie Christie) who throughout the movie is used and abused, but finds a true love in Dr. Zhivago (Omar Sharif). From their union comes the niece our narrator is searching for.

One can read many books in hopes of visualizing Russia, its people, their conditions, and their struggles at that time. But the movie presents this vividly! In essence it portrays a Russia of the early twentieth century that contains very rich people at one end of the social order and starving people at the opposite end. In between are individuals like Lara (a young student) and Dr. Zhivago (a young doctor), neither of whom is rich or starving. Nor are either much interested in the affairs of those on the extremes. They are just trying to live their own lives as best they can.

Lara initially, however, has a young idealistic revolutionary boyfriend, whose revolutionary politics Lara shuns. But Lara's life is interrupted after she is seduced by the older, urbane boyfriend of her widowed mother. That character, played by Rod Steiger, is the polar opposite of her own boyfriend. He is an abusive, opportunistic double-dealer. Zhivago—from beginning to end—is simply a befuddled but humane doctor and aspiring poet, an individual who is buffeted continually by the world-shaking events taking place around him. It could be that Zhivago's character was written in such a way as to allow the viewer a respite from the harsh and brutal realities that the movie exposes—starving wimmin, children, and workers being massacred by mounted, saber-swinging soldiers while peacefully demonstrating for food; Lara being seduced, abused and raped by her mother's boyfriend; the poor of Russia being led into World War I and subsequently slaughtered, or left to freeze to death on the battlefield, and on and on—a snapshot of how harsh conditions must become in order for there to be a revolution.

Here we need to return to the narrator's quest to capture a "Green Destiny" weapon. Long before becoming a general, the narrator was a simple worker or peasant member of the Russian Bolshevik Party, led by V.I. Lenin. That group was a tiny organization, perpetually persecuted, its members imprisoned and exiled by the Russian secret police. And the czar of Russia himself was an absolute ruler, with a huge, brutal, and efficient police-intelligence and military establishment to back him up.

By comparison our narrator's organization was like a flea on a dog.

Yet the Bolshevik party had a vision of how they would like to reinvent the commons, a pretty clear analysis of what was wrong with their society and what could be done to correct those things. Like Frederick Douglass several generations before, they too recognized that the czar's dragging of the starving and brutalized Russian people into a world war would provide them an opportunity to capture their Green Destiny weapon.

Thus we witness our narrator as a young man standing on a street corner, while the czar's soldiers parade by. Cheering crowds of well-wishers beckon the young men on the sidewalk around him to join the soldiers, receiving pats on the back and flowers from pretty girls. Yet in his narration he says that his Bolshevik party had *ordered* him to join the czar's army, a force of the very government that was brutally suppressing them, and starving and massacring its own people.

Indeed, he explains how his party had reasoned that the war the Russian people were being led to was sheer folly. Eventually it would end badly, and when it did he (and apparently other Bolshevik party members) needed to be near enough to events to take advantage of what would happen, while in the meantime learning how to fight from professional military personnel who were commanding the czar's forces.

The narration continues through scenes of the war being waged in the harsh Russian snows, the soldiers becoming demoralized, being led into slaughter over and over until finally giving up and deserting in huge numbers. Here our narrator details how he led a large contingent to desert, saying it was the best work he had ever done. He had entered the czar's army as a persecuted political opponent of the czar, and left that army as a professionally trained combat veteran, with a large contingent of others who were also ready for the struggle that lay ahead—to *reinvent the commons*; and they took their guns with them.

We switch scenes to see other Russian soldiers who had also deserted the czar's army by the hundreds, and who go on to provoke still more soldiers to desert and mutiny. Finally, Dr. Zhivago, who had been drafted into the czar's army, asks a deserter if he is going home to be with his family. He is told no; that this soldier was in fact going to join the Red Army instead. That Red Army was the Green Destiny weapon. Our narrator's Bolshevik Party had created it by organizing the deserters, mutineers, and revolutionary workers and peasants—a force led by professionally trained personnel, in which our narrator would one day become a general.

Throughout this movie, Lara and Dr. Zhivago are buffeted by the momentous events occurring around them. They attempt to share their love for each other, trying to ignore the efforts of the masses of previously starving workers and peasants to reinvent their commons by utilizing the Green Destiny weapon that they had created.

A lesson learned from these examples—of the United States Civil War and the Russian Revolution—is that both groups of oppressed people would have found it extraordinarily difficult to reinvent the commons *without* the Green Destiny weapons they forged. In both cases those weapons were the products of a massive *prefigurative project* to help people see the necessity of obtaining positions in their societies that would provide them with opportunities to become *professionally trained*, and to win over others to join them in those highly trained arenas.

Prefigurative Matriarchal Ecosocialist Self-Defense

Building on our two examples from the U.S. Civil War and the Russian Revolution, we take issue with those who have argued for building People's Self-Defense in the twenty-first century using methods utilized by countries like China, Vietnam, and in African anti-colonial struggles—in particular, the organizing of fighting groups that would wage guerrilla warfare to defend their efforts to reinvent the commons.

Creative revolutionaries know that today's technology has made such techniques and tactics extremely problematic, despite the dogged efforts of small groups in various parts of the world to continue to use them. The panopticon that encircles the entire globe, with its satellites, drones, interwoven military intelligence and private security with surveillance cameras, is daily being strengthened and expanded to a point where—without exaggeration—one can visualize this panopticon as something out of the *Matrix* trilogy!

The primary problem is that the old Chinese, Vietnamese, African, and other anti-colonial struggles relied on *space, time,* and *will* in order to forge their Green Destiny weapons. They asked: how do we use the available *space* (primarily rural and with heavy undergrowth) to allow us the necessary *time*, to be able to recruit, organize and train a fighting force that has the *will* to overcome any obstacles that might prevent us from reinventing the commons? And this specific reinvention, we must remember, never *fully* aimed at a commons that would be a matriarchal order, though each of these struggles still relied heavily on wimmin for success. The establishment of a panopticon, however, has circumscribed that old method. The guerrilla formations today find that it is extremely difficult to find enough *space* in which to maneuver and conceal themselves; curtailing the *time* they need to recruit, organize, and train enough people in order to give themselves a real chance of developing the force and *will* needed to overcome all obstacles to reinventing their commons.

Instead we must emulate our shero in CTHD, by daily living in the "compound" of the oppressive ruler—under the eye of the panopticon—while *still* training ourselves. We must do so *without* seeking to engage in any direct physical conflicts with that oppressor. We will start with the training methods laid out here, but *also* work to develop *wimmin and girls* as the spearhead of efforts to obtain *professional* training in all of the armed forces, intelligence, counterintelligence, and police organizations open to them. This would involve wimmin and girls who have developed enough consciousness to commit *fully* to working to reinvent the commons along matriarchal, ecosocialist lines. Such professional training will then *be passed on* to the matriarchal, ecosocialist groups in grassroots communities who are *also* struggling to reinvent the commons along those same lines. And finally these wimmin in the armed forces and other organizations must *also* seek to win over others there to their revolutionary goals.

Only by establishing a core of professionally trained, matriarchal, ecosocialist, conscious, and fully committed individuals, can an effective foundation be laid to reinvent the commons in a world where the potential for overwhelming violence on the part of others is ever-present. Such a professionally trained and committed formation will be able to develop a twenty-first-century way to utilize space, time, and will to forge and wield its own Green Destiny weapon.

Afterword
Let Us Not Rest
Until Justice Is Done
Nozizwe Madlala-Routledge
and Matt Meyer

n the late 1960s, as organizations for civil and human rights were rapidly recharacterizing themselves as "Black Power" and "Black Consciousness" movements, Russell Maroon Shoatz was presiding over Pennsylvania's Black Unity Council, a grouping which merged with the Philadelphia chapter of the Black Panther Party in 1969. We note this long-past fact here, at the end of this book of Maroon's writings, not to begin a history lesson but to set a clear context for our collective future work.

In the forty-plus years since those heady times, the vision and leadership of the Panthers and Steve Biko, of the South African liberation movements and the international peace and justice movements, has produced social change hardly imaginable back then. That a teenage girl named Nozizwe Madlala Routledge, who grew up in Africa under the repressive apartheid regime, interested in radical organizing and women's rights, could become—before age sixty—a parliamentarian in the land of her birth, a deputy minister of defense and of health; why that could be no more than a whimsical dream. We remember well the lectures which admonished us, in our different geographic spaces and political settings, that no such changes could take place in South Africa without a tremendous amount of bloodshed, and probably not in our lifetimes. And yet, we learned that dreams, when combined with the proper amount of fortitude, strategic planning, intense organizing, tactical considerations, and combined local, grassroots, door-to-door campaigning along with international solidarity, can have a startling way of coming true.

Contrast that with the fate of so many former Black Panthers in the United States, and those influenced by the Panthers and their predecessors—Malcolm X, Martin Luther King, Rosa Parks, Fannie Lou Hamer, Stokely Carmichael/Kwame Ture, Ella Baker, and so many others who fell victim to the illegal counterintelligence program (COINTELPRO) which the Federal Bureau of Investigation waged against all of the people's movements in the United States. Contrast that with the fate of Russell Maroon Shoatz:

- Forced underground in 1970 due to increased repression against the Black liberation movement;
- Captured and arrested in 1972 on charges relating to years-earlier "attack" on a police station;
- Disproportionately sentenced to life-plus in prison;
- Transferred and locked-down in solitary confinement in over a dozen state, county, and federal prisons, from 1977 to 1979;
- Transferred to the maximum-security prison "Fairview" in 1979, where he was forcibly drugged and at one point hospitalized due to a forced overdose of these drugs;
- Kept on twenty-three-hour-a-day "lockdown" at various institutions throughout the late 1980s;
- In solitary confinement since 1991!

The ongoing torture of Russell Maroon Shoatz, defying all international standards of criminal justice and human rights, is a clarion call to all peace-loving people. In addition to the questionable continued imprisonment of a close-to-seventy-year-old man, whose major life work has been for justice and the freedom of his people, the silence surrounding the cruel, unusual, and life-threatening conditions faced by Maroon raise questions about more than simply the U.S. court and legal systems. It raises questions about us all.

We are, and have for many decades, been active in explicitly nonviolent organizations, advocating Gandhian direct action responses to the imperial, colonial, and oppressive policies of the corporate and political world. From the secular-pacifist War Resisters International to the newly formed women's rights-oriented Embrace Dignity to a Pan-African Nonviolence and Peace-building Network that we have helped found in 2012, one might wonder why the plight of Russell Maroon Shoatz is of concern to us.

The answers, we hope, should be clear:

We believe deeply in the axiom popularized by Dr. King, that injustice anywhere is a threat to justice everywhere.

We believe that it is the responsibility of every human rights activist to spotlight horrific crimes, especially when carried out by nation-states purporting to be democratic and just. The ways in which Maroon, and too many of his fellow inmates, have been deprived of all meaningful social interactions, of environmental stimulation, of all forms of intellectual, educational, vocational, or therapeutic activity, and subject to physical and psychological abuse, racial discrimination, deprivation of food, showers, use of outdoor spaces—all of these constitute urgent reasons for our immediate attention and action.

We believe, as outlined in the appeal to United Nations Commission on Human Rights and acted on by Juan Méndez, the United Nations Special Rapporteur on Torture and Other Cruel, Inhuman or Degrading Treatment or Punishment, in an official inquiry to the U.S. government, that the treatment of Maroon constitutes persecution based on his political beliefs and remains a human rights crisis.

We believe, as asserted by prominent U.S.-based legal authorities— the Center for Constitutional Rights and National Lawyers Guild—that the policies and continued imprisonment of Maroon defy even U.S. legal precedent and standards.

We believe this because the United States is now incarcerating males of African descent at a rate more than five times greater than South Africa at the height of apartheid. With more in the prison system than were enslaved in the United States in the 1850s, there is a related crisis of unprecedented proportion. The fact that an estimated eighty thousand men, women, and even children are being held in solitary confinement in U.S. prisons constitutes systemic torture.

We believe that the most egregious case of this policy is Russell Maroon Shoatz, whose thirty years in solitary is nothing short of a slow-motion death sentence.

We believe that the policy of political imprisonment that targets former Panthers and radical activists has created, in the words of a recent Al Jazeera article, "Torture Chambers for Black Revolutionaries."

We believe the words of former political prisoner Nelson Mandela (words that hang in the halls of the old jails adjacent to South Africa's

Constitutional Court where Mandela was once imprisoned): "A nation should not be judged based upon how it treats its highest citizens, but on how it treats its prisoners. No one truly knows a nation until one has been inside its jails." Political prisoners have long been the backbone of every major movement for social change in every corner of the globe.

We believe, on purely humanitarian grounds, that all prisoners who have served lengthy terms without incident and who have reached a certain "elder" status should be released. There is no security or rehabilitative rationale for continued jailing of people in their late sixties or seventies, with deep ties to their communities and decades of good time served behind bars.

We believe in truth and reconciliation, and a process that understands that in order for there to be lasting peace in our twenty-first-century societies, we must face the truth about the uprisings of forty years ago. Russell Maroon Shoatz is *not* in jail because of any criminal activities. He is in jail because he is a revolutionary.

We believe that all people who believe in peace and nonviolence must work for justice, especially in these most grievous cases of injustice and especially at times when oppressive forces would have us distanced from colleagues and comrades such as Maroon, who are cast as "violent criminals" unworthy of our support.

The writings in this book give ample evidence as to why Maroon is so much more than a simple criminal, so much more even than a former Panther or prison-rights activist or wronged person. Maroon's ongoing contributions—about the nature of power, the role of matriarchy, the connections between environmental concerns and human liberation, and so many other issues—suggest why he is an exemplar of a "revolutionary maroon." He challenges us all to think deeper and work harder for our own and everyone's true and complete liberation.

Russell Maroon Shoatz must be freed now. His release must become a priority for all human rights activists, peace activists, prodemocracy advocates, environmentalists, anti-imperialists, students, churchgoers, even progressive Parliamentarians. Were our geographic and political settings just a little bit different, Russell Maroon Shoatz would be our Minister of Information, attending global summits and helping to raise the standards of all the peoples of this fragile, resilient, rainbow planet.

This afterword is our pledge to make the campaign to free Maroon a part of our work. From online petitions to local educational events to emergency call-ins to the prison to internationally coordinated actions, there are and will be many ways to get and stay involved. Now that you have come this far with us, reading Maroon's words and reviewing his call to work, let us go from the book to the cell block, and from the cell block to freedom. Let us not rest until justice is done.

Appendix 1
A Summary of the Case Russell Maroon Shoatz: More Than Twenty Years in Solitary Confinement

This document was originally drafted by Bret Grote and submitted by the signers to the United Nations Special Rapporteur on Torture and Other Cruel, Inhuman, or Degrading Treatment, Mr. Juan Méndez, asking him to investigate Maroon's case as an example of torture.

Factual Summary

Russell Maroon Shoatz (Maroon), a sixty-nine-year-old political prisoner, has spent the last twenty-one years in solitary confinement within the Pennsylvania Department of Corrections (DOC). During this time, he has not violated prison rules and has not been issued any misconducts in more than two decades. Despite his impeccable record, prison authorities continue to hold him in twenty-three to twenty-four-hour lockdown at the State Correctional Institution (SCI) Greene based on acts that occurred more than thirty years ago.

Background

During the 1960s and early 1970s, Maroon had been a dedicated human rights activist and community organizer in Philadelphia with the Black Unity Council and the Black Panther Party. In 1970, Maroon and five others were accused of an attack on a police station that resulted in the death of a police officer. The attack was carried out in response to the well-documented, pervasive assaults, beatings, and killings perpetrated against the black community in Philadelphia by police forces. Maroon was captured in 1972 and subsequently convicted, sentenced to serve multiple terms of life without the possibility of parole.

Maroon managed to liberate himself from prison on two occasions, once in 1977 for a period of twenty-seven days, and a second time in 1980 that lasted three days before he was recaptured.

During the 70s and 80s, Maroon was frequently placed in solitary confinement in order to repress his organizing ability, as he was and still remains an influential figure both inside and outside of prison. Maroon was placed in solitary after being elected as president of the DOC-approved lifers organization in 1982. In 1989, after a prisoner uprising at SCI Camp Hill in central Pennsylvania, Maroon was temporarily transferred to the federal penitentiary in Leavenworth, Kansas, although he was not confined at SCI Camp Hill during the uprising and played no role in it. During his eighteen months in federal custody, Maroon was held in the prison's general population without incident. Upon his return to Pennsylvania, he was immediately placed in solitary confinement, where he has remained to this moment in violation of his right to be free from torture and other cruel, inhuman, and degrading treatment.

Conditions in the Restricted Housing Unit

Prisoners in the PA DOC's typical solitary units, known as "Restricted Housing Units" (RHUs), are held in tiny, windowless concrete cells that are approximately 64 square feet. The cells contain a concrete slab for a bed, and a thin foam mattress is provided to sleep on. The cells also come equipped with a sink and toilet. The cell remains constantly illuminated, twenty-four hours per day.

Prisoners in the RHU are deprived of all meaningful social interaction, deprived of environmental stimulation, and severely restricted in the forms of intellectual activity that they can engage in. There is no educational, vocational, therapeutic or other programming in the unit. Reading material is often censored in order to control the ideas a prisoner has access to. Prisoners in solitary confinement have substantial limits on the amount of property they are allowed to possess. All visitations are noncontact, conducted through a thick pane of glass, during which the prisoner is handcuffed. Prisoners are served meals three times a day in their cell by guards who deliver the food through a tray-slot that is present in the middle of the solid steel door of the cell. The door has two thin glass slits for windows, providing limited ability to see outside of the cell. Exercise is permitted for one hour five days per week in a caged area not much larger than the solitary confinement cell itself. There is no exercise equipment or recreational items available to RHU prisoners.

Showers occur three times per week. During escort to showers and yard, a prisoner may be subject to a visual strip search and will be handcuffed prior to leaving the cell. Often prisoners are placed in leg shackles as well.

Solitary confinement units throughout the PA DOC, including those Maroon has been confined in, are often populated with mentally disturbed and sometimes psychotic individuals whose incessant screaming, talking, ranting, crying, banging on walls and furniture, and so on make it difficult to concentrate, sleep, and hold onto one's own sanity.

In addition to these general conditions of confinement, the solitary units in the PA DOC are rife with human rights violations, including physical and psychological abuse, racial discrimination, deprivation of food, yard, showers, routine retaliation, sexual harassment on the part of staff, refusal to provide competent and prompt—or even any—physical and mental health care, and more. Over his twenty years of solitary confinement, Maroon has experienced or witnessed others who have been subject to these further human rights violations.

During his time in solitary confinement, Russell Shoatz has experienced several serious health problems that have been exacerbated by the intense stress of the RHU, and by the inadequate health care provided to prisoners in solitary units in Pennsylvania. These conditions have included hypertension, prostate infection, damage to his muscles based on his being provided inappropriate medication, and development of cataracts in both eyes. Although he received surgery for one of his cataracts, he is currently in need of surgery to remove the other.

The imposition of such conditions of confinement for more than twenty years constitutes a flagrant violation of Russell Shoatz's right to be free from torture and other cruel, inhuman, or degrading treatment.

Rationale for Continued Placement in Solitary Confinement

There are two classifications for prisoners placed in the RHU by the PA DOC: disciplinary or administrative custody. Disciplinary custody is for those found guilty of violating prison rules. Administrative custody is a catch-all that has broad criteria capable of justifying virtually any decision to hold a person in solitary confinement. In Maroon's case, he has been kept on administrative custody status for more than twenty years under the pretext that he poses an escape risk if removed from the RHU. This rationale overlooks the reality that Pennsylvania prisons are far more fortified than when Maroon last escaped more than thirty years ago, along with the fact that Maroon is nearly seventy years old and less capable of posing a threat. Preventing escape, however, does not explain the extreme sterility, isolation, and deprivation of his current confinement, which is instead punitive in design and function. Maroon and his supporters are also aware of instances of other prisoners who have escaped or attempted to escape who have since been released into general population. Finally, this rationale overlooks the fact that Maroon has been released into the general prison population by the PA DOC and the federal prison authorities since his 1980 escape without incident.

The PA DOC has placed Maroon on something it refers to as the "Restricted Release List" (RRL), which is a list of approximately eighty-five prisoners (as of August 2010) who may not be placed into general population at any prison without the express authorization of the Secretary of the PA DOC, John Wetzel. In order to be removed from solitary confinement, Maroon must first be granted authorization by the prison at which he is held, in this case SCI Greene, then by the Regional Deputy Secretary and the Secretary. His classification status is nominally reviewed every ninety days, although he is always presented with the same rationale (escape risk) and never told what is necessary for his release.

Further, during a visit with SCI Greene's warden, Louis Folino, a visitor was informed that Maroon is being kept in solitary confinement due to an alleged plot to take over a prison in the 1980s and his role as an organizer. A mental health staff person asked Maroon about this alleged plot during a psychological evaluation a little more than a year ago. Maroon has no knowledge of any such plot, and if there is information regarding such in his file it is a fabrication. To the extent that Maroon is being held in permanent, life-long solitary confinement on the basis of secret and fabricated evidence his rights to due process are being violated.

Signatories:

Theresa Shoatz, Sharon Shoatz, Russell Shoatz III (on behalf of their father, Russell Maroon Shoatz), and the Campaign to Free Russell Maroon Shoatz (http://russellmaroonshoats.wordpress.com/), **along with the following organizational and individual cosigners:**
Center for Constitutional Rights; National Lawyers Guild; Human Rights Coalition-Fed Up! Chapter, Pittsburgh, Pennsylvania; Matt Meyer, War Resisters International, International Peace Research Association UN representative; Jihad Abdulmumit and Paulette D'auteuil, cochairs, National Jericho Movement; Dequi Kioni-Sadiki, Malcolm X Commemoration Committee.

For those interested in fighting for Maroon, please write letters or make phone calls to demand Maroon's freedom to:

Secretary of Prisons John Wetzel, 2520 Lisburn Road PO Box 598, Camp Hill, PA 17001. Phone: 717.975.4918

State Correctional Institution SCI Greene Superintendent Louis Folino, 169 Progress Drive, Waynesburg, PA 15370. Phone: 724.852.2902

To write to Maroon: Russell Shoatz, AF-3855, 175 Progress Drive, Waynesburg, PA 15370

To join the Campaign to Free Russell Maroon Shoatz, contact: freemaroon@gmail.com.

You can join the campaign by helping with fundraising, legal assistance, outreach/education, publicity/media, volunteering at events, etc. When you contact the campaign, please include your name, phone and/or email, city in which you live, and the type of help you can offer. Someone from the campaign will get in touch.

Appendix 2
Manifesto for Scientific
Soul Sessions

SCIENTIFIC SOUL SESSIONS

SSS members are united by the drive to prefigure a new society free of imperialism, colonization, racism, heteropatriarchy, and capitalist exploitation. We stand up against all forms of social inequality, and we stand for the dignity and self-determination of oppressed peoples. The leadership for this movement will first and foremost be women and oppressed nationalities. It is based on excellence and experimentation.

Together, as members of Scientific Soul Sessions:

1. We promote ecosocialism: the unity of humanity with the planet's ecosystems. As aspiring ecosocialists, we aim for existence based on the same respect indigenous peoples have always had for the earth and returning to producers the rightful share of the fruits of their labor. We respect our Mother Earth as provider of all life on this planet. We take concrete steps to lessen our ecological footprint for the health and well-being of all beings and future generations.

2. We are building toward a matriarchal future, which will be the opposite of patriarchy, not its mirror image. Matriarchy will be a revolutionary future, in which the social construct of gender is eliminated and humanity is re-socialized, in which the values of caring, nurturance, creativity, compassion and collectivity dominate.

3. We denounce gynocide—the ways that capitalism and white supremacy have attempted to break the spirit of struggle by inflicting violence upon and de-valuing women and all we represent. Our decision-making process emphasizes imagination, improvisation and intuition leading the way into the new and unforeseen; perception, wisdom, communal balance, and the art of listening and reception, as ways to overcome brute power.

4. In all decisions, we keep the seventh generation of our descendants in mind (as taught by many indigenous peoples).

5. We recognize spirituality as an essential element in the struggle for liberation. Our name is Scientific Soul: "Scientific" because we seek answers and solutions; "Soul" because we believe in each self moving beyond its limits, reaching out to people, natural creatures and to the cosmos, imagining and doing the impossible!

6. We bring art and politics together in provocative ways in our quest for excellence and the impossible dream! We see anti-capitalist analysis and anti-imperialist aesthetics as the paradigm for a new way of being and living that is not dictated by Western capitalist values.

7. Through forward-thinking artistic creation and political organizing we realize SSS leadership principles of commitment, capacity, and clarity.

8. Recognizing the self-determination of oppressed nationalities and the strength of a United Front, our leadership is principally composed of oppressed nationalities and women. Each of us checks our privilege and takes responsibility to change the ways we reproduce our internalized racism and oppression.

9. We refuse to compromise and be made mediocre by institutions such as the NGO/Non-profit Industrial Complex. We aim to be self-sufficient.

10. We are intergenerational. We acknowledge the experience and dedication of our elders. We respect the energy and fresh visions of the young.

11. We are internationalist. We seek to build a united front across boundaries and divides.

12. We are revolutionaries! We don't think capitalism is fixable.

Scientific Soul Sessions is proud to support the Campaign to Free Russell Maroon Shoatz.

For more information, visit: www.scientificsoulsessions.com.

Appendix 3
Ecosocialist Horizons

Maroon the Implacable is proudly copublished with PM Press by Ecosocialist Horizons. Ecosocialism is a vision of a transformed society in harmony with nature and the development of practices that can attain it. It is directed toward alternatives to all socially and ecologically destructive systems, such as patriarchy, racism, homophobia, and the fossil fuel based economy. It is based on a perspective that regards other species and natural ecosystems as valuable in themselves and as partners in a common destiny.

Ecosocialism shares with traditional socialism a passion for justice. It shares the conviction that capitalism has been a deadly detour for humanity. We understand capitalism to be a class society based on infinite expansion, through the exploitation of labor and the ransacking of nature. Ecosocialists are also guided by the life-ways of indigenous peoples whose economies are embedded in a classless society in fundamental unity with nature. We draw upon the wisdom of the ages as well as the latest science, and will do what can be done to bring a new society, beyond capitalism, into existence.

We recognize that ecosocialism on a global scale is a long way from being realized. But it is on the horizon: far off, yet rising; indefinite yet vital, a terrain to be mapped, explored, and brought into existence. Our mission is to facilitate a global movement toward the ecosocialist horizon. The whole future depends upon it.

Ecosocialist Horizons seeks to advance ecosocialism as a world-view and as a movement capable of offering real answers to the crises caused by capitalism. Whether these crises be social, economic, or ecological, an integrated approach is necessary. While we conceive of our work holistically, we can categorize our activities into three areas aimed at creating ecosocialist consciousness:

1. Providing news and analysis of ecosocialist concern through a multimedia website and other publications;
2. Educating and organizing to produce creative work and to organize events and actions;
3. Organizing convergences to advance diverse struggles towards an ecosocialist horizon.

Ecosocialist Horizons is proud to support the international campaign to Free Russell Maroon Shoatz.

For more information, visit: http://www.ecosocialisthorizons.com.

About
PM Press

politics • culture • art • fiction • music • film

PM Press was founded at the end of 2007 by a small collection of folks with decades of publishing, media, and organizing experience. PM Press co-conspirators have published and distributed hundreds of books, pamphlets, CDs, and DVDs. Members of PM have founded enduring book fairs, spear-headed victorious tenant organizing campaigns, and worked closely with bookstores, academic conferences, and even rock bands to deliver political and challenging ideas to all walks of life. We're old enough to know what we're doing and young enough to know what's at stake.

We seek to create radical and stimulating fiction and nonfiction books, pamphlets, t-shirts, visual and audio materials to entertain, educate, and inspire you. We aim to distribute these through every available channel with every available technology, whether that means you are seeing anarchist classics at our bookfair stalls; reading our latest vegan cookbook at the café; downloading geeky fiction e-books; or digging new music and timely videos from our website.

Contact us for direct ordering and questions about all PM Press releases, as well as manuscript submissions, review copy requests, foreign rights sales, author interviews, to book an author for an event, and to have PM Press attend your bookfair:

PM Press • PO Box 23912 • Oakland, CA 94623
510-658-3906 • info@pmpress.org

Buy books and stay on top of what we are doing at:

www.pmpress.org

MONTHLY SUBSCRIPTION PROGRAM

These are indisputably momentous times—the financial system is melting down globally and the Empire is stumbling. Now more than ever there is a vital need for radical ideas.

In the six years since its founding—and on a mere shoestring—PM Press has risen to the formidable challenge of publishing and distributing knowledge and entertainment for the struggles ahead. With over 250 releases to date, we have published an impressive and stimulating array of literature, art, music, politics, and culture. Using every available medium, we've succeeded in connecting those hungry for ideas and information to those putting them into practice.

Friends of PM allows you to directly help impact, amplify, and revitalize the discourse and actions of radical writers, filmmakers, and artists. It provides us with a stable foundation from which we can build upon our early successes and provides a much-needed subsidy for the materials that can't necessarily pay their own way. You can help make that happen—and receive every new title automatically delivered to your door once a month—by joining as a Friend of PM Press. And, we'll throw in a free T-Shirt when you sign up.

Here are your options:
- $25 a month: Get all books and pamphlets plus 50% discount on all webstore purchases
- $40 a month: Get all PM Press releases (including CDs and DVDs) plus 50% discount on all webstore purchases
- $100 a month: Superstar—Everything plus PM merchandise, free downloads, and 50% discount on all webstore purchases

For those who can't afford $25 or more a month, we're introducing *Sustainer Rates* at $15, $10 and $5. Sustainers get a free PM Press t-shirt and a 50% discount on all purchases from our website.

Your Visa or Mastercard will be billed once a month, until you tell us to stop. Or until our efforts succeed in bringing the revolution around. Or the financial meltdown of Capital makes plastic redundant. Whichever comes first.

Let Freedom Ring
A Collection of Documents from the Movements to Free U.S. Political Prisoners
Edited by Matt Meyer
$37.95 • 912 pages

Let Freedom Ring presents a two-decade sweep of essays, analyses, histories, interviews, resolutions, People's Tribunal verdicts, and poems by and about the scores of U.S. political prisoners and the campaigns to safeguard their rights and secure their freedom. In addition to an extensive section on the campaign to free death-row journalist Mumia Abu-Jamal, represented here are the radical movements that have most challenged the U.S. empire from within: Black Panthers and other Black liberation fighters, Puerto Rican independentistas, Indigenous sovereignty activists, white anti-imperialists, environmental and animal rights militants, Arab and Muslim activists, Iraq war resisters, and others. Contributors in and out of prison detail the repressive methods—from long-term isolation to sensory deprivation to politically inspired parole denial—used to attack these freedom fighters, some still caged after 30+ years. This invaluable resource guide offers inspiring stories of the creative, and sometimes winning, strategies to bring them home.

Contributors include: Mumia Abu-Jamal, Dan Berger, Dhoruba Bin-Wahad, Bob Lederer, Terry Bisson, Laura Whitehorn, Safiya Bukhari, The San Francisco 8, Angela Davis, Bo Brown, Bill Dunne, Jalil Muntaqim, Susie Day, Luis Nieves Falcón, Ninotchka Rosca, Meg Starr, Assata Shakur, Jill Soffiyah Elijah, Jan Susler, Chrystos, Jose Lopez, Leonard Peltier, Marilyn Buck, Oscar López Rivera, Sundiata Acoli, Ramona Africa, Linda Thurston, Desmond Tutu, Mairead Corrigan Maguire, and many more.

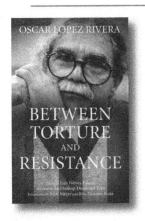

Oscar López Rivera
Between Torture and Resistance
Oscar López Rivera • Edited by Luis Nieves Falcón
Foreword by Archbishop Desmond Tutu
Introduction by Matt Meyer
$15.95 • 160 pages

The story of Puerto Rican leader Oscar López Rivera is one of courage, valor, and sacrifice. A decorated Viet Nam veteran and well-respected community activist, he now holds the distinction of being one of the longest held political prisoners in the world. Behind bars since 1981, he was convicted of the thought-crime of "seditious conspiracy," and never accused of causing anyone harm or of taking a life. This book is a unique introduction to his story and struggle, based on letters between him and the renowned lawyer, sociologist, educator, and activist Luis Nieves Falcón.

In photographs, reproductions of his paintings, and graphic content, Oscar's life is made strikingly accessible—so all can understand why this man has been deemed dangerous to the U.S. government. His ongoing fight for freedom, for his people and for himself (his release date is 2027, when he will be 84 years old), is detailed in chapters which share the life of a Latino child growing up in the small towns of Puerto Rico and the big cities of the U.S. It tells of his emergence as a community activist, of his life underground, and of his years in prison. Most importantly, it points the way forward.

With a vivid assessment of the ongoing colonial relationship between the U.S. and Puerto Rico, it provides tools for working for López Rivera's release—an essential ingredient if U.S.-Latin American relations, both domestically and internationally, have any chance of improvement. Between Torture and Resistance tells a sad tale of human rights abuses in the U.S. which are largely unreported. But it is also a story of hope—that there is beauty and strength in resistance.

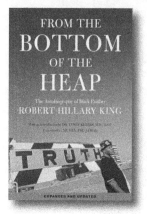

From the Bottom of the Heap
The Autobiography of Black Panther Robert Hillary King
Robert Hillary King • Introduction by Terry Kupers
Foreword by Mumia Abu-Jamal
$17.95 • 272 pages

In 1970, a jury convicted Robert Hillary King of a crime he did not commit and sentenced him to 35 years in prison. He became a member of the Black Panther Party while in Angola State Penitentiary, successfully organizing prisoners to improve conditions. In return, prison authorities beat him, starved him, and gave him life without parole after framing him for a second crime. He was thrown into solitary confinement, where he remained in a six-by-nine-foot cell for 29 years as one of the Angola 3. In 2001, the state grudgingly acknowledged his innocence and set him free. This is his story.

It begins at the beginning: born black, born poor, born in Louisiana in 1942, King journeyed to Chicago as a hobo at the age of 15. He married and had a child, and briefly pursued a semi-pro boxing career to help provide for his family. Just a teenager when he entered the Louisiana penal system for the first time, King tells of his attempts to break out of this system, and his persistent pursuit of justice where there is none.

Yet this remains a story of inspiration and courage, and the triumph of the human spirit. The conditions in Angola almost defy description, yet King never gave up his humanity, or the work towards justice for all prisoners that he continues to do today. *From the Bottom of the Heap*, so simply and humbly told, strips bare the economic and social injustices inherent in our society, while continuing to be a powerful literary testimony to our own strength and capacity to overcome. The paperback edition includes additional writings from Robert King and an update on the case of the Angola 3.

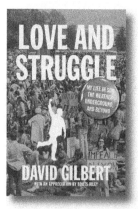

Love and Struggle
My Life in SDS, the Weather Underground, and Beyond
David Gilbert • Foreword by Boots Riley
$22.00 • 352 pages

A nice Jewish boy from suburban Boston—hell, an Eagle Scout!—David Gilbert arrived at Columbia University just in time for the explosive Sixties. From the early anti-Vietnam War protests to the founding of SDS, from the Columbia Strike to the tragedy of the Townhouse, Gilbert was on the scene: as organizer, theoretician, and above all, activist. He was among the first militants who went underground to build the clandestine resistance to war and racism known as "Weatherman." And he was among the last to emerge, in captivity, after the disaster of the 1981 Brink's robbery, an attempted expropriation that resulted in four deaths and long prison terms. In this extraordinary memoir, written from the maximum-security prison where he has lived for almost thirty years, Gilbert tells the intensely personal story of his own Long March from liberal to radical to revolutionary.

Today a beloved and admired mentor to a new generation of activists, he assesses with rare humor, with an understanding stripped of illusions, and with uncommon candor the errors and advances, terrors and triumphs of the Sixties and beyond. It's a battle that was far from won, but is still not lost: the struggle to build a new world, and the love that drives that effort. A cautionary tale and a how-to as well, *Love and Struggle* is a book as candid, uncompromising, and humane as its author.

CPSIA information can be obtained
at www.ICGtesting.com
Printed in the USA
JSHW042031190721
16992JS00002BA/2